DREAMS AND HEALING

DREAMS AND HEALING

Expanding The Inner Eye

How to Attune Your Mind-Body Connection Through Imagery, Intuition and Life Energies

Joan Windsor

DODD, MEAD & COMPANY · NEW YORK

A GAMUT BOOK

Published by Dodd, Mead & Company, Inc.
71 Fifth Avenue, New York, New York 10003.
Manufactured in the United States of America.

First Edition

1 2 3 4 5 6 7 8 9 10

Library of Congress Cataloging-in-Publication Data

Windsor, Joan.
Dreams and Healing.

Bibliography: p.
Includes index.
1. Dreams. 2. Spiritual healing. I. Windsor, Joan.
Inner eye. II. Title.
BF1099.S76W56 1987 135'.3 87-24565

ISBN 0-396-09079-6
ISBN 0-396-09150-4 {PBK}

To Jim, Jimmy and Robin Windsor and John and Elizabeth Hollis. Their presences brighten my days and illuminate my spiritual path.

To Ruth Montgomery whose wisdom and creative writings serve as an inspiration for my present and future work. I count her friendship among my highest blessings.

Contents

Acknowledgements

Books are co-creations of unified minds. *Dreams and Healing: Expanding The Inner Eye* could not have become a reality without invaluable contributions from my family, close friends, and spiritual mentors. Therefore, I would like to express my gratitude to the following people for their contributions in connection with the completion of this work:

Betty Hall, my secretary and friend, for her unfaltering support and patience given without reservation during the refinement of this manuscript.

Alan Vaughan, parapsychologist and intuitive instructor extraordinaire who continues to provide me with superior wisdom and serves as a spiritual model to emulate.

To my sister, *Arlene Helmus,* I owe a special debt of gratitude for the warm hospitality and loving indulgence afforded me during my frequent research expeditions to San Francisco.

Accolades to *John and Elizabeth Hollis,* our co-partners in all spiritual adventures. Without John's keen analytical mind and Elizabeth's exceptional intuitive talents, the current level of research achieved thus far would never have been possible.

Thanks to *Dr. Norman Shealy, Dr. Genevieve Haller, Mrs. Margit Nassi, Mrs. Virginia Light* and *Dr. Catherine Ponder* for the sharing of their "specialized brand" of healing philosophies and energies. I will stand forever in awe of their sense of mission and attuned sensitivities.

A special hug to all my friends and students whose personal experiences and anecdotes served to enrich the intensity and spirit of *Dreams and Healing,* expanding its scope considerably beyond the limitations of my own perceptions. You are my fellow co-creators.

My heartfelt thanks to all the participants of the Psychical Research Project. Their insightful responses and discerning commentaries provided us with an "evidential spiritual yardstick" for evaluating our work. We truly received in tenfold measure.

And finally, my husband Jim, the love and light of my life. The twin flames of our soul-mate relationship burn brighter with each passing year, and I am eternally grateful to The Father for bestowing upon me the richest gift he has to offer—*The Blessing of Love.*

Foreword

The belief that there is no separation between mind and body opens up limitless possibilities for the creation of our best possible world. But are the mind and body ultimately inseparable? That can perhaps be best understood with the aid of a scientific model.

Imagine a test tube of giant proportions, perhaps 5′10″ in height and about 1¼ feet in diameter. The test tube walls are made of a material with only a moderate resistance to the passage of an electrical current. This test tube is filled with a large amount of calcium, phosphorus, magnesium, potassium, sodium, and a generous supply of organic chemicals that contain carbon and nitrogen. If you have ever taken an introduction to chemistry course, you may recall that sooner or later, even without stirring this mismash, there will be a remarkable homogeniety of the mixture as long as there is water to allow the movement of the chemicals. If you have also had an introduction to physics course, you will recognize that the electrical conductivity of this test tube would be fairly great. This test tube and the mixture it contains is a crude representation of the human body. But because of specific physical characteristics of the human body, we do not just turn into one homogeneous mass. Nevertheless, all parts of the body are chemically and electrically connected even without a voltage system. And, of course, we have that marvelous creation, the human motor system, which allows us purposeful voluntary communication between the body and the brain. If you can, for just a moment, imagine the homogeneity of the human body both electrically and chemically; it should be much easier to understand that there can be no separation of body and mind.

The inseparability of mind and body can be examined on the level of "feeling" as well as on the purely physical level.

In the last five years, psychoimmunology has brought to scientific medicine for the first time the proof that hard-core scientists need to accept the concept of the unity of body and mind. The evidence is now overwhelming that depression essentially clobbers the immune system. There is no force more powerful than severe depression in initiating a wide variety of illnesses.

Interestingly, early in this century the nervous system, which controls actions and reactions in the muscles, glands, and organs, was known as the imaginative nervous system because it was recognized that it responded to imagery. Indeed, with relatively few exceptions, feelings are the result of words and images. Thus, if you are sitting or lying in a comfortable position without any strong external stimulation, almost all internal feelings will be the result of the internal thought processes—in both words and images.

Ambrose Worrall's wonderful little *Essay on Prayer* says what we want to say perhaps better than anything I have seen. "Every thought is a prayer. Thinking is what sets in motion spiritual forces to bring about changes in environment, body, companions, language, desires, hopes, despairs." He goes on to emphasize, "We should not concentrate on the elimination of a condition, but on the *creation* of the condition desired."

Each of us is on a personal pilgrimage in life and ultimately that pilgrimage will lead us to ponder our own purpose in life, to decide whether we really are creating our own reality as purposefully and correctly as we would wish. Joan Windsor's book, *Dreams and Healing,* is one of the tools that will help you take steps toward creating the reality you desire. My own personal search made a quantum leap forward in 1972 when I first visited the Association for Research Enlightenment in Virginia Beach. My life has never been the same in many, many *good* ways. The techniques presented in this book will help *you* in your own growth.

C. Norman Shealy, M.D., Ph.D.
Founder & Director
Shealy Institute for Comprehensive Pain and Health Care
Founding President, American Holistic Medical Association
Clinical & Research Professor of Psychology
Forest Institute of Professional Psychology

Preface

Dreams and Healing is the most important book you will ever read if you are at all interested in a practical program of self-help in relation to attuning your mind-body connection to total wellness. Within its pages lies the formula for the realization and maintenance of a harmonious and joyful balance between physical, mental, and spiritual states of being. What is the secret of this formula? Our attitudes and emotions can provide a protective shield for us against every conceivable type of illness or, if left unchecked, can be the procurers of pain and malaise. We do not have to accept these negative thought processes as inevitable, however, for we have the power within us to control, change, or recreate our entire life pattern. The concepts proposed in *Dreams and Healing* were originated in order to achieve that balance between our physical, mental, and spiritual states. They are a composite of personal experiences and professional commentaries, the central focus of which is the attunement of the mind-body connection through the inner eye.

Readers who wish to take command of their lives and work toward vibrant physical health and mental vigor can widen their vistas through the mediums of dream healing, the phenomena of shared and serial dreams, and dream creativity. The Twelve Dream Classification System initially presented in *The Inner Eye* is expanded upon. Fellow dreamers are charged to actively participate in the process of dream creativity to integrate and utilize its basic principles as a tool of transfiguration.

One of the uniquely exciting features of the book is the introduction of a new procedure for individualizing intuitive readings in the form of *The Holistic Life Reading.* With the inclusion of Physical Symbology, Current Issues, Future Trends, Character Analysis, Past Lives and Soul's Purpose, the term holistic counseling takes on an entirely new dimension. Step-by-step procedures regarding how to give a Holistic Life Reading are provided as well as the citation of five prime intuitive enhancers which, when mastered, elevate one's insights and self-healing skills to the highest levels. (All examples cited in the book are true although some names have been changed for the sake of anonymity.)

Of special interest to health professionals and emerging healers are the sections on *Spiritual Healing* and *Intuitive Counseling.* The healing process is examined in depth and five erudite healers discuss their own spiritual ideologies and how these relate to their healing philosophies. Psychiatrists, psychologists, and counselors can refine their professional skills through the study of innovative physical, mental, intuitive, and spiritual techniques, which is the subject of Chapter 11.

Why is it important to read this book? Dreams, intuition, and healing are the channels through which The Still Small Voice within communicates with each soul at the deepest level. The more highly attuned our minds and hearts are to spiritual truths, the more quickly the unification of the mind-body connection is empowered to become a transforming force in our lives both at personal and transpersonal levels. This is the natural birthright of each soul. Will you then join hands with me once again and witness the Magnificence of Creation through the clarity of the inner eye?

Joan Windsor

Introduction

Since the publication of *The Inner Eye,* Personal Development Services, Inc. has focused its attention on healing. This is a natural evolution from the study of dreams and intuition because the unconscious realm of mentation apparently plays a crucial role in both sickness and health.

Phil Nuernberger, in *Freedom From Stress, A Holistic Approach,* estimates that 70–80% of sickness in our culture is psychosomatic. We suffer mostly from "diseases of civilization" such as cancer, heart attacks, digestive failure, strokes, ulcers, hypertension, and mental illness. The significant involvement of mind and spirit, as well as body, in these conditions is now generally accepted. This was not the case in the recent past.

The holistic approach to healing was quite evident prior to the early decades of this century. It was assumed that the body healed itself with the assistance of medicine, positive expectations, and prayer. With the discovery of infectious diseases and antibiotics illness was viewed as something which invaded the body from the outside, and doctors who administered the appropriate drugs became the healers. The notions of prevention and self-healing were lost to the awareness of several generations.

In recent years there has been a renewal of interest in the body-mind-spirit connection. It is increasingly recognized that each of us must accept responsibility for preventing illness if we can and for our own healing if we cannot. In order to heal ourselves we need to be aware of the various healing modalities available to us, including our own unconscious minds. It is the purpose of this book to set forth alternative approaches to healing, recognizing that what works for one may not work for another, that each of us is responsible for our own healing, and that a combination of different modalities is frequently the most effective. Body, mind, and spirit are so closely intertwined that one cannot be out of balance without the others being affected. In my own counseling practice I have frequently seen hypoglycemia masquerading as neurosis; negative attitudes which cause digestive problems; and loneliness as the genesis of obesity. Effective therapy must treat the whole person—body, mind and spirit.

The term "holistic" is derived from "holy," which means to set apart for the service of God. We should seek healing not only for its own sake, but also in order to be of service to others. This is the spiritual path. I believe that this book will help us along the way.

Dr. James C. Windsor

I

Continuing Adventures in Transpersonal Consciousness

CHAPTER 1

The Transition

The truth is that nobody can be cured unless he is prepared to accept the need for a more or less complete reorientation of his life. To put it in a nutshell; the healed person is not the original person minus a symptom, but a newly oriented person in whom, through the new orientation, the necessity for the symptom itself has disappeared.

Gerhard Adler—*Studies in Analytical Psychology*

THE CHALLENGE: TRANSFORMATION THROUGH SPIRITUAL HEALING

This was one of those delightfully balmy spring days in early May which titillates the senses almost beyond endurance. Oscillating myriads of psychedelic colors and almost painfully pleasurable physical sensations waxed and waned much like the rhythmic motion of the emerald blue waves upon which my gaze had been intently transfixed for an indeterminate length of time. Far down the beach the sound of a child's echoing laughter broke through my reverie and once again I became aware of the thoughts that had induced such a state of contentment.

The date was May 5, 1983. My husband, Jim, and I had now been engaged in spiritual work for almost two years. There had been peaks and valleys in connection with our endeavors, but never in our married life had we experienced the joy and satisfaction that we now shared as a direct result of our newly fashioned spiritually oriented philosophy. This had been acquired from extensive investigation of both the Edgar Cayce readings, a composite of psychic and healing information channeled by one of America's most well-known clairvoyants, and voluminous reading of books, the focus of which was similar but the spiritual stance more broadly based. Although we spent most of our spare time involved in activities related to our spiritual awakening, as I review this period in retrospect, I realize now that we were only knee-deep in this work. Jim delivered learned speeches on parapsychology and religion while I attempted to evaluate and consolidate my newly acquired intuition and natural-healing ideas into our joint counseling practice. All of this would too soon become passé, however, and we would eventually find ourselves fully immersed in a research and spiritually oriented counseling work so broad that it would require us to delve into untapped resources and expand our unique individual talents to levels that lay far beyond the narrow perceptions of my logical mind on that dazzling sunny afternoon.

As I shook the sand from between my toes and gathered up my beach chair and partially read copy of Alan Vaughan's *The Edge of Tomorrow,* I pondered the possible factors that would have extended Jim's meeting this afternoon. Charles Thomas Cayce, grandson of Edgar Cayce and President of the Association of Research and Enlightenment (ARE), the educational arm of the Edgar Cayce Foundation (ECF), had requested this afternoon appointment. Present also was Eric Jensen, current Chairman of the Board of Trustees for ARE and ECF. There had been an air of secrecy surrounding the subject under discussion, and when it occurred to me to inquire about it intuitively, I had been made well aware that the "psychic doors" had swung shut on that issue. In fact, an edict had "filtered down" that I was not even to risk one eyeball to retrieve a clue. With a sigh of resignation that accompanied the knowledge that I was behaving myself *almost too well,* I gathered up the remainder of my belongings and headed toward Marshalls Hotel to change.

Three-thirty PM found me squirming in my chair at the far end of the ARE Library rereading page 46 of *The Edge of Tomorrow* for the fourth time and being well aware that my consciousness continually strayed toward the closed door of Charles Thomas's office in spite of my continuing efforts to resist. Another hour passed unrewardingly. I glanced at the number on the top of the page and saw the figure 60. For a speed reader who usually consumes 60–70 pages per hour, I had almost come to a standstill!

Then, it happened! Jim stood before me divested of his usual air of placidity. In its place I was amazed to observe an expression that could only be described as a marriage of "leo-lionish pride" and "soul indecision." This was completely out of character for the modest and decisively stalwart husband on whose wise judgment I had come to depend for so many years.

"What could have possibly happened in the past three and one-half hours to impel your personality to engage in this 180 degree turn?" I inquired teasingly but with genuine concern.

"Well," he began in a voice that brimmed with uncertainty. "I have just been offered the position of Vice-President of The Edgar Cayce Foundation. It would mean my taking a two-year leave of absence from Christopher Newport College. This would give us an opportunity to become more involved in the Edgar Cayce work, *but* it would also necessitate giving up our counseling practice and our Shellbank residence. What do you think of this proposal?"

For once in my life I was at a loss for words. The implications were farreaching, but there were also very serious problematic concerns that had to be worked through before any final decisions could be made.

I rose from my chair and gathering up my test folders, *The Edge of Tomorrow,* and other belongings that lay on the table, I turned to Jim and said, "Let's go sit by the ocean and discuss the pros and cons. We always think more clearly on the beach."

Jim agreed. We headed down the stairs and across the street to the patio that adjoins Marshalls Hotel. As we walked, I happened to glance at Alan Vaughan's title, *The Edge of Tomorrow,* and was struck by the synchronistic symbology connected with that title and how well it depicted the current situation.

Five minutes later we were settled comfortably at a circular stone table on Marshalls patio, fortified with banana fruit drinks purchased from the nearby bar and ready to dissect the issue.

Jim began. "We elected to become involved in spiritual work part-time and now because of progress and successes, an opportunity to be of more complete service is presenting itself. The choices, it seems to me, are relatively clear. If I become Vice-President of The Edgar Cayce Foundation, I will assume responsibility for administering the Library, the Readings, the Archives, and the Therapy Department. This is very exciting at first glance but on a day-to-day level it means long work hours and leaving our professional life behind for two years. It is very difficult to just drop counselees for that period of time and then pick up where you left off. The other true disadvantage I see is that we would have to leave our Shellbank home. You and I both agree that Shellbank is our source of stability and soul-serenity. How will we both fare without our retreat?"

Up to this point the anticipation of being involved full time with the Association of Research and Enlightenment/Edgar Cayce Foundation work had seemed very appealing. Now my practical Capricorn mind was beginning to perceive the full impact of the venture.

"Leaving Shellbank would undoubtedly produce real hardships on us," I responded in more alarming tones. Apprehension began to tug at my heartstrings especially where Shellbank was concerned. Shellbank was our haven, our place of peaceful seclusion where the world's travesties were left far behind. How could I give up that treasured sanctuary? Leaving the security of Christopher Newport College was also somewhat unsettling. Most frightening of all, however, was the spectre of closing up our counseling business to which we had devoted 11 years of our professional life! How could we possibly just shut the door on all of our clients?

I stared absently at the waves breaking in thunderous repetition one after another along the shoreline. I loved this place also, but it was so new, so full of humanity, so completely different from the lush green woods and the placid turquoise waters of the James River. Would I truly be able to adjust to this transition? And would I be willing to give up the additional hours that could be spent with my husband in doing the things we both enjoyed in order to serve more unselfishly in the realm of spiritual work to which I was almost certain we had been guided?

At this point our water-nymph seventeen-year-old daughter, Robin, fluttered into my view skipping across the beach with her blond hair bouncing to the cadence of her gait. With the day's activities at an end she and her young female companion had undoubtedly built up voracious appetites and, by now, were envisioning sumptuous platters of scallops, shrimps, and "autres bons moreceaux de mer" with which to satiate their gnawing hunger pangs.

Jim and I decided to table our discussion and immerse ourselves in the evening's festivities. *The time for arriving at the correct decision lay somewhere beyond us at a distant point in the Ocean of Time. When we arrived at that point, circumstances would crystallize our decision leaving no room for doubt. Until then the answer would remain suspended.*

The 50-minute trip to Newport News was prolonged by a 15-minute side trip to drop off Robin's well-tanned and equally well-fed friend. Then the three of us proceeded to Christopher Newport College to retrieve the Aspen from where Jim had parked it early that morning. By now it was several minutes after nine, and knowing how tired Jim must be as a result of the day's events coupled with the fact that he had done all the driving, I offered him the continued use of our Kingswood station wagon so he could make the rest of the trip in the best possible circumstances. He half-heartedly objected, but after the first mild protestations, he rebuckled his seat belt. I raised Robin from a semi-conscious state in the backseat, and she and I made our way to the Aspen.

"You go ahead and I'll follow," I called to Jim as I closed the door. This was the reverse of our normal procedure as Jim usually keeps me in view when we drive back to Williamsburg together to be sure I am safe. Tonight, however, I elected the position of protective escort, and Jim nodded in agreement.

I started the motor and waited for him to pull ahead of me. As we merged into the Friday night traffic of Interstate #64, I glanced toward the backseat of the Aspen and noted that Robin had resumed her "catnap."

This would be a quiet trip without her delightful chatter, but it would give me time to review the day's events and reassess all aspects of the offer in the solitude of my own mind. I switched the radio on and tuned in my favorite station. The familiar strains of an old classic *Dream* blended effortlessly with the black velvet tapestry of the warm May air.

"How appropriate," I mused. "The Guides must be with us."

I resumed my tranquil train of thought while my eyes continued to follow the dimly visible trail left by the taillights of our Kingswood wagon 100 yards or so ahead of me.

Suddenly, a merry-go-round of lights appeared off to my left. The night air was pierced simultaneously with the screeching of brakes and the terrifying response of my husband's blaring horn. I slammed on my brakes automatically and watched paralyzed as a vehicle now entered my full range of vision, veered crazily to complete a 360° revolution, and smashed head-on into the front of our Kingswood.

"Oh, Dear God!" I screamed as I witnessed the hood of the station wagon fold up like an accordion. My husband, Jim, slumped over the wheel. Instantaneously, the oncoming car spun sideways again and headed straight for the Aspen. I shut my eyes and prayed. It stopped five feet short of a second collision!

Adrenaline now began racing through my veins. I leaped from my car and rushed toward Jim's motionless figure. Never in my life have I experienced such terror. As I neared the demolished vehicle, I heard Jim moan. He raised his head and shook it as if trying to awaken himself from some horrible nightmare. A stab of pain dispelled that fantasy.

"Thank God you're alive!" I murmured. Tears of joy and relief brimmed over my eyelids and ran down my cheeks.

Jim examined his injuries, and except for a bleeding left calf and a severe pain in his mid-chest, there appeared to be no injuries. Again, I thanked God for sparing his life.

"I'm getting out of here!" were the next words I heard. I turned to see a man in his early twenties emerge from the twisted wreckage of the other vehicle. He began to head across the road toward a darkened field.

Fear now turned to rage within me. I rushed after him. Taking him (and myself) by surprise I grabbed his black tee shirt in my fist and with eyes ablaze, I shrieked, "You almost killed my husband. You're not going anywhere!"

The smell of alcohol from his breath almost sickened me. Here was another case of a drinking driver almost snuffing out the life of an innocent victim. I tightened my grip on his shirt. He must have been shocked by my brazenness; else he could have easily freed himself. I too was amazed at my continuing tenacity. This situation resolved itself quickly, however, as a burly 260-pound stranger emerged from the already gathering crowd and volunteered to give me a hand.

"You look after your husband and daughter now, Ma'am," he commanded as he grabbed my former prisoner's shoulders between his two big fists. "I have this situation well in hand!"

I breathed a sigh of relief and turned my attention toward my husband. By now, the rescue squad had arrived along with several policemen. They were attempting to free my husband from the wreckage of our old faithful Kingswood.

"You're mighty lucky, friend, you were driving such a heavy car and wearing your seat belt. Without both those protections I doubt very much that you would have survived such an impact!" commented one of the officers.

I had always loved our Kingswood from the day we purchased it. Jim always kidded me about it being a personal friend. Well, this night I was implicitly aware of the truth contained within that officer's statement. Had it not been for the strong protective hood of our station wagon absorbing almost the full force of the collision, the outcome of the accident could have taken an entirely different course.

"Daddy! Daddy! Are you all right?" Robin's voice was trembling with emotion. She must have emerged from the Aspen while my attention was focused on forcibly detaining my prisoner. She stood tearfully by as the police officers pried open the car door to free Jim from the wreckage. As he emerged relatively unscathed, she ran toward him throwing her arms around him and smothering him with kisses. I joined them. We three clasped one another to our hearts, fully realizing how close we had come to losing the one who is the central focus of our existence.

"Better get yourself checked out at a local hospital," advised the officer-in-charge after he had secured all the information necessary to determine the circumstances surrounding the accident. "There may be some internal injuries there that would otherwise go undetected."

"Good idea," Jim agreed. "I'll do that."

We decided to have this done at the Williamsburg Community Hospital as it was close to home. We knew several of the Emergency Room physicians there, having availed ourselves of their services several times. A thorough examination and x-rays revealed no further injuries or complications.

"You're *very fortunate,* Dr. Windsor," I heard the examining physician observe as he released Jim after taping his leg. "From the sounds of the accident you should have a dozen broken bones. Someone upstairs was watching over you." I agreed silently.

Later that night after Robin had retired, we reflected on the day's events. Being too keyed up to sleep, we reviewed all facets of the ARE proposal and how each would affect our present mode of existence.

The house question was resolved without much controversy. Virginia Beach would be our main residence four days per week. This would necessitate investing in a small apartment which could be used as home base during the time we spent there. Weekends would be spent at Shellbank where we could again find solace in the gentle ebb and flow of the tidal James waves and the soothing vibrations of our home's natural woodland setting.

The question of closing down our counseling practice was another matter entirely. By 4:00 AM we were no nearer a solution than we had been two hours prior.

"What happens to all the people with whom we have worked over the past 11 years if we just shut our doors and tell them we no longer are in the counseling business? What happens to their trust in us?" My question summarized our dilemma.

Jim shook his head in disheartment. "We would really be deserting them, wouldn't we?" he surmized realizing the full import of such a decision.

"Not only would we be deserting them, but what of future clients not yet seen? What happens to them? Do we say to them, 'Sorry. We're on our own spiritual path now. Let's reschedule in two years.' I don't mean we are the only counselors that can help people. What I am trying to convey is that we are a special brand of counselor. We are becoming spiritually-centered. This is a unique quality that makes this type of counselor different from the textbook variety who is not cognizant of availing himself of the multiplicity of healing skills and tools that a spiritual counselor has at his disposal. We have come this far in our joint counseling practice. What are our options now?" In the darkness of the morning hours Jim and I stared at each other in silent dismay.

I began again. "You know I almost lost you tonight. And I want to ask you *one* simple question. Since we have *both* been given the gift of the remaining portion of your life, what is the most productive use to which you can commend it?"

"To teach as many others as possible what you and I have just begun to understand," he stated without hesitation. I am convinced that age and past-life regression, meditation, self-hypnosis, telepathy, and prayer should all be integrated into the counseling process dependent on the needs of individual clients. I'm just now beginning to understand some of the dynamic soul connections inherent in each of these processes."

"And as for me," I responded fervently, "there is no doubt in my mind that intuitive impressions gained from readings could prove to be an invaluable asset to a person's own self-understanding and self-healing. But I don't understand enough about the process yet. Not only that, but dreams, laying-on-of-hands, diet, vitamin therapy, massage, and medical evaluations are all included in the healing process of counseling. What a frustration not to continue my investigations into these healing modalities. I have just begun to scratch the surface here."

Our eyes met and it was as it had been for the 26 years of our married life—we both knew exactly what the other partner was thinking. *This was that crystalline point in time when the* ***answer*** *had been revealed and the solution seemed almost too good to be true.*

"Our marriage has always been a sharing process. Now our work partnership can become one."

Jim now spoke enthusiastically. "I'll accept the Vice-Presidency of the Edgar Cayce Foundation for both of us. This probably will benefit our own soul evolvement and provide an opportunity for psychical research, spiritual understanding, and service. We are not going to close down Learning Development Services, however. Instead we shall christen it Personal Development Services, Inc. You can continue to see clients two days per week. I'll see clients occasionally when my counseling would be beneficial. Our research and investigation into hypnotic regression, intuitive readings, diet and nutrition, medical and chiropractic treatment, massage, and the effectiveness of various types of healers and their healing techniques should serve to enrich both our own healing skills as well as the healing skills of those professionals with whom we will work in both the present and the future. As we grow in understanding, so should the resources of Personal Development Services, Inc."

Adrenaline now pumped through my veins. "What we're talking about here," I interjected, "is really a transformation through Spiritual Counseling, isn't it? We can realize this most personally through our own counseling organization but it really isn't limited to just that. Transformations can be achieved through teaching spiritual philosophy in classes, lectures, and workshops in which we can report the evidence and results of our own work as well as the work of our colleagues. Counseling is not only effective in a professional relationship, but a confidential conversation with a good intimate friend—well, that sometimes is a form of spiritual counseling also."

A smile gently turned up the corner of Jim's lips. Although he tried to conceal it, it escaped his efforts, and he broke into a broad grin.

"You really do reach into the deepest recesses of my mind and know my exact thoughts and what I'm all about, don't you?" He threw his head back and laughed uproariously.

"You should know that as your partner in Spiritual Counseling that's what I'm all about," I retorted in jest. "Shall we embark on this great new adventure that awaits?"

"Could we wait until 9:00 AM tomorrow to begin? I think we have had enough excitement for one day." Almost immediately, his head dropped to the pillow and his sleep-laden lids closed tightly. I nestled down in his arms in serene contentment. I had almost lost him tonight and yet, in that brief instant of time, the course of our entire life had taken on a new dimension. There would be other days to share our adventures and our own personal transformation with others. For now I was content to be just where I belonged—safe within the circle of my husband's arms. Rays of light began to creep through the window and made their way across the bedspread to my pillow. A new day was beginning to dawn.

The question asked by my readers now is why are all these details of our personal lives and the spiritual course we have taken so necessary to include in this book? Throughout my counseling career the importance of a trusting and highly intimate relationship between my clients and me seems to have been the primary key toward unlocking the door to personalized development. This being the case, the same principle should be apropos with regard to spiritual counseling and teaching through the medium of writing. This would seem perhaps more expedient due to the lack of face-to-face contact. Thus, if my readers are presented the opportunity to establish personal ties with us by means of the written word and to develop an understanding and appreciation of events that have served as catalysts for the evolution of our own ideals and spiritual philosophy, might not they too begin to sense an awareness of its practical viability and adapt similar principles as standards by which to gauge spiritual progress in their daily lives?

Both my husband and I consider ourselves counselors—this being our chosen profession. Counseling, however, often has engrained within its perimeters the element of teaching. It is from this expanded viewpoint of teaching that the intent to write this book emerges.

The purpose of each soul is to educate itself through selected lessons. The Co-instructors in this University are Sorrow and Joy. Once wounded, spiritual growth is achieved through the healing of multiple afflictions. This healing assumes a variety of postures. *Dreams and Healing* is devoted to the examination of these healing orientations. Medical and miracle healings will be investigated. Cases of physical, mental, and spiritual life challenges will be presented and related to the concept of dream creativity. Other subjects for exploration are shared dreams, serial dreams, a novel and viable research approach to intuitive readings, and the possibility of the removal of physical anomalies through the applied energies of gifted healers. The final pages extol the merits of intuitive counseling and inspirational prayer as progressive methodologies for the probable realization of one's uniquely individualized pattern of soul development.

So come with me once again and let us venture together into realms as yet unknown, for all you possess of truth and wisdom is what you understand. And, according to Emmett Fox, true spiritual growth occurs only in direct proportion to the application and practice of knowledge already assimilated.

CHAPTER 2

Lessons in Spiritual Healing

The healing of the body is essential, but the thing that really matters of course, is the spiritual development of the soul. What is a physical healing but the outer evidence that a step in spiritual development has been taken.

Emmet Fox—*Power Through Constructive Thinking*

Several years ago I would have vehemently denied any suggestion that I would write a chapter with a title such as this. In fact, writing a book on this theme would never have ever crossed my mind. However, here I sit, pen in hand, about to embark on this educational and soul-stimulating venture. There are times I shake my head in laughter to think that I am so presumptuous as to believe that I have accrued sufficient knowledge to attempt such an undertaking. Yet, in more solemn moments of contemplation I am acutely aware of the depths of pain and suffering I personally experienced as I journeyed through my own episodes of ill-health and was equally touched with empathy as I recognized those same emotions reflected in the eyes of family, friends, and clients who were currently undergoing similar "baptisms by fire" in order to render their souls more spiritually resilient. It was in these more contemplative periods that I began to feel the urge to share with my readers three lessons in spiritual healing which exemplify the fundamental principles basic to my current holistic health philosophy. Each incident I am about to relate illustrates the pivotal role which attitudinal orientation plays in relationship to physical healing.

Section I entitled *Medical Healing* explores the question of the importance of medical practitioners in the field of spiritual healing. Section II, *Miracle Healing* discusses the circumstances surrounding instantaneous healings arising from "laying-on-of-hands." *Partnership Healing,* the final topic touched upon, extols the benefits realized as a direct outgrowth of complete commitment on the parts of the health professional, spiritual healer, and patient to participate cooperatively and totally in the healing process.

In many readings given by Edgar Cayce, the clairvoyant trance-healer of Virginia Beach, "the sufferer was admonished to change his attitude and outlook as a necessary precondition to physical improvement. So, we do indeed learn through pain and suffering. These handmaidens of karma serve to convert the soul."[1]

MEDICAL HEALING

In October of 1983 I had arrived at a point in time where I felt I had my life under control. I had learned the importance of daily meditation for intuitive development and practiced it faithfully with gratifying results. I appeared to have my cyst problems in abeyance having had no operations for several years. I determined that, so long as I watched my diet and adhered to the vitamin therapy Dr. Haller had prescribed about ½ the time, I would undoubtedly continue to enjoy good health. Mid-term reports from Jimmy, our son, and Robin, our daughter, contained evidence of above average scholastic performances and Jim was beginning to enjoy his part-time job with ARE. In short, I had grown smug and complacent with myself. When an attitude such as this obscures an objective view of life "The Forces" take a hand to assure that things move along at their proper pace again.

A dream recorded on October 18th targeted to make an impact on my soul hardly made a dent in my "armoured psyche" although I do recall feeling a mild sense of disquietment upon

1983 The Forces continued chiseling away my staunch line of defense bit by bit with the following series of dreams:

***Grandma La Bar's Advice* (November 14, 1983)**

Grandma La Bar says there is a lady who needs to go to the hospital. I say, "No, home is better." She says she has examined this woman and she is correct in her diagnosis.

***A Rust Spot on My Car* (November 15, 1983)**

A policeman points out a rust spot on the right front end of my car. I tell him it is repaired.

***The Operator* (November 29, 1983)**

Two workers have been putting storm windows on my house. Suddenly, they break in and are about to attack me. I yell, "If you don't stop, I am going to call the police." I try to dial the number but have to look it up. I am wasting valuable time. I call *The Operator* and I get the number—2557. A call will finally put a stop to this.

Finally, the Voice provided me with a Directive with regard to my choice of treatment in no uncertain terms. The transmission was:

"You have a good source of healing energy through surgery."

I now came to terms with myself, and made an appointment the following day to schedule a date for the operation.

Immediately upon affirming the appointment I was rewarded with two marvelous dreams which left no doubt in my mind that I had arrived at the right decision. The first was in the form of a type-written message. This was received on December 3rd and stated:

"No complications. She will be fine by the second week in December."

I found the contents to be of extreme interest due to the fact that my surgeon had scheduled the operation for December 12th *after* I recorded the dream.

The second dream viewed on December 10th relieved any anxiety about the success of being healed surgically.

A Successful Operator

> I am discussing my operation with Mr. Drake, my former principal at Franklin School in Rahway, New Jersey. I request Monday off from teaching for the surgery. Then, I am getting ready for it and find I have a piece of *Milky Way* in my mouth. I spit it out as I am not supposed to eat anything. Immediately, I see a bandage and realize the operation is completed. The physicians have *seared* the left breast also so no more cysts will occur. I say, "Do you realize how well I feel?"

This all manifested itself as previewed with the exception of the *searing* and, as I write these pages, there have been no reoccurrences.

What lessons were learned as a result of this bout of illness?

1. My surgeon informed my husband that there were two cysts that had to be excised, one being on top of the other. In rechecking my dream journal I noted these sentences. "I am visiting Dr. Haller. I seem to have several cysts. *One cyst is below the other.*"

When I discussed this turn of events with Dr. Haller later, she informed me that treating this type of problem nutritionally would have been very difficult. *Thus, I learned surgery is also a form of healing.*

2. *I also concluded that each illness must be evaluated individually and appropriate treatment then elected solely on the merits of the most efficacious method of cure.*

3. Of greater consequence, however, was my realization that, not only did I have to come to terms with the karmic patterns that were wreaking havoc in my life, but in the interest of self-improvement and growth, a drastic change in attitude toward healing was *mandatory!* Nutrition and vitamin therapy were not the sole source of healing nor was surgery and prescribed medicines, or for that matter, even healers who claim cures from "laying-on-of-hands." *It was rather a combination of each working in concert with another that provided True Healing.*

Mary Ann Woodward states my lesson succinctly in *Scars of the Soul* when she writes, "In each case . . . the actual transformation of these (karmic) patterns depends on the willingness of the individual to come face-to-face with himself or herself, accept it, and then begin working immediately to improve it."[3]

When a lesson is worth learning, it is re-taught. These points just cited were underscored a second time two years later. A dear friend of mine telephoned me with the distressing news that she had numerous tumors in her uterus which had probably been multiplying over a ten-year period. A hysterectomy was recommended. Since her doctor had determined these were not malignant, she postponed the surgery in the hope of somehow reversing the situation. In an effort to alleviate some of her anxiety I suggested she try the castor oil pack treatment as well as some nutritional measures. We also visited several healers in hope of reducing the size and number of the tumors. My friend made a valiant effort but there was always a seed of doubt in her mind when it came to actually believing that these methods tried would truly prove successful. Finally, in July of that year she came to terms with herself and sought healing through surgical removal of the tumors. She recovered rapidly and has since enjoyed vibrant health.

Here again the point is re-emphasized that a surgeon is a healer also. An additional insight was internalized from my friend's experience concerning the length of time the illness had been in existence. My "mental computer" suggests that the length of time needed to heal is in direct proportion to the length of time the illness has been in existence. Stated in concise terms—*the longer one permits the illness to devitalize physical being, the greater the healing time required to regenerate a healthy body. I have seen this statement evidenced time after time in our own counseling practice as well as reflected in the illnesses of personal friends. True healing occurs only when we are mentally and spiritually ready to accept it with open arms.*

MIRACLE HEALING

Miracle healing was a concept that was foreign to my logical mind until late 1983. From this time on, however, books on this subject began to make their appearance before me during browsing expeditions in bookstores. Incidents that aroused my curiosity even more came in the form of introduction to perfectly normal persons, and after a few minutes of polite chit-chat, the introducee would turn away to engage another individual in conversation, and the friend would draw me aside whispering in hushed tones, "He's a healer, you know." These days when events tend to happen in clusters, I pay heed. I determined to discover for myself exactly what miracle healing really was.

In Harry Edward's publication *A Guide to the Understanding and Practice of Spiritual Healing* I learned that "spiritual healing is a thought process."[4] A typical case would be when a sufferer of a disease of considerable duration is told by medical science he must live with his disease. In desperation he seeks a cure from a spiritual healer. The healing is set in motion through a mental request to "The Healing Forces" from the healer to effect a cure for the afflicted patient. "Within a comparatively short while the symptoms become progressively less, pain dies away, and the ill effects are overcome."[5]

Miracle healing is divided into two categories—absent healing and contact healing. "Absent healing is often considered to be the Cinderella of the healing movement, simply because it is intangible and impersonal, in so far as the healer may not know the patient or even see him at any time. In Contact Healing the body and facilities of the healer are used. The flow of healing energy to the patient is sensed . . . pain is less, minds are less 'harassed,' weak sight and hearing are strengthened, wastage is overcome and so on and so on. The benefit is tangible."[6]

In my experience extensive research into a specific area within the paranormal field is not conducted without purpose. This proved to be the case with miracle healing.

In September of 1984 my husband, Jim, was subjected to the rigors of a kidney stone attack. Anyone who has ever undergone a similar malady will attest to the excruciating pain of such an ailment. Jim was a veteran of several bouts having suffered three such attacks in a score of years. Usually, the jagged stone found passage from his body within a week or less. This instance provided the supreme test, however, as excruciating attacks occurred periodically during September and thereafter Jim was victimized periodically until November 30th when the ongoing affliction ended suddenly in a dramatic conclusion. Initially, neither of us had the slightest idea of the 180 degree turnabout Jim's illness would engender in our attitude toward the traditional methods of healing.

The first step necessary in the treatment of kidney stones is to determine the mass of the stone. Hospital x-rays placed Jim's stone size in a category that was vastly larger than the past three with which he had had to contend. This alarmed us due to the fact that if it would not pass or if it became lodged in the ureter, surgery might be mandated. Faced with these options we returned home and began to utilize all the natural healing remedies for dissolving kidney stones we could possibly locate. Pain was alleviated through application of a castor oil pack to the affected area. Jim consumed cranberry juice by the gallon and a healer friend of ours suggested parsley tea. This time-tested herbal drink served the dual purpose of acting as diuretic and "stone disintegrator." I brewed this daily and Jim swallowed it with a shudder. These treatments proved of some relief as the next set of x-rays revealed the stone had moved two inches down the ureter. We took heart and vigorously continued our home treatment program. Monitoring of the stone's progress several weeks later was disappointing. The stone had shown no further movement.

It was during this period that a physician friend of ours paid us a visit.

One evening the three of us elected to eat dinner at the Island House in Virginia Beach. The subject of our dinner conversation that evening centered around healing and our doctor friend, John, had an unbelievable story to relate. Through the psychic grapevine John had heard of a faith healer in Connecticut who was enjoying great success with incurable illnesses. On an impulse he sent one of his patients to her regular weekend healing service. The patient returned completely cured of a disease which John had treated for months with minimal success. Amazed by this turn of events he was determined to attend her healing service himself to view the "miracles" his former patient had recounted. He traveled to Greenwich, Connecticut, and to his amazement, witnessed healings which he would have considered beyond the realm of possibility. The deaf heard, the lame walked, and malignant growths seemed to dissolve under her touch. Invited for a visit backstage after the four-hour healing service, John set about gathering all the information he could about her personally and professionally. Her name was Grace Di Biccari. She and her husband had founded Grace N' Vessels of Christ Ministries, Inc., located in Brookfield, Connecticut. She did not classify herself as a healer per se but felt rather she was just a tool through whom God worked. She cited the many scriptural healing miracles of Jesus, and related her gift to the same Source.

"Does she dissolve kidney stones?" my husband, Jim, piped up after listening intently to John's animated discourse.

"Why don't you find out for yourself?" John replied with a twinkle in his eye. "It will be an evening you'll never forget."

Jim laughed skeptically at the firm conviction John's tone conveyed. "I'll check my schedule and let you know," Jim replied noncommittally. Later that evening, in the throes of a kidney stone attack, I saw him consult his date book. Stealing a glance over his shoulder, I noted, Trip to Grace N' Vessels—November 29th–30th.

Having been privileged to experience numerous paranormal episodes personally, I was undoubtedly more amenable to the concept of miracle healing than Jim. I was well aware of the belief many fundamentalists held concerning "miracle healers" being instruments of the Devil. I recalled a statement made by George Chapman, miracle healer from England regarding Dr. Lang, the psychic surgeon purported to work through him. He philosophized, "Even though Dr. Lang can quite obviously relieve pain and suffering in many people, some still believe he must be an agent of the Devil just because he is a spirit speaking through a medium. It always amuses me that the Devil is given credit for so much—particularly the bestowing of good health on sick people."[7]

On the trip to Greenwich a friend of John's, who had studied healing and was equally curious about the miracles Grace was reported to perform, Inga and I chatted about healing theories and our own spiritual philosophies. Before long we found ourselves deposited at the door of Greenwich High School in Greenwich, Connecticut, and quickly sought a seat while John parked the car.

The auditorium filled with an air of expectancy, was already crowded although the service was not scheduled to start for half an hour. John joined us shortly and immediately greeted a man seated three seats in back of us to the right. After a brief conversation, he turned toward Jim and introduced him to the small wiry man.

"Grace healed him of incurable lung cancer several months ago," John proclaimed. "Show them your x-rays." With that the stranger triumphantly produced a set of films from his coat pocket and proceeded to unfold them.

"Yep!" he agreed. "I was a goner but Grace dissolved the tumors. I'm a well man today!" If this were actually the case, Grace Di Biccari truly did live up to the appellation so frequently applied to her—*Amazing Grace.*

About that time a guitarist appeared on stage signaling the service was about to begin. Music filled the hall, and amid shouts, clapping, and hymn singing Grace Di Biccari made her debut. She was a small dark women in her 40s, although the youthfulness of her face belied her years. She began to sing "I Saw the Light." It seemed to me as if her voice could have belonged to a trained opera performer. (I found out later she had had a chance to go to Juillard on a music scholarship.) After a bevy of old time hymns were sung, the healing portion of the service commenced.

"There is someone in this section of seats who has been deaf since childhood," she exclaimed pointing to a young girl of 16. She motioned for her to come forward. At her mother's urging the astounded girl complied. Grace then placed her hands over her ears and prayed. Immediately thereafter, she whispered something in her right ear. *The teenager correctly repeated the first words she had heard in more than a decade.* A shower of tears burst forth followed by uncontrollable sobs. Grace clutched the child to her breast. Shouts of joy rang out from the audience at the miracle they had just been privileged to witness. This miracle was followed by other equally impressive healings involving glaucoma, arthritis, and paralyzed limbs. The service continued for three more hours. Heart patients, cancer victims, and diabetics were among the incurables invited to receive The Healing Touch. Many people swooned as the healing energies entered their bodies, and they were caught by Grace's assistants and gently lowered to the floor until their healing was complete.

Finally, at 10:45 PM Grace asked everyone in row two who desired a healing to come forward.

"That's you," I nudged Jim as she beckoned us to proceed to the front of the auditorium. Jim grabbed me by the hand. We walked down the aisle and joined the group already forming a line to become recipients of her gift. As she came nearer, I could physically sense the tremendous healing energies surrounding her. She stood before Jim and looked directly into his eyes.

"Why have you come?" she inquired softly.

"I have a kidney stone," Jim replied, "and would like to avoid surgery if possible!" Without further ado she placed one hand on his back where the kidney stone was lodged and the other on his head and prayed.

"God has dissolved it," she whispered in his ear.

Jim thanked her and we returned to our seats.

"Do you feel she healed you?" I pressed him intently.

"Probably not," Jim retorted with his usual healthy skepticism. "But she sure generated a lot of heat!"

Three days later we left the urologist's office with the answer. *The stone that had been visible on Jim's x-rays three weeks before was no longer in evidence.* The physician could not find a logical explanation for its disappearance other than it had broken up into tiny particles which then passed down the urinary tract and were eliminated. This, however, he felt was unlikely due to the size of the stone and the fact that Jim had felt none of the intense pain which would have accompanied such an occurrence. Since stones are not likely to move back to the kidney, the question remained—where had it gone?

Did Jim tell his doctor how he was cured? *No!* More important—Does Jim believe in miracle healing now? *Yes!*

In reviewing this story the point is this: In spite of the fact that faith is not an essential ingredient in all healings and a healthy, skeptical attitude was maintained by the analytical mind of my husband, Jim was involved long enough in spiritual work to believe that such a healing was possible. It was this small grain of faith "the size of a mustard seed" that served as a catalyst to ignite the healing energies and provide him with the healing for which he had prayed in order to avoid surgery.

PARTNERSHIP HEALING

"Many people hold the mistaken view that spiritual healers are against medicine and that they provide an alternative therapy to medical treatment. In fact, every responsible spiritual healer makes a point of ensuring that his patients have sought medical advice, and the majority believe that a combination of medical and spiritual help is the ideal."[8]

The above statement summarizes my own philosophical stance that has evolved over the years. This has been formulated through a studious pursuit of the subject as well as through experiences. As with most undertakings, a combining of several talents is far more efficacious than a solitary endeavor. Thus, the vigorous application of medical knowledge, spiritual healing, and patient involvement should effect a more rapid and permanent healing than any less complete combination.

In support of my healing philosophy I would cite the case of Mr. Terry Gemilere who, through partnership healing, was able to rid himself of cancer as well as avoid an unwanted ileostomy.

Terry was a student of ours in the first parapsychology class Jim and I taught at Christopher Newport College. He was an unassuming young man of 28 who spoke in class only when he had something important to contribute to the discussion and then presented it in such a way that everyone turned to listen attentively to his point of view. He sat in front of me in class. I often sensed marvelous positive energies surrounding him as Jim lectured and the students took notes. I pondered how he had acquired so much savoir faire for having dwelled such a short period on the Earth Plane. Then, halfway through the semester, I learned the source of his wisdom. The subject under discussion was healing and Terry volunteered to share his experience with his fellow students.

Terry had always dreamed of becoming a soldier. Therefore, after graduation from a military academy, he joined the army and became a member of the intelligence section. As part of his plan for advancement, he determined to seek full training in the School for Special Forces. A requirement for admission was a thorough physical examination. Routine x-rays revealed something that was anything but routine. A closer look at those mysterious dark shadows that presented themselves resulted in an initial diagnosis of ulcerative colitis. This was non-life threatening, but it did render Terry unfit for the Special Forces Program as well as an army career. Immediately thereafter he was released from the service. This was Stress #1. Within a year Stress #2 presented itself in the form of a divorce from his wife. Reeling from two knock-out blows from life, Terry began to drift aimlessly.

In July of 1980 Terry developed extremely high temperatures ranging from 100° to 104°. The first series stayed with him 30 days. After a number of these episodes, he entered the Veteran's

Hospital in Hampton, Virginia for another physical examination. Terry also realized that he was losing weight, but both the nurse and he were shocked when the scale registered 125 pounds. His normal weight was 165. *He had lost 40 pounds in 10 days!* Further tests revealed his blood pressure to be 70/90 with normal being 120/80. Most debilitating of all, however, was the fact that he was losing approximately ¼ of a pint of blood per month from internal bleeding. The previous diagnosis of ulcerative colitis was discarded.

On December 24, 1980, he received a call from the Surgery Clinic of the Veteran's Hospital to schedule a consultation. Arriving at the appointed time, he was ushered into the conference room where three surgeons were seated. The Chief Surgeon, speaking for his colleagues, informed Terry of his condition.

"You have developed cancer of the colon which requires surgical removal. It is necessary to perform an ileostomy to retard the spread. Even if this is done, there is no guarantee that it will provide a permanent cure."

Terry sat stunned. Then, he shook his head in disbelief. He was too young for cancer. Moreover, the prospects of having a bag attached to him for the remainder of his life was not a pleasant prospect. As he mulled the situation over in his mind, a Still Small Voice inside him seemed to be saying, **"If the body is opened up, the cancer will spread."**

The surgeons continued giving advice as he tried to pull himself together. "Why not attend a therapy group of patients who have already undergone the operation? This will acclimate you to the idea and the operation will not seem so ominous," one suggested. "We'll also start chemotherapy after Christmas. This will assist in the healing process."

During Christmas and the weeks following Terry walked through life in a dazed condition. He began chemotherapy in January and immediately became deathly ill from the side effects of the medication. He had yet to sign the papers agreeing to an ileostomy.

During a laying-on-of-hands service that Terry attended, he prayed fervently for spiritual healing. The healing did not occur instantaneously. However, within a week, the name of The Human

Services Institute located in Phoenix, Arizona was given him as a healing alternative to the ileostomy. The program offered by the Institute focused on regenerating health through a holistic healing approach. Terry contacted Dr. John McBride, Director of the clinic, and described his illness to him. Dr. McBride invited him to spend a week in Arizona working with his prescribed regimen and providing his body with a chance to heal itself naturally. Dr. McBride had contracted cancer several years before and had cured himself personally through the method he now advocated for the patients that passed through his center.

Terry discussed Dr. McBride's offer with the team of surgeons at the Veteran's Hospital. They agreed to Terry's proposal to undergo treatment. After all, it *was* his body. But, they advised him, "The longer the cancer remains in the colon, the less will be the chance of long-term survival." Terry weighed all the alternatives and decided to make the journey to Arizona.

The week-long program consisted of a combination of high fiber diet, proper vitamin intake, massages, biofeedback, stress therapy, and visualization. The program boasted an 80% rate of cure with the criteria for cure being remaining cancer-free for five years. The program's main thrust was the negation of the devastating effects of stress upon the body's immunological system. Lectures emphasized that acute and prolonged periods of stress turned off two of the body's three major defense systems. This rendered the individual extremely vulnerable to disease. The point of the relaxation and visualization therapies was to revitalize the body's natural defenses against illness. Relaxation techniques encouraged the glands in the brain to resume production of their natural immunity substances. Then, by visualizing the part of the system that was under attack, the body's own "defense agents" were marshalled and dispatched to wage war and ultimately defeat the debilitating intruders.

Since Terry's health problem was in the colon, his personal visualization technique was to have John Wayne walk through his intestinal tract with a fire hose and wash away all dark or "charred" areas where he sensed the cancer had assaulted the organ. As an end result of the cleansing, he envisioned his colon turning pink and assuming a normal state of health.

Terry entered into the healing process with a "partnership attitude"—attuned to both sets of doctors with whom he had a relationship. He also maintained a stalwart faith that he would absolutely triumph over his cancer. Terry proved to be an avid student, learning his lessons well and exhibiting a zeal for adopting a new lifestyle which several months before he would have considered impossible. In the weeks following his return to Virginia, he continued to faithfully practice the modes of his new life model.

Thirty days after he instituted the program the bleeding stopped. He began to reclaim some of the weight that had melted away from his ravaged frame. All signs pointed to a physical healing.

In July of 1981, the surgeons at the Veteran's Hospital pronounced him in official remission. "And," added Terry as his classmates gazed upon his broad physique with a new attitude of esteem, "I have no doubt that I will be completely well at the end of five years."

After a short period of time one of the more inquisitive students piped up, "Could you share with us an abbreviated form of the healing methods offered by The Human Services Institute?"

"Of course," responded Terry agreeably. "I'll cite the major points of emphasis if you'd like to take notes." Then, for twenty minutes he proceeded to outline the therapy that saved his life. "I am certain the primary key to cancer remission is the maintenance of a positive attitude on the part of each patient. At the outset of the program we were given books on the subject. These were entitled *You Can Learn to Live* and *How to Fight for Your Life.* The publications described how visualization and a healing orientation can change the immune system of the body.

"A second point of importance was the detoxification of one's body. Most surgeons who operate on colons find them coated with impacted foods from an improper diet. The detoxification process consisted of a liquid diet, internal cleansing, and vitamin ingestion. This tended to ready the body for the future therapies.

"Nutrition, of course is always important for good health, and we were instructed to eliminate all sugar from our diet, as cancer feeds on sugar. Additional dietary recommendations were a switch from red meats to fish and fowl, no ingestion of coffee, and one addition of bran and high fiber foods. High fiber acts like a sponge to soak up moisture and also sweeps the colon like a broom. One final thing—we were told not to mix vegetables and fruit, as this causes an adverse enzymatic reaction. A space of 2 hours is recommended between each consumption.

"Vitamin therapy is important. We were placed on specified dosages of B complex, which promotes relief of tension and muscle relaxation. Ingestion of selenium in combination with Vitamin E acts as an antioxident which protect the chromosomes from damage which lead to cancer. Vitamin A or Beta Carotene is another good vitamin defense against cancer. Since each individual's metabolism is different, one should see a doctor or nutritionist regarding the amount prescribed.

"Finally, my strong religious beliefs were a core factor in my healing. I had implicit faith in the Universal Force leading me and encouraging me to heal myself through partnerships with physicians, healers, and Guidance from a Higher Dimension. And as you can see, it worked!"

On November 23, 1985 I received a note from Terry concerning his progress. Several months ago his doctors had detected a small benign tumor. Optimistic as ever, he ended his correspondence with this statement. "As you would guess, I went into therapy and took a leave of absence from school. Luckily, the classes should be easy to make up. Present diagnosis—the tumor is gone. It was small to begin with, but no surgery was required. I did it again!!!"

The three types of healing that have been examined in this chapter are surgical healing, miracle healing, and partnership healing. The type of healing appropriate for you depends on the current condition of your body, the attitude you maintain toward your illness, and the lesson you have chosen to learn. An excerpt from Mikhail Naimy's *The Book of Mirdad* (Stuart and Watkins) summarizes the essence of this chapter.

Man invites his own calamities and then protests against the irksome guests, having forgotten how, and when, and where, he penned and sent out the invitations. Time does not forget; and Time delivers in due Season, each invitation to the right address; and Time conducts each invitee to the dwelling of the host—

Accept a misfortune as if it were a fortune. For a misfortune, once understood, is soon transformed into a fortune; while a fortune misconstrued quickly becomes a misfortune. . . .

There are no accidents in Time and Space; but all things are ordered by the Omni-will. (Quoted in *Surgeon from Another World,* by George Chapman and Roy Steinman, p. 128.)

CHAPTER 3

The Psychical Research Project

Akashic-Records **It is the record that the individual entity itself writes upon the skein of Time and Space, through Patience, and is opened when self has attuned to the Infinite and may be read by those attuning to that consciousness.**

Mary Ellen Carter—*Edgar Cayce On Prophecy*

THE CONCEPTION OF THE PROJECT

The Psychical Research Project was a direct outgrowth of a previous study—College Psychical Research Project—which was described in *The Inner Eye.* The new project differed in format and procedure due to the acquisition of more sophisticated intuitive skills coupled with a finer appreciation of the individual needs which must necessarily be met at the level of soul development radiated by each participant. The continuous intermingling of these two elements eventually culminated in a creation termed *The Holistic Life Reading.* The process of development of this individualized type of intuitive reading should be of particular interest to those who are engaged in developing their own unique style and form of spiritual channeling.

I had been the instrument through which psychical information flowed abundantly for over two years. Refinement of the reading process was a continuing "labor of love" for both my husband and me. We hoped to procure the best knowledge possible for the betterment of the quality of life of our clients. This is what counseling is about. There was no doubt in my mind that rapid advancements had already been made, but from my deeper subconscious I received periodic promptings that enormous sources of information remained untouched. We had not yet developed a precise formula for assembling responsible and non-prejudical feedback.

Another point for resolution had to do with a competitive attitude on the part of many of the intuitives Jim and I encountered as we engaged in our ongoing program of psychical research. Several of these supersensitives displayed awesome talents, but they had become so preoccupied with pride in their own accomplishments that their egos had become their greatest karmic burden. On the several occasions on which I had witnessed psychic rivalry between such individuals, the furiousness with which they entered into such competition was frightening. There were, however, several scientifically oriented, well-balanced intuitives we knew such as Alan Vaughan and Douglas Johnson. Making their acquaintance provided me with assurance that one could be the possessor of a supersensitive personality and yet retain some sense of humility.

These promptings surfaced intermittently as I drove back and forth to my counseling practice, when viewing a mindless television program, or in the rare moments when I sought the solitude of my Shellbank retreat and had time to reflect upon personal issues that really were of key importance for balance and harmony in all facets of my life. This situation remained static until the morning of January 1, 1984. It was then that the Forces determined I had stewed about this idea sufficiently and was, by now, malleable enough to be the co-designer and custodian of a completely new formula for restructing and refining our current intuitive reading program. As I awakened, I realized I had the entire format in my mind. I sprang out of bed, rushed to the phone, and forgetting the earliness of the hour, immediately dialed Elizabeth Hollis's number in Winston-Salem, North Carolina. She and John were about to become partners with Jim and me in creating what would later be known as a *Holistic Life Reading.*

Jim and I had known John and Elizabeth Hollis since 1982. Our friendship with them had proved to be a source of both joy and spiritual expansion. As each husband–wife team individually explored ever-broadening metaphysical vistas, they shared their newly acquired knowledge with the other partnership. Initially, Jim had taught John and Elizabeth the fundamentals of past-life regressions. This avenue of exploration felt so comfortable to their psyches that within a short period of time they became deeply enmeshed in their own unique form of "readings research." Working as a team, they were now quite adept at securing reincarnational sketches of past lives for friends and acquaintances who desired such information. Elizabeth served as "the channel" and John, her analytical guide. John and Jim maintained the identical focus—*If this phenomena is an actuality, how then can it be utilized to optimum advantage for the benefit of humankind?* To this end Elizabeth and I were never allowed to settle complacently into our intuitive work. Our husbands were always presenting us with new challenges to be met and new frontiers to be conquered.

During the two-year period that we had known the Hollises, I learned that not only did Elizabeth and John excel in past-life readings, but the personality analysis Elizabeth devised for each client could be counted among the most insightful tools with which I had come in contact throughout my fifteen-year practice. *In short, what Jim and I lacked, our counterparts, John and Elizabeth Hollis could provide. This was the catalyst that propelled me out of bed and sent me scurrying to the phone on that cold New Year's morning.*

"Hello," a sleepy voice answered after three long rings.

"Sister Elizabeth, Sister Elizabeth! Wake up! This is Sister Joan calling," I began excitedly. (We teasingly addressed each other in this fashion. The term Sister had originated when, through a past-life regression, we had discovered we shared a life together as nuns in sixteenth-century France.) "I just woke up with a marvelous new idea for refining our intuitive reading process. I just had to phone you and John for your input."

"Wake up, John!" Elizabeth's tone of voice indicated she was now wide awake and touting her slumbering spouse. "We are about to embark on another intriguing expedition with the Windsors. Grab your dream journal and pen on the nightstand and take notes."

"You know how much I detest competition among psychics and the degree to which I have been bothered by the incompleteness of our present format of intuitive reading," I continued. The words seemed to rush out before I opened my mouth. "Well, I believe these problems have truly served as an impetus toward achievement of a more sophisticated and polished type of product. Knowing me so well you are also aware that I administer not just one, but a complete battery of tests to the individual clients I evaluate. This approach provides me with a holistic profile of their personality rather than just examining intelligence, perception, and memory in isolation. Why not apply the same concept in the context of our readings?"

"That sounds like a truly viable approach to upgrading the quality of our work," Elizabeth replied laughingly. "Also, because we know you and Jim so well," she continued, "I know we shall soon be over our heads in this project before the week is out. What can we do to assist?" I could hear John pumping her for information in the background.

"Our readings should be all encompassing. Thus, a holistic reading should be comprised of six sections, each of which speaks to a significant portion of the client's entire life blueprint. Sections included would be Physical Symbology, Current Issues, Future Trends, Character Assessment, Past Lives, and Soul's Purpose. The justification of each section is as follows:

1. *Physical Symbology*–This is an extremely important section because the condition of our bodily health symbolizes the issues with which we are currently dealing as well as the soul lessons we have elected to pursue. This should not be viewed as a medical diagnosis, but merely an examination of one's bodily health as related to one's entire psyche.

2. *Current Issues*–The current issues section deals with subjects such as marital relationships, the acquisition of income, career choices, and life involvement with one's children and parents to cover a few areas. These seem to be the most frequent questions posed by our clients.

3. *Future Trends*–The future portion of each reading could contain predictions concerning the outcome of the matters discussed in the Current Issues part, as well as the prognostication of entirely new ideas of which the client is as yet unaware.

4. *Character Analysis*–This section shows us our attitudes and the variety of ways we can act and react in the world. Since our attitudes determine our actions and therefore our destiny, our understanding of these attitudes is important if we are to have an impact on our lives.

5. *Past Lives*–The past life information gives us clues to how our past behavior or life settings may be affecting us in the present. Understanding of behavior may lead to resolution of problems and the ability to let go of old habits. If we can make good use of the knowledge of strengths and weaknesses, this information can be very useful.

6. *Soul's Purpose*–Each reading should conclude with an explanation of the purpose chosen by the soul to be used as an ideal for this particular incarnation.

"A system for a numerical evaluation of the reading should be instituted so we can statistically determine its accuracy. In that way we can factor out the types of errors we are making and improve our 'batting average.' Any comments?"

"Just one," Brother John chimed in on the extension phone. "When do we start?"

The first order of business was to locate a population of subjects consisting entirely of strangers so there would be no way possible to contaminate the results with familiarity. Jim proposed we contact Paul Zuromski, editor of *Body, Mind And Spirit* and run an ad in that publication to solicit subjects for our experiment. The readers of *Body, Mind And Spirit* would undoubtedly be interested in participation in such a research project. Therefore, we felt our choice of subjects would be highly motivated to supply us with the type of information required for evaluating the validity of our Holistic Life Readings.

After the ad was placed, I composed guidelines for assessing a reading as well as an evaluation system to ascertain the accuracy of the document. These were to be sent out with each psychic manuscript. The Displacement item was added in 1985. Therefore, the scoring system was 1–3 initially. The guidelines read as follows:

Suggestions for Interpreting Your Intuitive Reading

The reading you requested has been completed. If properly utilized, it may assist you in gaining a better understanding of yourself and your present and future challenges. When reviewing it, the following guidelines should be taken into consideration:

1. The present and future events contained therein are "impressions" which have come through the intuitive's subconscious. As a result some slight changes may have occurred. Don't expect all information or predictions to be exact. These are only "tendencies" toward events.

2. There is a time distortion in the intuitive realm. Events perceived may happen within days, weeks, months, or even years after they have been seen initially. Therefore, your interpretation of the time element should be flexible.

3. Some of the thoughts picked up are truly "thought patterns." Therefore, these may never manifest themselves in physical reality.

4. *The physical and health portions of the reading should in no way be regarded as a medical diagnosis or prescribed medical*

treatment. The health suggestions given have a "natural healing" orientation and should be viewed as such.

5. *The reading is given for research purposes only and should not be used as a basis for decision making.*
6. Since some of the information contained in an intuitive reading is obtained from the individual, the more receptive one is, the better the quality of the reading.
7. Remember, there are few absolutes in the intuitive realm. There is, however, much to be gained and learned about oneself and life through intuitive sources. Generally, all that is given is needed and should be seen as constructive and helpful. If the reading is received with this attitude, considerable benefits and progress can result.

Evaluation Sheet

Please respond to the numbered items as follows:

1. Correct
2. Correct-*Displacement (Added 1985)*
3. Partially Correct
4. Incorrect

Following each rating supply the reason for the rating to confirm or deny the statement.

Please note a rating of (2) indicates the presence of displacement. This carries with the rating the implication that while the impression is not for you *personally,* it is correct for someone within your family circle or a close associate. This type of rating provides the reading with a more discriminating factor than if a rating system was merely 1, 2, and 3. Where it is not possible to rate statements (i.e.: Future Trends, Soul's Purpose), please write a short paragraph as to whether such remarks would fit your personality, life style, interests, etc.

We would be pleased to receive any additional insights that you might have to offer.

Now the stage was set for a response.

Within three weeks several applications arrived. Now our work began in earnest. I would forward Elizabeth a copy of the application blank containing the data necessary for her to complete her portion of the reading. Accompanying these were 4 questions asked by the participant on any subject of his or her choosing. She would then tape her Character Assessment and Past Life Reading and forward them to Betty Hall, my secretary, to type in numbered manuscript form. Betty would assemble her reading and mine and mail them out with accompanying instructions regarding the feedback requirement.

It might be of interest for my readers to review the process by which Elizabeth and I received our intuitive insights. In summary, each of us would place ourselves in a mildly altered state of consciousness, hold the client's picture or handwriting sample in our left hand, and view, hear, or sense the impressions that flowed into our subconscious minds. These would then be recorded on tape and typed in manuscript form. Impressions such as these can be received in a normal state of consciousness, but I find that in a relaxed state impressions flow more abundantly. (Detailed instructions regarding the procedure for developing advanced intuition are contained in Chapter 10.)

After four manuscripts had been produced, we received our first evaluation. We averaged about 70 percent accuracy over all, but our clients were very impressed with both the form and style of our Holistic Life Reading. We felt we were in the ballpark and had made it to first base.

As more and more readings were evaluated and returned, we reassessed our techniques and learned from our errors. (A summary of these revisions is contained in Chapter 9.) Our batting average began to soar so much so that after 3 months it was a rarity to score below a 75–90 percent rate of accuracy.

We never read one another's work until our personal analysis was completed. The overlap between the readings was impressive given the fact that Elizabeth worked in Winston-Salem, North Carolina and I in Williamsburg, Virginia. *The point to be made here is cooperation between psychics for the good of the client is an attitude to be courted rather than challenged, for in the spirit of cooperation, "miracles" became commonplace.*

There were, of course, occasional failures. One involved a man who requested a psychic reading for his wife and then responded to all the items for her himself. The reading pointed out she was a woman who was a victim of suppressed anger. He vehemently denied this saying *he* had asked her about this and she agreed with his point of view.

Another recorded failure was in connection with a woman who requested we read her future and then shot the entire reading down in one curt sentence which read as follows: "No one can read my future but me!"

There were several mediocre returns, but I can safely state the majority of the readings done within the context of The Psychical Research Project achieved high grades for accuracy. The primary point of value, however, was the degree to which our clients felt they had benefited from our service and the plaudits of gratitude expressed for the type of counseling provided. This, after all, was the crucial motivator for all of us on the Psychical Research Staff.

As with *The Inner Eye,* my husband, Dr. James Windsor will supply a more formal analysis of our research in Chapter 4. Before this formal presentation, however, I have selected for inclusion within the pages of the Psychical Research Project Chapter several sample readings so that the reader may judge for himself the quality of our Holistic Life Readings. (Names have been changed for the sake of anonymity. Responses are in italics.)

Laura Allen—September 30, 1984

Physical Symbology

1. There is a very fine, highly developed brain. A very clear, well-formed brain free from any insults. There is well-developed thinking.—*Thanks. I think so.*

2. She had excellent vision at one time, extremely precise both at near and far point. An infection of the eyes in her late teens occurred. She was ill with perhaps the flu leaving her body in a weakened condition. Soon thereafter, the germ within the body migrated to the eye area weakening the eyes and allowing infection to set in. This lasted two or three weeks and caused some concern about loss of vision.—*Yes. True. This was after the car wreck. I lost my vision for an extended time period. I was very weak with various infections while in the hospital.*

3. I get the impression she was taken to a vision specialist—Dr. Howard——baum (?) He switched medications from what had been prescribed and the infection cleared up in four days.—*Yes. After car wreck.*

4. This is important at this point because she needs to watch this area of weakness when she becomes tired, stressed, and run down. The eyes "have it" meaning from the weakness the problems show up more in the eyes than in other areas.—*Very True.*

5. Eating lots of carrots with the Vitamin A (Beta Carotene) is suggested.—*Thank you.*

6. I get the impression of a muscle balance weakness in the left eye when she was younger.—*Yes. Even today, but right eye is weaker than left as time has progressed.*

7. There may have been a minor operation when she was younger. The impression is that there should have been, or there was. A muscle weakness seems to have been present. *I poked a metal stick into my eye at about age 7 or 8 and this required work by specialists (the left eye).*

8. It seems that Laura uses her eyes a lot as she does a lot of reading, not just for educational need but just likes to read—an avid reader on many subjects and this use of the eyes tends to weaken an already weak area—over use.—

Very True. This was in part from the times when there was nobody with which to play. I live on books to this day.

9. It appears she has reduced her allergies with a change of diet. There are some fall-backs, but her change of diet within the past year has been of great benefit to the body.—*This is really not reliable. I have never had any diagnosed allergies. I have, however, had health problems that well could be food-related.*

10. I see at one time the nasal passages were stuffed up and clogged. At the present they are clear with free breathing. It seems she may indulge in *breathing exercises* also for the body which has brought a balance in energies. She should continue in this aspect of the healing arts for this has been and will continue to be of great benefit to this body—the breathing purification of the body.—*I have had a lot of work done on my nose, this is very true. The last operation was to correct the deviated septum that was totally blocking one side of my nose.*

11. Some tendencies toward allergies continue. This is concerning chocolate (she loves chocolate—gets high ingesting chocolate so there is a weakness here.) She is allergic to chocolate—a reason she likes it so well.—*Very, Very, True—Only never diagnosed.*

12. There is still a tendency to be allergic to pollens in the air at certain times of the year. This was severe enough at one time to consider or to have shots. This is greatly improved but there is still a tendency toward this.—*Not True. I have in the last year had some small problem by moving here perhaps. Nothing that has bothered me to any great extent. My sister had a great and still has a great problem with allergies. As a child I did have enormous problems with throat infections and ear infections even after the removal of my tonsils. At this time there was little knowledge about allergies and I was never tested.*

13. I am getting that she has this tendency to eat fruits high in Vitamin C—tomatoes especially. This will help to counteract the pollen problem. Ingest bioflavanoids—orange and lemon peels also in the raw state, not the bioflavanoid pill, but peelings of oranges and lemons are suggested for the pollen problem.—*True. I love spagetti as well as pizza and ketchup. I eat large amounts of acid fruits as well.*

14. She has had some trouble with her teeth—abscesses on the teeth—one is coming up within the next six months. The problem will be on the lower back right of the mouth (middle of December comes through.)—*This was found about one and one-half years ago. I had my wisdom teeth removed and by the time I got the nerve to go back for cavities, I was pregnant. Thanks for the advice.*

15. Laura needs to increase her calcium intake. I am getting that there may be a calcium deficiency in the body. She needs to increase milk—dairy product intake in her diet.—*True. I try but I never developed a taste for dairy products. My mother refers to the fact that if I was bad as a very young child, my father would dump my milk on my head as punishment. I am trying to get milk into my system.*

16. She must have had a lot of vaginal infections—yeast infections. The area of reproduction, the vagina, the ovaries, and all, the uterus are another area of weakness. There were lots of infections in the past. It was very persistent reoccurring, weakening the areas of reproduction organs.—*Very True.*

17. She is very prone to reflexology and balance. She is sensitive in the sense that her body responds very quickly to treatments. Therefore, foot reflexology or just a good massage of the feet will balance the polarities in the body and send healing energies to distressed areas.—*Very True. My husband gives superb foot massages and now I don't have to look hard for excuses.*

Current Issues—Laura Allen

1. A carry back to the past with a boyfriend. His name pops up here . . . I get the basic thread through his reading is a tendency to do what people who have cysts do—hold on to things long after they are useful.—*True.*

2. The purpose that the boyfriend served in this life was to be a motivator. Apparently he was able to get her to focus on things that she would not have otherwise. He served as a catalyst getting her interested in subjects she would not have otherwise pursued.—*My marriage with him was the main reason that I began to change my diet. The other interesting thing is the fact that I may never have moved to this area if not to be with him and look at all the good things that have come from this move!!!*

3. He served as a catalyst and steered her in that direction.—*True.*

4. He got her interested in healing and helping other people—to serve others. He taught her pain which in this case was not bad because through pain one grows. When one can understand pain oneself, then he can empathize with others and therefore be a better counselor.—*True.*

5. He was the motivator, the catalyst, the pain provider, but the growth provider. This was his role in this life.—*True.*

6. This individual is a healer in the finest sense of the word. She is an energy provider rather than a laying-on-of-the-hands or a nutritional prescription or chiropractic healing type of individual. *True. It has been mentioned at several points that people feel that I am a very bubbly or energetic person.*

7. She processes energy extremely well and passes it on to others so when one "is in her care," the energies flow well and persons who come to her or are assigned to her, benefit from the kindnesses, the extra energy flow, the intuitive insights to know what that person needs to feel better physically, mentally, and lately spiritually. Through reading she is now able to provide spiritual insights to people that she was not able to do without the background that she has come to possess in just the last three or four months. This is a new insight. Before she was providing the physical healing with the passing of physical energies, now it is more mental and the newest again is the spiritual.—*True. I share things that I feel are important with others out of my caring nature as well as the fact that I tend to enter into other's personal affairs. If you are in my house, then you do as Caesar does and I must admit that I make a great Caesar.*

8. I get the impression that she was a very lonely child when she was 7, 8, and 9. She felt like an outsider. I see her sitting on a three-step-stoop while other girls are playing nearby while she just sits and watches. She buries herself in books. She was very much a loner which is not all bad as sometimes in solitude one gains more than if one is constantly with others. There is a tendency to look inwardly and to examine oneself so it is not a negative aspect of her life, but a time of looking inwardly at her personality better and to utilize the time constructively when she is alone. This pattern probably has carried on through her existence although she began to be more friendly and more outgoing. She made friends in her teenage years and growing up, but as a child I see her as very lonely.—*True. I used to sit about three steps high on the back porch (there are a total of nine steps) and watch the children play through the hedges. Even as a child I remember reflecting on why people were so mean.*

9. This brought the pattern into existence to constructively use times of isolation for growth rather than be down or despondent. She didn't, she learned how to use her time productively.—*Very True.*

10. I feel that she may have been an only child—isolated from her family in some way when she was young. I see the house. She appears to be perhaps with an aunt whom she stays with for long periods of time. I don't mean that she is completely away from the family, but seems to spend extended periods of time away from them—with a relative. This was good and bad.—*Although I have a sister, we are seven years apart and we're far from being close. She was only two when my mother and stepfather began dating and they were more of a "family" due to the fact that she called him daddy and was accepting of him. I spent as much time as possible with my aunt (mother's sister). I have adopted several of her qualities (good and bad).*

11. She developed a good relationship with this relative—(Aunt?) Seems to have somewhat of a feeling of being unwanted. This carries on through life.—*True. No matter how good things seem to be there is still a bit of skepticism in each relationship that I have due to the past.*

12. Her past all ties into the present. What she has done with her adversities is that when confronted with this, she is determined that it not defeat her, but to grow through this. I get the words "grown through pain and adversity." Each time she has worked out a solution to these problems. She is a highly inventive and intuitive soul who has used the adversities to her own purposes.—*Very True.*

13. In reference to the questions concerning her vocation—I get the word "therapy." I see her working with people, massaging their legs as with stroke victims. Rehabilitation—therapy connected with this. People being taught to walk again, I see them using the rails, stretching the arms with mechanical apparatus for improvement of muscles and balance types of activities.—*I have two things that have gotten my interest. The first is working with older people and the second (more recently in the last year) working with special children. I love children and have talked with my roommate (the person in my future reading?) about opening either a day care center* *for the aged, or for the special children. Either will have persons with the description in #13.*

14. It seems to be a long time before she comes to this. It will come about in a roundabout sort of way later in her life—perhaps in her late thirties. She has some trouble getting this degree she is pursuing but she will succeed.—*Probably. Gee Thanks.*

15. She has two things going for her that others don't have in this rehabilitation or therapy she will provide. She has developed her own healing besides the energies. At this point she is so well into the psychic healing and the *homeopathic* and *neuropathic* therapies that she can advise people in dietary remedies which is an added bonus for these individuals. This doesn't come through graduate school. *True. I'm working on this as I can.*

16. Another thing that most therapists do not have: She visualizes the healing that she wants to take place. In her mind, she is such an energy producer that not only does she surround them with this energy, but pictures the effects of the healing in her mind, and it will take place within the person. Excellent visualization skills and can transfer the picture in her mind into the reality of the person. She is not so much a laying-on-of-hands person—she does the massage well, but the energies don't flow through the hands for instant healing. Her real healing comes from surrounding the person with her energy and thoughts and picturing in her mind sent to the person in need—incorporating it into his aura and becoming healed.—*I hope to learn more of this.*

Future Trends—Laura Allen

1. There is a lady in her class that she is working on—teaching her the dreams, passing on health ideas. Why? She sees in her things that she has healed in herself. Because she is doing this for this lady, the energies flow back to her tenfold and provide her with a healthy atmosphere for her physical health.—*True. This is Ann. This explains part of the closeness although we are not as much interested in the same things as far as recreational time activities.*

2. This lady weighs about 220 lbs., curly brown hair, and is single. There appears to be a physical handicap—a limp, or a strange walk. It seems to be a temporary thing probably from an injury.—*Ann? Sprained her leg.*

3. Laura is worried about money. The aunt is going to provide her with help. I see additional money through the family somehow. Unexpected money—several thousand dollars. It will be timely when it is needed the most—through family ties—no strings attached. A relief.—*Same aunt who is helping now?*

Character Assessment—Laura Allen

1. This individual tends to keep a certain amount of distance between herself and other people that she comes in contact with. She is a friendly person and full of kindness, yet finds it difficult to become close to others and fears too much intimate contact.—*This is true. Although I am friendly, I have few friends that are extremely close to me. I am, by nature, very cautious in my dealings with others. This is what I refer to as a basic mistrust of people. They have to "earn" the privilege of my closeness.*

2. She is independent in some areas, yet finds herself wanting to be depended on by someone else.—*This is seen in my clear need to have a man in my life. I am not comfortable when I am single and not involved with a man.*

3. Her mind is very quick and very intuitive. She is a very intelligent individual.—*I have knowledge in many areas. This is reflective of the reading that I have always done. This was* *mentioned in the current life reading. When considering the Jungian type scale, I am very intuitive. This was measured on the Myers-Briggs type indicator test.*

4. She doesn't always go through the same rational thought processes as others do, and she might be hard-pressed to explain how she came to some conclusion, yet she very often comes to the right conclusion.—*This is true and I become frustrated when others question my judgement. I fully expect others to just accept what I say.*

5. In her partnerships she seems to have more of a sisterly relationship than a strong intimate partnership.—*I have very few intimate relationships. I have been hurt in the past. Although I do not hold resentment, I am not easily accessible to people.*

6. She is a hard and ambitious worker. She has a good deal of energy and endurance. She sees what she wants to achieve and works until she completes it. There is a lot of strength in her work, and she is one who should always work and never be without a project to keep her occupied.—*I am often hung up in the notion of getting something done. It is not unusual for me to ignore other responsibilities to get the supplies for another project. I often wonder if I want to complete the project, or just have the necessary supplies at hand.*

7. It is important to her to grow and expand. She has an interest in higher education, and in all its facets . . . understanding of philosophy, and the universe, as well as simply achieving a degree of some sort.—*Very True.*

8. She has an interest in the metaphysical, a desire to understand what makes the world go round, and what she can do to understand herself better.—*My self-improvement projects are perhaps the things that are most important to me now.*

9. I feel that she will do best, and learn most, when she is associated with someone else while she does it—a companion with the same interests. In working with others, somehow she will be able to gain the most understanding about herself through others.—*There is very little that I do alone in my life. I don't understand this part of me, yet in all honesty I get little done when I am alone. When I do things with others, I get much more done.*

10. There is a great deal of intensity in her relationship with her children, and in her experience of having and raising children. She may wish to have more than one. It is an expanding type of experience for her, one that helps her understand herself better, but not one that she takes lightly at all.—*I have a need to have more children. I am fascinated with this entire process. I am not sure, however, how many more times I can give birth to children that go to heaven before I can know them, and have them to be with me. I guess God will give me the strength.*

11. She is more than normally awed and impressed by the mystery of childbirth and having children. She is one that should be very cautious about using drugs, or any kind of substance that affects a baby as she is unusually sensitive to these.—*I crave sugar and sweet things. I used sugar substitutes with the last pregnancy. I am on a yeast-free and mold-free diet. This does not allow for any natural sweeteners.*

12. I would caution her to take care that she is eating enough protein foods and excluding foods that have no value except caloric value. The intake of protein is very important and a sufficient quantity is recommended.—*I am often called a left-over flower child. I dress differently and am, in fact, very hard to buy clothing for.*

13. Her taste in possessions is a bit unusual. She may be a person who fancies objects that are strange in some way. It seems that she is not conservative in her choice of material possessions. She may wear clothes that are unusual or present herself to the world in a different sort of way.—*#12 applies here also.*

14. One method of presenting one's self to the world is through writing. She may have an inclination, or an ability to write. I don't see this as a creative fantasy as I see it as non-fiction, practical sort of writings—something useful to her. If she keeps a journal of some kind, or a dream diary, she will find it very helpful to her.—*I keep a dream diary. I do this more intermittently than I prefer. Although I enjoy and have benefited from working on my dreams, I don't take the time that I should.*

15. She has a knack for being able to look forward into the future and feeling comfortable with the future, and yet she treasures the past in a special sort of way. She is interested in history and her traditions, her origins. This shows itself sometimes in her ability to get along with persons of another generation—both younger and older people. She is able to span generations in her understanding. She is not caught with only her own generation.—*This is all true except one point. I am not comfortable with the future. In contrast, it often scares me. I see life as working in cycles.*

16. I see her health picture changing frequently. Events may occur which surprise her at the time. She may be subject to some kind of a stiffening condition—arthritis possibly. This will be mirrored by a freezing, or an unchanging mental condition also. Once she starts becoming very set in her ways, then it tends to be reflected in the physical.—*I am a very firm person. I have principles that often get in my way. When I try to be flexible, I take the stress inward. I am trying, but this has not been an area of success for me.*

Past Lives—Laura Allen

1. I get the impression of a very open, sandy place like a desert. It is very flat and hard packed. There are little dunes and hills and much loose, soft sand. There is some brush.

2. I see a caravan of a small group of people—12 to 15.

3. They are dressed in desert robes.—*One of the things that is very interesting is the fact that I dislike tight clothing. Although I was brought up in an open environment, I particularly enjoy loose robes. Since my travels in East Africa, I have adopted robes as a part of my wardrobe. In particular, I dislike anything tight around my neck. I do not wear turtleneck items. Although I will wear loose shoes, I prefer lightweight shoes.*

4. This seems to be the Near East.

5. The people are tall and rather dark. The men are bearded and the women have dark, braided hair, or rather just twisted so that it hangs in kind of a ponytail long down their backs.—*Many psychologists state that women with long hair are independent. I am very independent and I enjoy my hair long. I have often thought that my biggest mistake was when I cut off my hair that streamed down my back. I am still trying to grow it back.*

6. I get the impression here that she is one of these women—the one who is in charge—the oldest woman.

7. She is tending a fire and seems to be giving orders for packing and arranging food. It appears they are moving from this area. They are nomadic people.—*It is important that many people have a home, a base so to speak. I, on the other hand, have never felt that I have a real home in that I would prefer to move again someday. My life is where it takes me. Perhaps that explains my particular hold on material things.*

8. She is in her early to mid-forties.

9. The group consists of four or five women, their men, and some children—three or four children ranging from 8 to 12.

10. This is a special group of people. They are traveling and gathering information for a much larger band—perhaps an actual caravan. I don't know why the women would be with the group, but they are a small group with a special purpose.

11. This woman has an odd sort of name. It starts with M—Mehlhengh—lots of h's here. She is in charge of the other women—the grandmother. She is accorded a lot of respect for her age and her children.—*One of the characteristics that I have relates to being in charge. I am a leader. I have respect to the others in a group, yet I have no patience for a leaderless group. I rather naturally take charge.*

12. She is kind of a healer or a doctor. She knows medicines. She is the one people go to if they have been injured, or if they have something in the eye that is festering. I see her dealing with eyes, helping people with poultices, etc.

13. I see them rejoining their caravan. A huge group of people—hundreds of people. They split up and go to their own families. Some of the women among them have left small babies, and they go back and retrieve their babies that were too small to take on this special trip.

14. When Mehlhengh comes back, she and her husband go to the great-grandfather of the group—the leader of the group. They tell him about what signs they saw—two or three of them interpret.

15. They are sort of like priests or priestesses. They are individuals who have the spiritual care of their caravan.

16. Based on the information that they came back with, the caravan prepares to go off. They have decided to go west and stay near a mountain for the winter season. The signs were that it would be a hard winter so they will head for a protected area rather than staying on the open desert.

17. I see her training younger women to work with the medicines. She is also a midwife. She attends the women who are giving birth.

18. She has been hardened by her life, and although she did not seek to become an elder and a person of respect in this group, as she grew and learned it was evident that she was an appropriate choice.

19. She had to suffer in the training to become a spiritual leader, and she was denied many things that others were able to have. She was deprived in a way, making her become hardened. This was necessary for her, but it also shut her off from some pleasures in life.—*This is very evident in this life as well. I suffered a lot so far in this lifetime. Thank GOD not physically, but more so emotionally, and materialistically. I feel that those are the things which have made me the individual that I am today. I don't think that I would change many things in this life, even if I had the chance. I have a blind trust in GOD. I feel that all things have a purpose in life.*

20. There are many new babies each season. Taking care of them and especially the birthing is a big responsibility for her. She is responsible not only for delivering the babies, but also for determining whether or not they can survive. She is the one responsible for helping them out of the world if she determines that they won't survive. A great responsibility on her.—*I have a special part of me drawn to this topic. We are hoping to start our next child in February. I have a great understanding of medical things, birth in particular. With my first husband, we had an agreement that I would not go to the hospital to bear our children. We both felt that we wanted to have a midwife and ourselves.*

21. Occasionally a woman will have twins and the tradition is not to keep both babies unless there can be found another woman in the tribe who so recently lost a baby that she is still able to nurse. If there is no wet nurse available, then one is killed and left while the band of people travels on.

22. Occasionally she is feared and hated by women in the group because she is seen as the one making the decisions and although for the most part her decisions are fair and appropriate, she incurs some animosity from the distraught women.

23. This is one of the hardnesses, one of the difficulties, restrictions that she is obliged to accept by her position. Someone has to make these decisions for the good of the tribe.

24. When she gets old, and it is time for her to die, she has given the power into the hands of a prodigy. This woman tells her she is unable to travel with the group any longer. She finds her a place to wait for death by a rock or a cave. She waits there and dies within three or four days from no water. She was near 60 which is very old in this time.

25. She spent this lifetime obeying laws. Her whole lifetime seems surrounded by laws, requirements, and duties she was fulfilling. She did this well.—*I have a good orientation to rules. I respect them yet I am definitely into free choices. I often "assist" the rules in getting what I want or need. Making choices is hard for me sometimes, and with major changes, I feel insecure. I will often seek outer imput to make myself secure. This may relate to my need to prove myself to others.*

Soul's Purpose—Laura Allen

Through adversity, frustration, and in a sense of futility at times, this soul has achieved a pattern of growth and a positive focus toward each major issue of life with which she was confronted.

The major task this entity has chosen in this existence for herself is to overcome physical abnormalities, or weaknesses, these being the challenges, and thereafter, utilize her knowledge for the benefit of all of those with whom she subsequently comes into contact. This purpose is now being achieved—has been, is, and will be.

Joanna Hunt—December 11, 1984

Physical Symbology

1. This is a soul with gentleness surrounding her—*Incorrect. My life is on tension most of the time.*

2. The hair falls in short, soft ringlets, signifying tender caressing thoughts involving not only herself, but those closest to her.—*Incorrect. Permanent only. My kids only.*

3. This person is well-groomed with an air of cleanliness also. Clean thoughts of mind and body and a spiritual cleansing frequently takes place.—*Correct.*

4. With regard to this, the basic health of this entity is very good to excellent.—*Correct.*

5. The hair appears well-groomed with very few strands of gray. Dark hair runs in her family without graying until very late in life.—*Correct.*

6. In regard to the brain the IQ range is from 115 to 125–130. The higher ranges are the verbal. She is not as proficient with her spatial relations and manual aptitudes as she is with the verbal concepts.—*Correct. Not very good at typing either.*

7. The eyes appear quite normal. The lenses are somewhat thickening with age but there seems to be almost normal vision present.—*Correct. Need my reading glasses more often.*

8. This entity has long, dark lashes, an aspect of beauty of the face.—*Partially Correct. Medium eyelashes and big eyes.*

9. There are a few tendencies toward allergic reactions—*True. Have to use hypoallergenic cosmetics and hairspray and* *sneeze a lot. Had the hives for seven weeks from too much honey.*

10. The skin occasionally has dry patches. A suggestion of skin beautification is a mud pack every two weeks. Nightly scrub the skin face with a mixture of equal parts of lemon juice and peroxide to cleanse and fade age spots. An emollient substance to promote healthier skin would be a mixture of two parts lanolin, two parts rose water, one part glycerin, one part olive oil, one part liquidified cucumber. This should be used after the lemon-peroxide mixture on a daily basis. An occasional teaspoon of olive oil taken internally to carry the toxins away from the body, cleansing the skin internally would be of benefit also.—*Thank you for the suggestions.*

11. This entity tended to have fluid build up in the ears when younger. This was caused by infections of tonsils and adenoids. One of the main weaknesses of this entity is in the throat area.—*Incorrect. Had bronchitis bad as a child, anemic, and lots of colds. Sinus trouble also.*

12. I don't believe there has been an operation for tonsils and adenoid removal although there was discussion about doing so when she was younger.—*No operation. Mother had too much trouble with hers so none of us had tonsils removed.*

13. This entity is subject to severe strep throats and has been throughout her Earth Plane existence.—*Mother claims not.*

14. When younger these strep infections were as frequent as two to three times a year with one relatively severe.—*That was the bronchitis and took many shots for this.*

15. These have improved to some degree recently, but there is still a tendency toward sore throats.—*Coughing phlegm from sinus trouble and smoking too much.*

16. There was a fear with the strep throats of affecting the heart with rheumatic fever when younger. I feel there may have been a mild irregularity with the heart in the past, but there seems to be none of this presently. It was a worry that the strep infections may cause a heart difficulty. This never materialized.—*Incorrect. Muscle spasms from nerves.* (Acknowledged tendency toward this in later correspondence. See *JoAnna Hunt Psychic Research Update.*).

17. To reduce the likelihood of sore throats re-occurring, gargling with a mixture of glycothymoline and water on a regular basis is recommended.—*Thanks for the remedies. I will pass them on to others.*

18. An apple cider vinegar-soaked cloth across the throat and tonsil area when signs of a sore throat appear would alleviate, or at least minimize the condition.—*Sounds good to me. Will try it.*

19. High intakes of fresh orange juice accompanied by ingestion of mangos, kiwi fruit, passion fruit, and an occasional persimmon would maintain a good balance.—*Thanks.*

20. Oil of eucalyptus vapors are healing for the sinuses.—*Again thank you.* (In Psychic Research Update extolled success of the treatment.)

21. This is a person with healing hands. This skill will be commented upon later in the abilities discussion.—*Correct.*

22. The only problem I feel is the area of the reproductive organs. I get the impression that either a virus has attacked these organs from the other parts of the body, or within the fallopian tube there was a stoppage from infection—perhaps a combination of both. These occurred frequently in her early twenties, and in her early married life.—*Correct. Now you've hit the nail on the head.*

23. I feel there was some difficulty in getting pregnant because of this.—*Correct.*

24. There seems to have been a clearing, or an opening, or healing measures taken to assure that the fallopian tubes were open and the ovulation process occurred without impediment. This, combined with the tipped uterus, made it quite difficult for her to become pregnant for the first five to eight years of her marriage. Thereafter, with medical assistance, she became pregnant first with a boy and then with a girl.—*God must have done it when I prayed to get pregnant. I do have a tipped uterus and 5 years is right. No assistance medically, and I had a girl first and 11 years later a boy.*

25. The suggestion is given for osteopathic or chiropractic adjustments in the neck and shoulder area to improve the throat infections. This is optional.—*Correct. I need to go back and get a few adjustments for neck and back.*

26. This entity had achieved a high degree of holiness in communication with the Godhead.—*Correct. At least I feel I do.*

27. A final remark—this entity has extremely good auditory discrimination of fine sounds and musical pitches. This symbolizes also the hearing of higher communications than the average person.—*Correct. High pitches I hear and low pitches I cannot hear clearly. I feel a pressure or high-pitched sounds when contact is felt.*

28. This excellence in pitch seems to be connected with musical ability in this life.—*Sang in choir, played piano and baritone in the band. Even went to contest with the baritone. Bothers me to hear someone sing off-key.*

29. I get the impression of ringing bells—is she a bell ringer?—*This is like a ringing in my ear when I hear the high-pitched sounds. Not a bell ringer! I have them use the left ear for male person and right for female contact. Also the left means yes and the right no.*

30. She also seems to engage in some musical instrument with strings. Perhaps a harp but I am uncertain of this. It is hard to see. It doesn't seem as large as a harp. Maybe she just possesses the aptitudes to play these instruments in this life if she so desires. It depends upon her wish to develop this.—*Incorrect. Although I've always been drawn to a harpsicord, love stringed instrument music especially the mandolin. Always wanted one since the time I saw* Dr. Zhivago *and heard "Lara's Theme." Still my favorite song and type of music.*

Current Issues—Joanna Hunt

1. Joanna seems to live a rural rather than an urban existence, although she is certainly not isolated from people.—*Correct. Picture shows this.*

2. I am told to tell her that they have been having trouble with their car—a car and a truck recently. One will break down and then the other. This has continued for a period of months. It will be alleviated in late January, early February. Conditions will improve. This is apparently a financial and transportation worry. This comes through rather pronouncedly.—*Correct. The communication radio wears down the battery all the time when it's very cold out. Just had the carburetor fixed and new brakes put on, and the tires are bad. John got a new truck so we couldn't afford to get a car too. You are so right and thanks for the good news.*

3. Joanna seems to be well educated—a widely read person.—*Love to read and will pick up anything and search it out to a point.*

4. Her training seems to be in the health service field—connected or related to medicine. This was before she was married and she still maintains an active interest in this although she does not practice the art any longer.—*Incorrect. No training in this field except what I read.*

5. This is where the aspect of her healing hands comes in. I feel there are physiotherapy or massage-like abilities in which

Joanna had been trained. I get that she uses this on muscles that are atrophied, both adult and child.—*No training. Have watched others heal and use invisible needles. A chiropractor showed me how to press out muscle spasms and use pressure against pressure for a stiff neck. My father has Guillion Barre' disease and we were shown how to exercise him at the hospital rehab unit before he came home so that we could help him. This I did do and still help him to walk yet. I tried healing on him, but it didn't work. Guillion Barre' just is a difficult disease to help.*

6. She has apparently already done some research into the healing area.—*Correct. Every book and herb that I can find information on.*

7. She could be quite apt at acupressure. She is already into massage it seems, but I get that a good book on acupressure on the various pressure points in the body to relieve pain in other areas would be of great benefit to her. If she will research a bookstore that carries health and metaphysical materials, she might procure such books providing training in this skill.—*Correct. I push tight muscles out of my husband's back all of the time. I glide my hand over his back and when I feel a warm spot, I find the tight muscle and push it out while he is exhaling the big breath that I tell him to take. Thanks.*

8. My impression is, however, that the healing hands that she possesses are one of her foremost abilities to help people who are ill.—*OK.*

9. In addition to the healing ability she has two other skills that should be developed and utilized in the service of others. The initial one is a precognitive skill which is indicated by the fact that she has precognitive dreams that frequently come through.—*Correct. About all of them come true, but a few are mixed up as to what I thought was going to happen.*

10. She is able to predict the future through dreams and small intuitions with approximately 65 to 75% accuracy of development.—*Correct as before.*

11. This is a secondary skill with the healing hands being her most precious ability.—*Thank you. I wondered which I was to concentrate on.*

12. The third and final ability she possesses lies in the skill of being able to get intuitive impressions for friends and associates. This can be accomplished in this manner. Hold the person's right hand cupped in both of her hands and then ask for guidance. This can be done in the conscious state. She will receive insights of a health service involving health impressions and also of a precognitive bent. Therefore, she can give suggestions to improve health and also indicate the direction this person's future might take. These are short intuits, rather than a long discourse such as this being given. This is primarily an adjunct to the other things that she practices. This is why this is being given as the third skill.—*Correct. Only I have used psychometry for this. I will try your way also. I get pictures that aren't clear to me, and the other person relates to the object I see. Spooks a few people who don't understand this kind of thing.*

13. I am getting the impression that Joanna is extremely capable at cooking. Now the picture contains pies but what I am seeing beyond this is as if her family has been somehow connected with bakeries or restaurants or the preparation of food.—*Correct. I can make a little of everything and it tastes good most of the time. Yes, my father has a bar-restaurant.*

14. I feel that this is perhaps her father and brother who run this establishment.—*Correct on father.*

15. She has been involved in this on and off all of her life.—*Correct. As a child we went up there and when I turned 21,*

I started helping him off and on. Taking over when he would get sick, which was seldom for him.

16. This restaurant is some distance from where she resides, 75 to 100 miles away, but there are frequent trips there so the contact is still maintained.—*Incorrect. It's exactly 7 miles to town and, yes, now that Dad has Guillion Barre' my sisters and I will run it for him till he gets better. Mostly I do the book work.*

17. I also get the impression that she is aware of good diet and nutrition rules. Much of the time she adheres to these in preparation of meals for the family, but the weakness, which is understandable, is in the preparation of the desserts, which frequently require a high amount of sugar for delectable tastes. This is where she forgoes the understandings and the strict health regimens that she often stays with on a daily basis and indulges in the preparation of delectable desserts with the sugars. She is also able to prepare these with honey and fructose and raw sugar, but I feel that when she really wants to bake something that tastes good, she uses the sugars.—*Correct, but no more honey after the hives I had for 7 weeks from using so much in everything. Back to sugar—have to eat most of the baked goods or give them away because my husband's sweet tooth is only for candy. Maybe pumpkin pie or strawberry in season. Have to eat what I make or give it away. Sometimes the birds and dog get it.*

18. I am seeing Joanna's husband. He likes to wear baseball type caps—I assume they are farm caps.—*Correct.*

19. He wears big, heavy, flannel shirts and very warm plaid jackets for outdoor work.—*Correct.*

20. Her husband is between 5′10″ and 6′ and 180–185 pounds. Well built.—*Incorrect. He is 6′5″ and weighs 300 lbs. average. Was this way when I met him. Cooking sustains this I guess.*

21. I get the impression that he had very blond hair when in his late teens and early twenties. It is sandy-colored now and thinning but he still has a vestage of good healthy hair remaining.—*Correct.*

22. He has a nice easy-going personality. He laughs easily.—*Partially Correct.*

23. He possesses a great love for Joanna and I get the impression that Joanna is a gentle soul who returns his love which is abundant for her and the relationship is probably 75–80% of the time very loving and cooperative.—*Correct. Says he does.*

24. This man's name is John, but they call him Johnnie.—*Correct. By some old friends, but not by me.*

25. His occupation appears to be twofold and he seems to be well-educated also, but perhaps Joanna is the more well-read of the two. Johnnie is more involved in the work-a-day world and doesn't have the time or the inclination to devote to lengthy studies of spirituality.—*Correct.*

26. The fact that their residence is rural suggests that there is some farming involved here but it is not the sole source of income.—*Correct.*

27. There is a small vegetable garden in back of the house from which Joanna cans and preserves much of the food that they eat during the winter months.—*Partially Correct. Used to before we attended fairs, but this work came at the same time the garden came ripe.*

28. One of her specialities is a very sweet pickle with a red garnish contained within the glass jar also.—*Correct.*

29. Getting back to the farming occupation of her husband; Johnnie seems to raise animals on the farm which he sells for the purpose of slaughtering for both their own needs, but more for financial profit.—*True. Raising club calves that is. Raise some beef for our own.*

30. He farms one plot of land and rents another. He grows hay and fodder in the winter months, while in the summer the farm is devoted to raising potatoes, different types of corn, and some special type of bean—for producing farm feed for livestock. The bean contains an oil used in cooking when it is crushed and processed. I mentioned so many crops because they seem to vary from year to year depending on what he wants to plant in relationship to the best use of the soil for that year.—*Correct.*

31. In addition to this, he has recently gone into some kind of business with a male partner.—*Funny you should pick this up already. Only the building is in process of being built to do just that. The neighbor will do the welding. Building is not done yet. Just started on it in December.*

32. This involves the selling of policies for maintenance of farm equipment. Something on this order.—*It's hay wagons and feeders, small sheds, etc. Small work.*

33. He and the partner do not necessarily do all of the maintenance. They may occasionally be involved in a job but they have hired mechanics to do this work.—*Partially Correct. Both men will do the work with maybe a helper.*

34. There is a type of policy sold here which is of benefit to their customers. Equipment is maintained when needed.—*Correct. Welding is one.*

35. I get the name John Deere—this is either my conscious thought, or it is a farm equipment somewhat like that. The policies are sold and this is becoming more profitable for him, and will be so in the future. This is necessary to supplement the farm income as it is so variable that sometimes they are rich, and other times nearly broke. So this is a subsidy to maintain a normal standard of living. This will be more profitable in the future.—*Correct. He has a John Deere collection in* *miniatures—tractors, etc. Maybe contracts you see for orders. I hope.*

Future Trends—Joanna Hunt

1. A warning is given here to be careful of ice and snow and low temperatures this winter. There is a tendency for some kind of equipment in the livestock area to break down. It must be involved with heating, or—I'm uncertain—but I get equipment broken down because of the temperature being so cold, and a danger of some of the livestock freezing. If precautions are taken to check machinery to be sure that all things work well, this could be avoided.—*There is no heater in the barn except the waterer that has a thermostat on it. We put in a new one this year because the old one kept going out and water had to be carried from the house. Thank you, we will watch for this because we have 22 head of cattle, one bull, a club calf, and 9 horses besides the dogs and cats and a few chickens. My husband checks this daily now and keeps a close eye on it because of the trouble we had last year.*

2. I get the impression that there may be a separate freezer and there is something wrong with the refrigerator which is very frustrating to Joanna. Therefore, within the next year or so, there will be a replacement of the refrigerator with a more abundant capacity in the freezer. Apparently, the freezer space is too small. In spite of the fact that she home-cans, or freezes, she is always running out of space in the freezer so this new freezer will provide more space and alleviate the crowded conditions. This is given because this heralds the release somewhat of the financial burden that has plagued them in the past. This is due both to an increase in the policy business on the husband's part, as well as a small inheritance the husband receives and shares with Joanna. She is able to improve their household furnishings and especially purchase the new refrigerator which is a great source of delight to her.—*We just got a new refrigerator this year as well as new washer and dryer. Everything goes at once. We have an upright freezer in the garage and a chest type in the basement now. You are right about it being full, but with his hog ribs and deer ribs right now. Deer meat takes up one freezer alone and I don't even like it. What we are having trouble with is the furnace right now. He's been here twice to fix it and as I sit here typing, I had to go down and throw the switch to get it to kick in. This has been a real pain for about 2 months. He's going to call back tomorrow morning to see if what he fixed did the job. It hasn't, so I guess it needs the new switch behind the new fuel pump that he already put in. We have a wood-burning stove on the other side of the house and I want floor vents put in so the heat comes upstairs to the family room and bedrooms. This has to be done yet.*

3. I get the impression that one of the readings given for Joanna contained a lot of negative suggestions, especially in the area of her personal health. This was completely read from the subconscious of the intuitive rather than any spiritual physicians. Much of this was negated by Joanna herself, in that she refused to accept this reading which was done three or four years ago. This is to re-emphasize that her health is good to excellent. She has negated the forces that this person tried to set in motion, and the reason this is given is that within the next three years a period of great spiritual growth in the health field will occur for her, in that she can provide healing suggestions and remedies for others through her own understandings and personal development. This is so she will rest assured and focus upon emphasizing the development of her spiritual talents.—*Thank you for the health reading. I've always felt that my health was fine. They're trying to get me to stop smoking. I keep saying I have to die from something. I should cut down though, sometimes my throat is very phlegm-*

filled but I say that's sinus draining. If I had a reading like that I've put it out of my mind. For as I sit here I can't remember such a reading. I use to argue with my teacher on the Spiritualism she taught because some things just didn't sit right with me. She injected too many of her own fears on us and had me scared to death to close my eyes and see anything black. Even a hat or something like that. I'm sure she meant well but she and I would get into it on a lot of things. This is not why I quit, though. She gave me a lot of insight that I needed to get started on why my dreams were coming true and other things that happened. Thank You. I needed to know my strengths and weaknesses and which vein to follow. I needed to know my hands can heal. I lost my pictures in meditation because I didn't believe what I saw or use what I saw. I thought I had misused what I saw and gave wrong explanations instead of what I saw. For three years they stopped, and I thought that was why they were taken away. Since then I've found out that they want me to use healing and go the way all of you have explained to me in this reading.

Character Assessment—Joanna Hunt

1. This is an individual with a great need to search within for a source of power.—*Correct.*

2. She has an intense need to understand herself, the world around her, and how she fits into the scheme of things.—*Correct.*

3. This is a person who feels a need to be at the head of something—to be a leader in some way or another. To be not necessarily admired, but perhaps to be looked up to by others, and to know that she is doing a good job and accomplishing something with her life.—*I am a leader of Cub Scouts, Committee Chairman, but I enjoy what no one else will take the time to do.*

4. She is a practical individual—not easily swayed by flattery or any insincere attempts to turn her head or get her attention.—*Correct.*

5. An idea has to have a practical base for her to consider it, and she tends to turn toward the more practical applications of any philosophy, religion, or theosophical subjects that she investigates.—*Correct.*

6. She is at ease with a wide range of people, and one of the most important things to her is that a person be sincere, truthful, and honest with her.—*Correct. Say it to my face not behind my back.*

7. She has a great fixity of purpose, and could be called stubborn on occasion. It is difficult for her to change her mind, or for people to change her plans in mid-stream. It takes her time to adjust to new plans, new ideas.—*Correct. Stubborn Dutchman.*

8. She believes strongly in fairness and justice and has a humanitarian bent. She has great feelings for masses of humanity and yet is not very knowledgeable about people on an individual basis. She doesn't know human beings very well, but she knows how she wants human beings to behave and to be treated.—*Correct. I always fight for the underdog if he's in the right.*

9. This lesson is one that is coming to her today—the contrast of how people really are in the real world and how great the world could be if people were to behave and attune themselves appropriately.—*Correct.*

10. This contrast is presented to her in this lifetime so that she can give herself better understanding of how to deal with the world.—*Correct.*

11. This is an issue in her life that juxtaposes close emotional ties that people need to have with others and the more broad-reaching humanitarian feeling for people in general.—*Correct.*

12. She may have a good deal of idealism in this area—a hope or wish that things could be perfect.—*Correct.*

13. She has a good deal of talent and creative ability that could be brought to the resolution of this problem in the world.—*Correct. I try.*

14. The career, or the life work, that she has made for herself or that she will be making for herself, if she has not already started on it, is going to be unusual in some way. It will involve communication with other people, whether this be verbal or physical or mental—in some way it will be one that emphasizes communication. It could even be an overt communication work. For example, computer work, telephone communications, or it could be on a more intimate personal level as in counseling or therapy through massage, or some kind of manipulation.—*Correct. As a Den Leader and Committee Chairman, you take a lot of training, and then pass it on. In fact, the best job I ever had was selling radio advertising. A new FM Station started up and it was a real challenge to sell, versus paper ads. The massage work is done on my husband's back and legs.*

15. She has an intuitive ability that is expressed through physical contact through one of the senses. This could be the sense of touch, or whatever, but she is able to operate with vibrations that are helpful to others and to receive vibrations from others, which could be helpful to her or not depending on the vibrations. She needs to be aware of the fact that she can pick up others' vibrations and protect herself if necessary. This I am sure is helpful to her in her healing work.—*Correct. I can glide my hand over his back and when I feel a warm spot I know where the pain is and push the enlarged muscle out with pressure. When I feel bad vibrations, I protect myself with a shield or invisible wall.*

16. She may have occasions when her energies are scattered or dissipated through emotions somehow, when she is not able to be as effective as she would like to be because she is not focusing on one thing—not concentrating well enough to accomplish it.—*Correct. Always too many irons in the fire at one time.*

17. A positive side of this is that she can put energy into a number of different things and to keep track of a number of different things going on at the same time.—*Correct. My mind keeps better track of more things collectively than of a few things.*

18. She is a person willing to work hard at educating herself, becoming more knowledgable in a broad range of subjects. Particularly the ones that touch on society as a larger whole, such as philosophy, politics or metaphysical subjects, higher education, law, etc.—*Correct.*

19. Because she is interested really in defining herself in relation to the world and because she has a strong sense of order, the study of these subjects gives her a feeling that there is a good deal of order in the universe.—*Correct. Only there isn't a lot of order in the world.*

20. I get that she has had to be somewhat independent in her study also—forge her way alone into the subjects that she chooses.—*Correct. I want to learn the good and bad of all things and decide for myself which way is right for me.*

21. I am getting the impression that perhaps she has had difficulties in relationships with other people that came about because of money or financial situations or because of work or career difficulties or interferences from these areas somehow. In some way relationships were changed or terminated because of these things.—*Correct.*

22. It could be that the reason why she has a tendency to avoid close relationships is that she instinctively wants to investigate every aspect of a relationship and to feel it very intensely, but she is not willing to let herself go to this extent.—*Not sure of this one.*

23. I feel that in the last two years she may have been having a difficult time, or for some reason has been feeling that she is terribly burdened without enough time for herself, or is not able to do what she wants to do. This will probably continue for another six to eight months. There will still be things that she feels are not going exactly right, but the heavy burden will be lifted off her shoulders and she will feel more able to cope with things.—*Correct.*

Past Lives—Joanna Hunt

1. I get the impression of an older woman who is dressed in a long, tan gown or coat of some kind.

2. She is short and very bent.

3. She is involved in fishing, or gathering shellfish of some kind along what looks like a river. It is salt water.

4. She just kind of blends in with the ground; the sand and even the water is somewhat brown—has a brownish cast to it. She moves slowly throughout that environment and is very much in tune with it.

5. She gathers these shellfish and has them in buckets—shallow buckets and carries them somewhere to be sold. I see her selling them in the mornings and again in the evenings. The rest of the time she just walks along this muddy area.

6. She is a very quiet and a very gentle soul. She talks to the birds and to the critters that she sees.—*I've always talked to animals.*

7. She has very little contact with other people although she sells what she has caught; she does not talk to the customers very much. She is more at ease in her fishing environment. She is friendly, but people feel that she is shy.

8. I see that she was an only child of her parents, and I see her as a young girl spending a lot of time out at the water. She continues to do this.—*I still like to be by the water but not on it.*

9. She is not married. She does not marry in this experience.

10. There seems to be great contrast in the types of lives that she leads.

11. Several hundred years before this she has had a life as a man, and is very extroverted, outgoing and authoritarian. One who is always at odds with his environment—one who creates waves and brings up disharmony with others. He is very self-centered and tuned only to himself with no ability to view life from other's point of view. This is in contrast to the woman who is the fisherwoman because she is very much in tune with her environment—she adapts herself and creates harmony and lives in harmony.

12. In the previous life as a man, I think she was a Roman. I see him wearing arm bands with metal bands around his wrists and arms—jewelry with a significance like military designations for rank. He is associated somehow with the military. It is his career and the more he is in it, the worse he gets, the more authoritarian and the more he likes to throw his weight around.—*Strange that you should say this because I've felt I lived in the Roman days as a gladiator or soldier. In fact, in a meditation I saw a row of people on each side of me, and one of them was a Roman soldier with the helmet and gold nose plate. I've seen the ring in meditation also. It's red and blue in block pattern but a little different pattern.*

13. His name is something like Ectutus. His lesson in this lifetime as a soldier is to learn the affects of imposing his will on others, and his life is to present to him the consequences of only seeing things from his own point of view. He doesn't progress very much in this particular lesson in this lifetime.

14. In later experiences, the same lesson was presented in different guise and he was able to internalize it.

15. In the present time, it manifests only occasionally as urges to have a leadership role, or just to be admired or appreciated by others. It is not an ingrained pattern as it was previously.—*Correct.*

16. I see her lifetime as a fisherwoman simply as a desire of her soul to experience harmony with nature in the Earth Plane. There were many experiences previously that did not incorporate harmony. Not so much a life of a specific lesson as one to simply enjoy being in tune with this plane.

17. Her husband was also present in the Roman period as a fellow soldier. One who made efforts to temper her arrogance with only occasional success. He was a friend in that existence.—*He still makes efforts to temper my arrogance.*

18. I get an impression of the father, mother, son, and daughter being out together in a small boat, row boat, and are making a common effort there in some difficulty. They are working very hard together there to reach land I would guess. I see them spending a long period of time together under adverse conditions. This situation makes them stronger together. I don't know if this is symbolic for previous lifetimes of hard work, reaping benefits presently, or perhaps it is an actual experience.—*We're always under adverse conditions now. Guess we didn't learn it in that lifetime either. Hard work is normal yet. John has always wanted a boat but I'm not that fond of being on the water yet.*

19. She has been incarnated more times than I can count. It is not a question of three or fifty—it is innumerable, not on just this plane but on other planes.—*I feel I've been here many times, but thought that was more than my share and couldn't* *have been that many different people as I've seen or felt. As to other planets . . . yes, those dreams are so real.*

20. The nature of the experiences on the Earth Plane are not really such that one can identify them as the best experience for this soul or the worst experience. The measurement is different. Best cannot be identified in terms of most successful or learned the most. The times where she may have made the tiniest bit of progress could be more important than a lifetime where she may have seemed to improve by leaps and bounds in her development. The task could have been harder, the task could have simply been more important to her or more necessary.

21. I get the impression she has made great progress. She is progressing all the time. This is not ever a subject of being competitive and comparing the best or the worst lives to have lived.

Soul's Purpose—Joanna Hunt

This entity possesses a gentleness and a charm found among only a limited few upon the Earth Plane during the current era. She is among those who has elected to return bringing with her a myriad of spiritual talents and creative understanding to be used in the alleviation of the sufferings of those with whom she comes in contact and provide positive affirmations and directions for those who wish to enter discussions with her where she then becomes the procurer of spiritual wisdom and insights.

The purpose this soul has selected is to become a part of the spiritual band of disciples who will disseminate and elaborate upon the determinism of spiritual truths in the everwidening interests of the population in general.

Quite a few will be touched by this entity's spiritual enlightenment, and her purpose shall be realized more and more as the New Age enters in upon us. This is an entity who will gain more and more in the discernment and clarification of spiritual truths.

An example of an unusually accurate health reading can be observed in the Physical Symbology section of one done for Grace Waters.

Grace Waters—March 3, 1985

Physical Symbology

1. I get the impression that this entity has trouble with far vision. This has been going on since puberty, but it seems to come and go so that at times she has perhaps improved vision to some degree and there was a necessity for wearing glasses but she refused often to wear them. She felt prettier without the glasses. As of late she wears contact lenses, and this is a satisfactory solution for removing the frames from the face. It seems that she often has trouble with the lenses. They are more of a nuisance than they are a boon. She can see well with them, but she is either losing them periodically, or they slide around in her eyes—problems are connected with the contact lenses. Often, she feels like "The heck, I'm not going to wear them." At times it is essential that she have them and so does.—*Correct. Correct. I am nearsighted. I have been wearing glasses since I was 22. I have been wearing contact lenses on and off for the last ten years. Right now I have soft contact lenses (there had been marked improvement in my vision last year) and the right lens drives me crazy, but I am totally at a loss without either glasses or lenses. I have said recently that I might switch back to glasses because the lenses are more trouble than they are worth, but there is vanity of course.*

2. I get two suggestions for the vision problem. One is the head and neck exercise which involves three dips of the head forward, three backward, three to the left, three to the right, three clockwise, three counterclockwise once in the a.m. The second is that I am sending her an absentee healing and it is hoped that with this there will be considerable improvement in the vision. If this is the case, it would be wise to let us know in the results or the reply to the reading if an improvement occurs and she wishes additional absentee healings. These would be done several more times upon request.—*I will try your suggestions. And yes, please send an absentee healing. Actually, in the last two weeks there have been changes in my vision, but I can't tell whether positive or negative, only that my vision is not 100 percent with corrective lenses.*

3. She seems to be blessed with lovely skin. I see a small red mark above the nose on the forehead which seems to come and go rather than being a permanent fixture. I'm not sure whether she puts a dot there or it is a beauty mark or a mark that fades from dark to lighter, but I see a small round mark in that area.—*Partially correct. I used to have nice skin, for the past couple of years have been getting blemishes, something I never had before in my life, but my skin is soft and relatively smooth. There is no mark on the forehead, there is a scar on my left eyebrow close to the nose.*

4. This individual appears to be extremely healthy so there are not many things to comment on in the physical section.—*Correct. I am really quite healthy.*

5. The composition of the blood is extremely healthy with an abundance of red corpuscles—iron-carrying vessels. This contributes to the high level of energy of this individual.—*OK.—I'll take your word for my blood count. You've been right so far.*

6. She seems to be always on the go, involved in quite a few things, many projects, and she seems to handle many of them quite well. There are occasional times when she sits back, retreats, but generally the energy level seems to be quite high.—*Yes.—I'm quite busy, I feel like I work 7 days a week. I get no time for myself and I resent it. I don't have time to retreat, but I wish I could. That's what I used to do.*

7. The lungs at one time had considerable residue. I believe she was a smoker from an early age.—*Partially correct. I didn't start smoking until I was 20, but I had pneumonia when I was 11 years old (a severe case) and lighter cases of it 2 or 3 times since.*

8. I see this as somewhat of a cross she bears. She has quit and then gone back to smoking several times. I feel that she has hypnotic training to help with this and uses meditation and positive thinking to try to rid herself of this habit. She is either in the process of winning the battle, or has it won. This is good as smoking is not a healthful habit to maintain.—*Absolutely Right. I have quit and gone back. I am an oral person. I smoke out of boredom and nervousness and yes I have had hypnotic training with this. I was in therapy from 1982 until 1984, and my therapist was a psychologist who practiced hypnotherapy.*

9. There seems to be a problem with the nails. She likes to grow long nails, but they break off easily and the nails are soft and seem to be scarred. This indicates often that there is too much polish and the nails cannot breathe. More basic than this is that there is a lack of calcium and phospherous in the body.—*Very Accurate. Correct. I have nice hands and I like to wear jewelry so I like to have long nails, but they will grow for a month or two and then just peel off and yes, some of them are ridged. I have added a calcium supplement to my vitamin list.*

10. I would recommend an increase in calcium with calcium supplements and an increase in dairy products—cheese more so than milk. I get that the ingestion of nectarines, peaches, and green grapes would be extremely beneficial for her metabolism.—*Correct in suggesting cheese rather than milk. I have a lactose intolerance and have not had milk since I was three months old and my mother stopped nursing me. Cheese*

I love and it has often been my total diet. The fruits you suggest are some of my favorites, but they are seasonal.

11. At one point in her life it seems that she had an injury to her spine in the lower lumbar area. This involved a disc problem which caused an injury to a vertebra. An operation was considered. I see her hanging in some sort of traction or treatments with bed rest and perhaps even followed by a mental healing, whether through her own strong will not to have the operation, or through healings through prayer. The mental healings contributed to the elimination of the necessity to have an operation. The injured area has healed well with little scar tissue present.—*Correct. Extremely accurate! I have suffered with my back all my life. It wasn't until last June when I went to an orthopedic surgeon that I finally found out what was wrong. I have a fractured vertabra in my lower back, and I have had it since birth or at least early, early childhood. Because of the fracture the disc has been eroded. An operation was never suggested; I have never been in traction, but I did, and on occasion do, wear a back brace.*

12. This lady has an extremely shapely and beautiful body and is often complimented about this.—*Thank you for the compliment.*

13. She moves gracefully and I wonder if she isn't into some kind of dance. She likes to dance, or she has had dancing lessons in the past. I see grace, charm, and beauty of physique connected with her.—*Oh yes. I love to dance. I love music. My parents wouldn't let me have dancing lessons or music lessons, but I am always dancing. I always have music around. I'm told I'm a good dancer, and I'm never still.*

14. It is my feeling that her name was chosen carefully matching her personality and physical stature.—*I don't know about my name. It was supposed to be Graziella, after my mother's mother, but my mother couldn't spell it so I became Grace which is the closest translation from the Italian.*

THE PSYCHICAL RESEARCH PROJECT UPDATE

In early September of 1985 Jim and I composed a letter requesting an informational update and mailed it to all participants who had received readings through the Psychical Research Project over the past two years. The responses we received added considerably to our already favorable statistical and factual data bank. Space dictates the inclusion of only a select few cases. Therefore, I have chosen four of the most definitive examples to further annotate the evidential aspects of the validity of intuitive readings.

Case #1

In an intuitive reading for Joanna Hunt, item #3 in the Future section was marked Incorrect in the initial reading. Information received through the updating request rescored that item as Correct with this commentary:

> I've recalled an audience reading when we went to Chesterville, Indiana, back a few years ago since I answered your question. This lady claimed it was a message from a grandmother and that I had heart trouble. I denied it at the time and also thought that if this were true either one of them would have told me before this. I do get pains around my heart, but I attribute these to stress and nerves.

Case #2

In a reading done for a lady we shall call Bonnie Myers, items #17–19 under the Current Issues section were given *4's,* (incorrect).

17. For the daughter—she appears to be the happiness child—much indulged. She has a physical ailment. This is one of the reasons for the indulgence.

18. It appears she has difficulty forming red blood cells. A tendency to be anemic. This stems from a problem earlier in her existence. This condition occurred when she was around three years of age. It was an acute attack—an abnormality of an organ which required hospitalization, medical measures—perhaps even surgery to correct. I feel that Bonnie was afraid of losing this girl also.

19. I am having a great deal of trouble seeing what it was that caused this blood condition that exists presently. It seems that the reason I am having so much trouble seeing this is that Bonnie blocks it from her mind and therefore I cannot read it in her aura. It is blocked out from being so terrifying to her. I get only the general condition that exists. This is one of the reasons for the over-protectiveness. Usually I can read these things, but not in this case because of the blocking as though it never existed.

Character Assessment #10—She does a very efficient job at her own nurturing. If she has children, I have a feeling that she is rather strict with them and insistent that they learn the proper way to behave. She may have to do some kind of nursing with them. Perhaps their health is not as good as she would like and is obligated to care for that.

Upon receiving Bonnie's updated material we were amazed to read this statement:

> Although what was given at the time did not apply—my younger son "the girl" fell on a nail with his right knee this summer. This resulted in a septic knee joint requiring three weeks' hospitalization and four weeks' IU antibiotic therapy at home. He became anemic during this and remains slightly so. Also, his platelet count elevated directly with the sedimentation rate causing a few moments of consideration that "something else" might be going on. My son also had surgery during this time and indeed has had a lot of the "nursing care" mentioned in the Character Assessment portion.

The difficulty in reading this was due to the mother actually "blocking" the probable future from her patterns of thought, and indeed, the event did not "exist" in reality at the time the reading was done.

Case #3

In the same category of viewing health problems previously not present or unknown, Physical item #12 of Bonnie's reading contained this information:

> **12.** This lady is subject to night blindness. Ingestion of carotene supplements and/or the eating of large quantities of raw carrots would improve this situation to a degree at this point and time. With the metabolism of this entity, the elimination of this problem is highly unlikely.

Item #12 was denied initially, but her updated reply supplied the confirmation originally lacking.

> Since my last reply, I have seen an opthamologist and had a radial keratotomy performed. He told me also that I had chronic blepheritis. From the symptoms, I know I have had it for several years, if not my entire life. Some of what was previously diagnosed as sinus problems was in fact the blepheritis. I will begin treating this in October if I pass my surgical check-up. I feel my photosensitivity has improved since the surgery also. I have taken the carotene also—but again not regularly.

It is interesting to note that night blindness is often due to a Vitamin A deficiency which regulates the light sensitive retina of the eye and also is involved in the visual mechanism responsible for distinguishing various shades of gray. Blepheritis is an inflammation of the eyelids at times associated with either a bacterial infection, allergies, or seborrhea of the face and scalp.

Case #4

In a lighter vein, a residence was described for Lana Marsh which in no way fit the description of her residence at that time.

Therefore, items #17, 18, and 19 of the Current Issues section were scored 4's, (incorrect). The description was given thusly:

17. The place where she lives seems to be a one-story house. The roof is unusual in that it seems to have red tiles—one over the other, which is not the normal fashion for rooves in this neighborhood.

18. This is a low extending house, going in several directions. It is not just long but seems to have two extensions off the back of the house. Perhaps one is a screened-in porch and the other is as a patio arrangement. There may be a swimming pool connected to this patio when you step down three steps—it seems that there is a swimming pool to the back of the house.

19. The front door is not in the center of the house, but rather when looking at the house, it is off to the left. The walk curves out to the right and then ends at the driveway where two cars are often parked.

The update revealed this description was indeed correct, but read for the duplex into which she had recently moved.

17. I now live in a duplex apartment.

18. The duplex is constructed in two directions/extensions. There are three back steps, and when I moved in there was a child's swimming pool in our adjoining back yards. (Let's upgrade that 4 to a 1!)

19. The two front doors are off center; the walk does go to the right and ends at the driveway where my son's and my cars were parked most of last year. (He's now gone to college.) (Let's upgrade the 4 to a 1!)

The readings presented were chosen for inclusion in the Psychical Research Chapter because, in the opinion of my husband

and me, they appear to exemplify what can be accomplished when intuitives work in concert with one another combining the very best of their own native talents. When such an attitude is adopted, a veritable intermingling of minds is achieved through which only high caliber blessings are channeled.

I would like to conclude this chapter with a short poem by Amanda Bradley entitled "Our Dreams Are Within Our Reach." These lines are truly representative of the creative influences available to us in the form of intuitive readings if we would but attune our soul vibrations to the Universal Blueprint of which we ourselves are the architects.

Within our reach lies every path
we ever dream of taking.

Within our power lies every step
we ever dream of making.

Within our range lies every joy
we ever dream of seeing . . .

Within ourselves lies everything
we ever dream of being.

CHAPTER 4

The Psychical Research Project: Implications*

***Ignorance* is the key factor. *Not knowing why* creates the frightening private hells. Therefore, the very first step towards establishing some degree of stability is to replace ignorance with knowledge. To succeed in implanting into the mind of the sufferer understanding of the *pattern* of the 'illness' and the reasons *why* it is happening is to establish a vital bridgehead, from which a slow but certain build-up towards a mental stability and an eventual permanent cure will be achieved.**

Tom Johanson—*First Heal The Mind*

The College Psychical Research Project described in *The Inner Eye* was only a limited probe into the world of extrasensory perception. At that time we were primarily interested in identifying the kinds of abilities utilized to get the information. We were satisfied that telepathy, clairvoyance, retrocognition, and precognition do indeed exist. There are ways of perceiving other than through the traditional five senses.

The present Psychical Research Project, which is ongoing, was designed to continue this research on a more systematic basis using two readers to produce a "holistic" reading and to quantify the feedback in order to identify areas of strength and weakness. To date 103 subjects have participated, providing a wealth of data.

Since a holistic reading consists of sections on Physical Symbology, Current Issues, Future Trends, Character Assessment,

* Dr. James C. Windsor

Past Lives, and Soul's Purpose, it would seem prudent to comment on each.

PHYSICAL SYMBOLOGY

Intuitive impressions of someone's past health history and current conditions are especially interesting to the scientists because they can be checked out empirically. The impressions are either right or wrong. It is quite astounding that such information would have *any* degree of accuracy. To achieve a relatively high level of correct impressions suggests the operation of a phenomenon which we do not yet comprehend. When accurate information is somehow acquired with the subject hundreds of miles away, it becomes even more remarkable. The evidence from this research project is very persuasive and poses various questions:

1. Where is the information on past health history stored? Since specific events are frequently not in the conscious memory of the subject, are they preserved on the unconscious level? Is there a universal storehouse of memory where all events are kept?
2. How does the reader look into the body of a subject and become aware of *current* conditions? Is the unconscious mind privy to what's going on all over the body? Does each cell have an awareness of its own?
3. Can intuitive impressions become a useful adjunct to traditional medical diagnostic procedures?

Although we do not yet have the answers to these questions, we no longer have any doubts about the existence of the process. It is possible, through a procedure we do not yet understand, to get, from a distance, accurate information on past health history and current conditions. Intuitive impressions, like medical diagnoses, are not always correct, which leads us to proceed with great caution in their application. At this point, investigating the phenomenon itself is a source of great intrigue.

The following are examples of accurate impressions of past health history.

1. Laura Allen (Chapter 3) was described as having had various difficulties with her eyes, caused by infection, which "caused some concern about loss of vision." Laura confirmed that this was true: "I lost my vision for an extended time period."

   Laura also confirmed that the infection cleared up after a change of medication.

2. The reading said that Laura's nasal passages were at one time stuffed up and clogged. Laura replied, "I have had a lot of work done on my nose, this is very true. The last operation was to correct the deviated septum that was totally blocking one side of my nose."

3. According to the reading, Laura had suffered from chronic vaginal infections. This was "very true."

4. Joanna Hunt was told, "The only problem I feel is the area of the reproductive organs. I get the impression that either a virus has attacked these organs from other parts of the body, or within the fallopian tube there was a stoppage from infection—perhaps a combination of both. These occurred frequently in her early twenties, and in her early married life." (Note information from the past). Joanna replied, "Correct. Now you've hit the nail on the head."

   The reading went on to describe Joanna's difficulty in getting pregnant, partially because of a tipped uterus, and her efforts for five to eight years before having a boy and a girl. Joanna replied, "I do have a tipped uterus and five years is right. No assistance medically, and I had a girl first, and 11 years later a boy.

5. The physical impressions for Grace Waters included a description of her frustration, over several years, with contact lenses and her indecisiveness about wearing glasses. Grace responded, "Correct, correct. I am nearsighted. I have been wearing glasses since I was 22. I have been wearing contact lenses on and off for the past ten years. Right now I have soft contact lenses, and the right lens drives me crazy, but I am totally at a loss without either glasses or lenses. I have said recently that I might switch back to glasses because the lenses are more trouble than they are worth, but there is vanity of course."

6. Grace's reading identified a past injury to the spine which "caused an injury to a vertebra." Grace explained, "Correct. Extremely accurate! I have suffered with my back all my life. It wasn't until last June when I went to an orthopedic surgeon that I finally found out what was wrong. I have a fractured vertebra in my lower back, and I have had it since birth, or at least early childhood."

The above examples confirm that there is indeed recorded somewhere the health history of each individual, and that this information can be accessed by certain individuals who possess the ability to view the body clairvoyantly.

Equally interesting are the examples of accurate impressions of currently existing conditions.

1. Laura Allen was told that she had a calcium deficiency. Although this was not confirmed medically at the time she responded, Laura told an interesting story which explained why she had not developed a taste for dairy products. "My mother refers to the fact that if I was bad as a very young child, my father would dump my milk on my head as punishment."

2. Joanna Hunt received a rather interesting, instant, IQ evaluation. "In regard to the brain the IQ range is from 115 to

125–130. The higher ranges are the verbal. She is not as proficient with her spatial relations and manual aptitudes as she is with the verbal concepts."

Joanna replied, "Correct. Not very good at typing either."

3. Joanna had "tendencies toward allergic reactions." Joanna confirmed that this was true. "Have to use hypoallergenic cosmetics, hairspray, and sneeze a lot. Had the hives for 7 weeks from too much honey."

4. Joanna was described as having "good auditory discrimination" with musical ability. She confirmed that she sang in the choir, played piano and baritone, and that it bothered her to "hear someone sing off key."

The reading said that Joanna "seems to engage in some musical instrument with strings." Joanna described her interest as follows: "Although I've always been drawn to a harpsicord, I love stringed instrument music, especially the mandolin."

5. A detailed description of a current condition of Grace Waters is rather amazing and worth repeating. "There seems to be a problem with the nails. She likes to grow long nails, but they break off easily and the nails are soft and seem to be scarred. This indicates often that there is too much polish and the nails cannot breathe. More basic than this is that there is a lack of calcium and phosphorus in the body."

Grace replied, "Correct. I have nice hands and I like to wear jewelry so I like to have long nails, but they will grow for a month or two and then just peel off, and yes, some of them are ridged."

6. The reading said that Grace likes to dance. "I see grace, charm, and beauty of physique connected with her."

Grace wrote, "Oh yes. I love to dance. I love music. I'm told I'm a good dancer, and I'm never still."

An interesting aspect of these examples of current conditions is that they include a wide range of information on physical manifestations, underlying causes (blood analysis), and various talents and interests. The impressions are truly "holistic."

Is it possible to get, over distance, accurate impressions of current physical conditions and personality characteristics? The answer is clearly yes. How is it accomplished? This will be the subject of future research.

All of this information received was not accurate. Sometimes there seems to be an outright miss. For example, Joanna Hunt was told, "This is a soul with gentleness surrounding her." Joanna replied, "Incorrect. My life is on tension most of the time."

At other times there is "displacement." This is when the information is incorrect for the readee, but very accurate for someone with close emotional ties to the recipient of the reading. Laura Allen was told that she was severely allergic to pollens. Laura said this was not true. "Nothing that has bothered me to any great extent. *My sister had a great and still has a great problem with allergies.*"

Displacement is frequently not recognized because the recipient of the reading may not be aware of the physical problems of those who surround him.

The time element seems to be the least accurate in intuitive impressions. What is described as present may be past or future. Laura was warned of trouble with her teeth "within the next six months" (lower back right of the mouth). The response was "This was found about one and one half years ago."

The final source of inaccuracy which I wish to mention in this context is the reading of "thought forms." The sensitive frequently picks up on not what *is,* but what is in the mind of the person being read. A person was told she had an oval rug in her living room. She did not have such a rug but wanted to own one and had visualized it in its place for several months.

In summary, it is possible to get accurate information on past health problems and current conditions. There are inaccurate impressions, usually in the form of displacement, time distortion, or the perception of thought forms. The usual 75–90 percent accuracy, however, is impressive.

CURRENT ISSUES

Current issues usually focus on relationships and vocations. The extent to which the impressions focus on "core" problems rather than periferal matters is impressive throughout.

Laura Allen's reading described a past relationship which served the purpose of introducing her to important areas of interest which she now pursues. Laura confirmed that his influence led her to pay more attention to diet and to metaphysical philosophies, although he also caused great pain which led to the demise of the relationship. The reading summarized his purpose, "He was the motivator, the catalyst, the pain provider, but the growth provider. This was his role in this life." The comment reminds us of Viktor Frankl's point, that we can find meaning through suffering.

The reading used the term "therapy" in describing Laura's future vocation, especially rehabilitation treatments. Laura affirmed her interest in working with older people and special children. Perhaps this information will encourage her to continue her preparation.

The reading for Joanna Hunt contained some bad news on a mundane matter. She was to have much car trouble. The reading said, "This comes through rather pronouncedly." Joanna's reply explained the problems in detail: "The communication radio wears down the battery all the time when it's very cold out. Just had the carburetor fixed, and new brakes put on, and tires are bad."

The reading also observed correctly that Joanna was a good cook and that her family was connected with the "preparation of food." It turns out that her father owns a restaurant. Joanna's husband, Johnnie's, vocation as a farmer was discussed in detail, including the statement that he had recently gone into some kind of business with a friend. Joanna's response included the following,

"Funny you should pick this up already. Only the building is in the process of being built to do just that."

In her follow-up report, Lana Marsh described an interesting "current event" which turned out to be in the future. The reading described in detail Lana's residence which was incorrect. Several months later she moved into the house previously described. This was especially interesting since Lana had no knowledge of her new residence at the time of the reading.

The greatest contribution of the current issues section of a holistic reading is to help the recipient identify and solve problems of living and working. *It is counseling at its best, because the information not only presents the facts, but also the underlying dynamics of the relationships involved.* Our experience to date suggests that this is one of the most practical and helpful elements of a reading. If the suggestions are followed, the quality of that person's life usually improves.

There are significant implications here for the counseling profession. It is well known that certain counselors are gifted in the sense that they have a special talent for empathy and understanding. This is an intuitive skill, both given and developed. *Future counselor education programs will take such skills into consideration in selecting students and in their training programs. The intuitive aspect must be recognized, accepted, and developed if counselors are to realize their full potential!*

FUTURE TRENDS

Future trends are impressions of what the future may hold if present inclinations persist, unencumbered by an act of will. The person's right to choose can wreak havoc with a prediction about the future. For this reason, impressions of the future must never be seen as deterministic.

Since the time element seems to be the most nebulous in the intuitive realm, it is also difficult to predict with accuracy when an event will take place. It may be a day into the future. It could be a year, or more.

Checking out the validity of future trends is also more difficult because the follow up required may come long after the initial reading is given and interest has waned or the connection with the reading forgotten. Nevertheless, there is persuasive evidence that it is possible to perceive future events in a person's life with some measure of success. This is probably the most mind-boggling of the intuitive skills! Also, we resist believing it is possible because we do not like the inference that the future is fixed. It may be that the explanation is fairly simple, and the process quite scientific. It may be that our view of time as linear is severely limited.

Let me share a few examples of future trends from our current research.

Laura Allen, who was worried about money problems, was comforted by the following prediction:

"An aunt is going to provide her with help. I see additional money through the family somehow. Unexpected money—several thousand dollars. It will be timely when it is needed the most—through family ties—no strings attached."

Laura responded to the statement. "Same aunt who is helping now?" Several months later, she confirmed the same aunt had provided her with a sizeable financial gift.

The reading for Joanna Hunt warned of the possibility of heating equipment breaking down which would result in livestock freezing (see Chapter 3, Page 69), but Joanna was told that this could be avoided if precautions were taken.

Joanna confirmed that they owned a barn in which there were housed ". . . 22 head of cattle, a bull, a club calf, and 9 horses. . . ."

This reading is especially interesting, because it had not been revealed through correspondence or conversation that Joanna and her husband even owned livestock. The "trend" also served as a warning of events which could be prevented.

An update response from Bonnie Myers described an interesting turn of events (Chapter 3, Pages 83–84). The original reading described a daughter with a tendency to anemia which Bonnie said was incorrect. She wrote several months later:

> Although what was given at the time did not apply—my younger son "the girl" fell on a nail with his right knee this summer. This resulted in a septic knee joint requiring three weeks hospitalization and four weeks IV antibiotic therapy at home. He became anemic during this and remains slightly so.

The sex of the child was incorrect, but what was given as a current event was apparently a glimpse of the future.

Joan made an interesting observation when commenting on this report: "The difficulty in reading this was due to the mother actually 'blocking' the probable future from her patterns of thought, and indeed, the event did not 'exist' in reality at the time the reading was done."

This remark implies that this future event was in the unconscious mind of the mother, but that she was reluctant to see it herself or let anyone else observe a probable traumatic event.

In a recent reading a young lady named Susan was told that someone would buy her a car and pay cash for it. There was to be no obligation on her part. This prediction was judged "very unlikely."

Several months later Susan reported:

"You did the reading in September, 1985. I met Richard about January 9, 1986. He bought me a 1978 Toyota Corolla on February 26. He simply told me to find a car I liked, and when I did, he brought me the $1,200 in $100 bills!"

Can we see into the future? It appears that we can discern tendencies which materialize if an exercise of will does not intervene.

CHARACTER ASSESSMENT

Our "character" consists primarily of the manifestation of our values in everyday life. Our attitudes and behaviors are the outward expressions of what we treasure most highly. An understanding and appreciation of our character, therefore, is essential to good mental health. Self-knowledge is the most important kind of wisdom. We need to know our strengths, weaknesses, and motives. A "holistic" reading includes an assessment of character which can provide significant insight as a basis for change.

Laura Allen was described as a person who finds it "difficult to become close to others and fears too much intimate contact." Laura felt that this was because she had a "basic distrust of people." This observation and her insight bring to the surface an attitude that could be worked with and changed to Laura's advantage.

There is a comment in Laura's reading which suggests a strong relationship between one's attitude and one's physical health. The reading says, "She may be subject to some kind of stiffening condition—arthritis possibly. Once she starts becoming very set in her ways, then it tends to be reflected in the physical."

This is a powerful message and a helpful warning. The development of a more flexible attitude could save Laura much physical discomfort.

Unlike Laura, Joanna Hunt is "at ease with a wide range of people." Joanna is a leader. She is self-confident and productive, also stubborn. She believes strongly in fairness and justice, and has a strong sense of values.

Joanna is also a healer. Her hands are sensitive, and her commitment to service is sincere.

According to Joanna, these statements describe accurately her personality. What is the benefit? If Joanna is reminded that she has gifts for which she is responsible, she is more apt to realize her potential.

The above examples indicate the usefulness of character assessments. They provide an opportunity for growth when a contrary view must be defended.

PAST LIVES

To speak of past lives is to introduce the subject of reincarnation, which is controversial to say the least. Although two thirds of the world's population take it for granted, the idea of living more than once is foreign to Western thought.

Although we do not have hard data to support reincarnation, much of the research such as that of Ian Stevenson at the University of Virginia, is persuasive. My own experience with hypnotic regression has left me very impressed, even if not entirely convinced. Almost every good hypnotic subject can come up with a vivid description of a former existence. Elizabeth Hollis and Joan Windsor, without exception, have described former lives for the 103 subjects included in this current report. Where does this information come from? Let us consider some of the possibilities:

1. The subject, or the intuitive, may simply have a vivid imagination.
2. There may be buried in the subject's mind an unconscious memory of a scenario from a forgotten novel or movie. The information may be brought to consciousness under hypnosis or read telepathically by the sensitive.
3. The intuitive may "pick up" the information from another person or even a book.
4. Or the past life memory, or information, may be *real.* It may represent an actual experience in a past existence.

Why are we interested in such information? Because there seems to be a cause-and-effect relationship between one life and another. Knowledge of our strengths, weaknesses, and motives, which are remnants from the past, may be of great assistance to us in understanding the present and planning for the future.

Most of the subjects who participated in the Psychical Research Project were apparently helped by the past-life information.

Whether or not it was true seemed to be less important than that it provided insight into current personality characteristics. For example:

1. In the Past Lives section of Laura Allen's reading, presented in Chapter 3, there is described a nomadic existence of extreme hardship. Laura identifies in her present life tendencies which could relate to this previous life. She is partial to robes and loose shoes; she prefers long hair; she has never felt she had a real home ("My life is where it takes me").

In addition, like Mehlengh, Laura said, "I have a great understanding of medical things, birth in particular." Laura and her husband prefer a midwife to a hospital.

These similarities could be coincidental. They could also be a carryover from the previous life. In any event, Laura feels that she gained in self-knowledge.

2. Joanna Hunt's past life reading is especially interesting because it describes the relationship between two previous lives—the gentle fisherwoman who talks to the animals, and the authoritarian Roman soldier who was brash and at odds with his environment. We can understand how the soldier would seek the harmony with nature and the solitude, which the fisherwoman enjoyed.

Joanna talks to the animals, and she has caught a glimpse of a Roman soldier in her meditation. She dreams of sojourns to other planets. Does the story make any sense? It does to Joanna. Perhaps that is enough.

The past-life readings are fascinating stories. Every one is absolutely unique, which, in itself, is astounding!

Do past lives exist? *We don't know for sure—yet. Are past life readings helpful to those who receive them? They are.*

SOUL'S PURPOSE

The use of the term *soul* connotes a particular point of view, namely, that there is a non-physical part of us which is separate and different from those substances which make up our physical bodies. Edgar Cayce has described the soul as being composed of spirit, mind, and will.

Spirit is a portion of God which is within each of us.

Mind is the capacity to act.

Will is the ability to choose a course of action and to sustain it.

The soul with these attributes survives death, and continues to grow and develop in a different dimension. It may return again, occupy another body, and continue its journey back to a oneness with God.

The term *purpose* connotes that each soul is here to fulfill a special mission. The Soul's Purpose section of a holistic reading suggests that this special mission can be identified and communicated to the person who has requested the information.

If each soul does indeed have a unique purpose to fulfill, there could be no more important knowledge for each of us to have, if we are to realize our destiny.

The statements of soul's purpose in the readings are usually quite eloquent, sometimes poetic, and always focused on spiritual growth rather than material success. Character development, therefore, seems to be much more important than accumulating wealth.

The following are examples of statements which describe a soul's purpose:

1. "The major task this entity has chosen in this existence for herself is to overcome physical abnormalities, or weaknesses, these being the challenges, and thereafter, to utilize her knowledge for the benefit of all of those with whom she subsequently comes into contact."

2. "This entity possesses a gentleness and a charm, found among only a limited few upon the Earth Plane during the current era.

"The purpose this soul has selected is to become a part of the spiritual band of disciples who will disseminate and elaborate upon the determinism of spiritual truths to the ever-widening interests of the population in general."

These examples have elements which seem to be guiding principles in most of the statements of soul purpose:

1. Whatever the challenge, there is always a transcendent quality which involves service to others. It is through giving of ourselves that we grow spiritually.

2. Some souls are farther along the path than others. There are individual differences in soul development.

3. The soul itself selects the situation into which it is born in order to maximize its opportunity for growth.

II

Exploring Advanced Dream Techniques

CHAPTER 5

Dreams and Healing

Any physical ailment is symbolic of an inner reality or statement.

Jane Roberts—*Seth Speaks*

As I have advanced along the spiritual path through the investigative pursuit of dreams and their interpretations and significance, it has become obvious to me that one of their primal functions is that of healing physical, mental, and/or spiritual aberrations. All facets of the soul operate in unity. Any malfunction or deviation from the norm in one unit eventually is reflected in all other aggregates. In the words of Ronald Beesley, spiritual teacher-healer and the author of *Substance of Thought,* "any disharmony between body-mind and soul-spirit is an imbalance at the centre of our being, and balance and health are one, therefore, the degree of health is determined by the state of balance between body-mind and soul-spirit. Occult teachings maintain that all sickness is relative—that the basis of all illness is soul-sickness or frustration."[1] Thus, when an illness such as asthma or ulcers strikes, it is judicious to explore the possibility of disharmonies in the mental and spiritual aspects of our personalities which may explain the physical manifestation. If such aberrations are in evidence, a viable plan should then be designed to reduce and resolve these existing conflicts.

This chapter is based on the aforementioned principle, but I intend to take the concept one step further, focusing not only on the causative aspects of body-mind-spirit disharmonies as envisioned through the dream process but also the curative properties of dreams. Affecting a cure through dreams is far more productive than merely possessing an awareness regarding the cause of one's infirmity. The former serves as a catalyst for spiritual progress as well as for bodily healing.

In the course of gathering material for *The Inner Eye,* I was astounded by the degree to which the dreams I recorded dealt with bodily health and healing. The majority of these related to my own health, but a considerable number were concerned with the problems of friends and relatives. In both types, remedies were suggested to alleviate physical suffering.

While reviewing material for *Dreams and Healing* I observed a similar pattern. Through intensive study and scrutinization I was able to discern with marked clarity four categories of healing dreams. Through the internalization and usage of these categories, each one of us will expand our current dream horizons, thus increasing the likelihood of healings in our own lives and in the lives of those closest to us. The four categories of dreams of healing and physical health are:

- Advice dreams for maintenance of personal bodily health.
- Healing dreams for companion souls.
- Shared healing dreams with one another.
- Healing insights carried over from the dream state to consciousness.

ADVICE DREAMS FOR MAINTENANCE OF PERSONAL BODILY HEALTH

The most elementary type of healing dream focuses upon the refinement and maintenance of personal bodily health. Insights received from dreams may not involve major health issues or grandiose healing schemes, but they do usually offer the dreamer statements designed to tune-up the body to the point where it will operate at peak efficiency. The advice given ranges from short one-liners or a miniseries of visual images, to rather extensive physical examinations of the bodily dysfunction. In either case the message is clearly transmitted along with the corrective measures to be adopted to assure physical improvement. If the advice is put into practice, changes begin to take place within several hours or a week or two at the most. Permit me to cite several prime examples of this subcategory to illustrate my point.

During the third week of March 1983, a minor pain made its appearance across the small of my back. I could not recall how I hurt myself but began applying heat and massage to alleviate the condition. As if to assure me that no major disaster loomed on the horizon, on March 27th as I awoke, I received the following sentence of explanation and vote of confidence in my choice of treatment.

"You hurt your back picking up the brown suitcase. You'll be ok."

Another message received May 29, 1984, stated in no uncertain terms what my sedentary work life was accomplishing with regard to my circulatory system.

"Your blood does not circulate well. You need to jog."

From September to November of 1984 my husband Jim suffered from intermittent but excruciating episodes of pain brought about by his bout with kidney stones. After sitting up with him from 3:00 to 4:00 AM on September 28th, I returned to bed in a state of exhaustion wondering when he would be released from his agony. A healing dream transpired that contained advice for pain reduction.

The Analgesic Quality of Rosemary Tea

It is raining and a man is ill. I read a book that discusses the healing quality of rosemary. I think I should use it in hot water.

Knowing next to nothing about herbal cures I looked up the medicinal properties of rosemary. I was surprised to find that not only does rosemary improve circulation but is also *antispasmodic.* Thereafter, Jim drank sizable quantities of rosemary tea, and while it did not offer him a complete cure, it reduced his discomfort to a more tolerable level until the final healing was accomplished.

Before leaving this topic I would like to touch on one final point which is worthy of further consideration. The subject in question is spiritual responsibility in connection with personal healing and development of a higher level of awareness. *Namely, when an individual receives a "healing reading" or a physical healing, a spiritual responsibility is also incurred. The healing carries with it an obligation to share with others one's newly acquired wisdom and healing energies. This is especially true in cases involving similarity of issues or diseases.* If this personal responsibility is not shouldered, chances are the healing will be of a temporal nature and a resurfacing of the condition will occur, which ultimately may prove more devastating than the initial circumstances. This idea will be dealt with in depth in the chapter on Spiritual Healing.

HEALING DREAMS FOR COMPANION SOULS

Not only is the dreamer able to invoke physical guidance and healing for himself, but given that all minds are in contact with one another, we are often assigned the task of personally healing our friends and acquaintances. This is accomplished through the medium of dream revelations which contain transmissions commenting on aberrant conditions regarding their physical health. When companion soul revelations are received, the most important consideration is how the dreamer should communicate the health and healing information effectively without summoning up undue alarm and pronounced anxiety for the companion soul. To bluntly state to your closest friend that you envisioned him in the hospital suffering from severe heart failure is most *unproductive.* In addition to asking for direction from higher realms, try applying the following questions to the situation. The concept of *balanced introspection* (examining the material transmitted from all angles) is the key here.

- Is this truly information that will prove fruitful to the companion soul involved, or was it merely given for your own understanding of his situation?
- If the healing dream merits communication, in what ways will it provide assistance?
- Are there prescriptions suggested as well as an assessment of the physical disorder?
- Is a cure likely, or is this a non-healable karmic condition with which the companion soul must contend?
- Are there specific ways by which you can be instrumental in the application of your friend's healing?

The concept of *balanced introspection* in dreams of this type is essential to assure oneself that the most positive healing course and methods are selected and realized.

Two prime examples of this healing type of dream evolved through the precise interpretation and utilization of precognitive and health information by two of our former Christopher Newport Parapsychology students. The theme of both is pregnancy and childbirth, and in each case, significant lessons were learned and incorporated into the individual's life pattern. The outcomes of each were radically different, however.

The first case in point involves Kara Andrews. A parapsychology student in the fall of 1983, she quickly acquired the knack of sifting through her dream material to retrieve nuggets of wisdom and self-knowledge and then translating these valuable ideas into goal-oriented plans of action. The outcomes of her plans proved fruitful. She lost a considerable amount of weight, guided herself through an ill-fated love affair, and eventually married a likeable young man several months after completing our course. Immediately thereafter, she became pregnant, and because miscarriages had plagued other female members of her family, she requested an intuitive reading from Jim and me. I observed what I felt were twins, but one was malformed and departed while the other was born without incident.

The interpretation later proved to be inaccurate in light of what transpired. In retrospect, I now feel this was the death of the *first* child I was witnessing, and the second infant will be born without complication.

To continue with the story, Kara's pregnancy was carefully monitored until the final few weeks before birth. Just before the predicted date of delivery she experienced this dream.

The White Coffin

> My baby is born, and I bring it home from the hospital. I hold *it* in a *car* seat on my *right* shoulder. Then, I observe I am holding a *small white coffin* instead. I carry it up to the second floor, but our nursery is on the first.

The car seat suggests the physical body, and the right shoulder indicates a future event. (For those of my readers not familiar with dream symbology, please refer to *Guidelines for Healing Dreams* at the end of this chapter as well as Appendix D.)

Three days before the birth, she dreamed her baby was doing the dead-man's float and then smiled at her and waved good-bye. She woke up crying hysterically, and requested an immediate examination. The doctors could find no heartbeat. Eventually, the baby was born dead. The event was extremely traumatic for both parents, but several weeks later she confided to me that, without the warning signs of the impending danger presented in the initial dream and the spiritual assurance of happiness portrayed by the smile and wave of that brave little soul as he departed this life, she doubted she would have survived such an ordeal and remained emotionally stable.

The second case has a more positive outcome. Diane Thomas, a student who had enrolled in our first parapsychology course in the spring of '83, stopped by my office in April of 1985, and bouncing her cooing 6 week old baby daughter on her knee, she related this inspirational episode to me.

Diane's blood is Rh negative. During the first trimester of her pregnancy her doctor checked the amniotic fluid in her uterus and noted the bilirubin reading was dangerously high. This usually means damage to the unborn infant if it continues at the same or higher levels. The doctor suggested introduction of labor or a caesarean section. Faced with these dismal alternatives, she silently retreated to an isolated room in the hospital where she worked. She prayerfully entreated God to grant her three things. She prayed for a normal child, a daughter, and finally, that she be sweet. After what seemed an interminable length of time, she felt a peaceful serenity encompass her being. Intuitively, she knew she would have a dream that night that would contain the response to her plea. She did not. Coincidently, the following morning *her husband* remarked that he knew they would have no difficulty locating a suitable home when they moved to Washington in June. When she inquired why he felt that way, he related this dream.

The Perfect Room

> We are looking for a new house in Washington. There is quite a bit of dirt in the doorway of the one we are considering buying. We are given a choice of various rooms to decorate as we move down the hall, but we refuse some of them as they are not appropriate. At the end of the hall is the master bedroom. On the left is a blue room and on the right a *pink* room which is sparkling clean and bright.

(*Interpretation:* Washington means a cleansing of the burdens. Washing = cleansing; ton = burdens. Dirt signifies the initial rise of the bilirubin level. Note during the state of transition in the hallway, the choices of induction of labor and the C-section are refused. The Thomases already had a young boy which is depicted by the blue room to the left of the *master* bedroom. The pink room on the right (future) signifies the birth of a beautiful and healthy daughter.)

Diane's prayers had been answered in her husband's dream. This was a more powerful Truth because his unknowing mind had no way to slant the information she desired to receive. The most mindboggling part of the story is in the third trimester. Her bilirubin count went down and, at birth, her baby daughter's blood showed no signs of erethro blastosis. "And," she added, "she certainly is sweet!"

SHARED HEALING DREAMS FOR ONE ANOTHER

As we advance in dream work, we develop the capacity not only to dream *for* a companion soul but, as a result of consciousness expansion, eventually participate in shared dreams *with* intimates and with members of groups formed for the purpose of pooling their dream resource material for the evolvement of the group as a spiritual whole. "One of the most valuable things a dream group offers is simply that, like 'two heads,' several heads are better than one. Each of us has our blind spots, and sharing and working on our dreams with others who know us well makes up for the natural limitations of solo dreamwork."[2]

Through intensive review and interpretation of dreams, expanding minds realize that not only are dreams soul flights into higher realms in an unquenchable thirst for esoteric knowledge, but they may also be the vehicle for achieving physical healings for others while the body lies at rest. All that is really required, after the processes of dream incubation and interpretation have been perfected, is the strong desire on the part of participating friends or members of a dream group to become a true instrument of healing for the afflicted soul. To quote Phyllis A. Koch-Sheras, author of *Dream On,* "You don't have to wait for your dreams to offer you health advice spontaneously. You can educate them to provide this advice when you need it, through dream incubation. If you wish to help a friend by incubating a telepathic dream of her condition, it may help to get a personal item, such as a scarf or piece of jewelry, to help you focus on her. You can then take this item to bed with you and suggest to yourself that you are going to dream for your friend's benefit."[3] Shared healing dreams are among the most powerful tools that can be evoked by beginning spiritual healers because of the intensity of focused energies generated by like-minded souls.

For the past several years an evidential technique I have employed to verify the existence of telepathic dreaming among our Christopher Newport College Parapsychology students is this healing dream exercise. The class is divided into groups consisting of 6 persons each. One member of each group volunteers to be the subject of the experiment. This person is preferably someone who is the victim of a physical dysfunction, but the other participants of the group do not know the nature of the disorder. On an appointed night the "dream healers" request health information for the physical healing of that soul. All dreams received are recorded and shared among the group during the next class meeting. The results have proved to be amazingly accurate not only in fact, but also in accrued healing benefits. Examples of two such cases provide provocative insights into this phenomenon.

Janice Day suffered from a diabetic condition. During the day her blood sugar would elevate to a relatively high level and then plunge dramatically with the approach of evening. Her physical condition was one of constant exhaustion because of the variation in blood-sugar levels. Three shared healing dreams and intuitive impressions recorded by members of the group honed in quite precisely on Janice's condition.

***The Dead Battery* (Student I)**

> I see a pale blue station wagon has car trouble. The lights flicker on and off. The driver attempts to start it three separate times and then realizes the car battery is dead. This happens at night at the edge of a ditch near some woods.

Note the weakness present in Janice's "physical vehicle" as connoted by the pale blue color. This is associated with the dramatic drop of blood sugar nocturnally. The lower energy level is depicted also by the dead battery. Although no cure was given, the general condition of debilitation is clearly evident.

The Dark Blue Skirt (Student II)

A young woman in a clothing store wears a dark blue skirt. She looks down at her skirt and appears upset.

The Dark Blue Skirt (Janice's Dream)

I am wearing a new dark blue skirt in a store. A man comes along and pulls at my slip. I am upset by his gesture.

Janice related afterward that litmus paper turned *dark blue* in the presence of high blood-sugar levels. The tugging at her petticoat reflects the "slip" in the amount of glucose in the system. Note in both dreams the condition upsets each dreamer—thus, Student II also telepathically assumed the emotional drainage caused by Janice's illness.

Student III did not dream, but was discussing the problem with Jeanne, another parapsychology student who is a spiritual healer. Jeanne picked up the impression that there had been some problem with vitamins. Janice confirmed this, mentioning that she had changed her vitamins to a different brand recently and had noted an improvement.

The second case concerns a student Sara Hatten. The deviation from perfect physical health was a minor but an unusually irritating one. Small warts appeared intermittently on her eyelids, neck, and top part of her arms. Both dreams presented below contain healing remedies for Sara's condition.

The Salmon (Student I)

We were in an old rural house typical of those of the 1860s. The house was on a *slight hill* or *rise* with a forest area near the left of the house.

> A resident of the house has fallen ill and a physician is called in. I am dressed in old work clothes. The doctor arrives wearing a tall stovepipe hat. He sees the patient for *45* minutes. He then states that the patient needs to eat a particular kind of fish to recover. I get my fishing equipment which is homemade and proceeded to the river to fish. Soon, I appear to snag what looks like a large-mouth bass. After a considerable struggle, I land it. It is a king salmon. I give it to the doctor who says it contains necessary ingredients to cure the patient.

There are several interesting aspects in connection with this wonderful health dream. The warts are suggested by the house being situated on a slight rise. The physician's wearing of a tall *stovepipe* hat indicates the incubation of heat resulting from the usage of healing energies. The time of the examination is important—4 = a test; 5 = a change of activities. I marvelled at the eagerness of the dreamer to be of service. The conclusion of the group was that salmon contains a dietary substance that might prove beneficial to the elimination of Sara's warts. This is probably due to the fact that salmon contains a large amount of Vitamin A, which is essential for the proper healing of skin blemishes.

Healing Plants (Student II)

> A girl goes to a friend and asks for help. She takes the friend by the hand, and they walk through some beautiful woods. The friend tells her she will help her. She relates how her dead father used to walk in those woods. She says that one day an old lady had approached him and described all the plants and herbs that had healing powers. She had warned him that some of them were poisonous. Therefore, it was essential to pay close attention to one's selections. The father assimilated this wisdom and related this knowledge to his daughter, who, in turn, told it to her friend.

Student II spoke with a counselor friend about her dreams and was thrilled to find out that the counselor and her father often walked in the woods. After his death, the counselor found a book in his attic containing home remedies for herbs and healing plants. She gave it to Student II who delivered it to Sara the next week.

Student II felt sure that the book contained the information to dissolve Sara's warts.

In dreaming for one another one can easily observe that healing is a natural talent for those who demonstrate empathy for the suffering and the afflicted. Merely turning one's thoughts to those in pain can generally stimulate the flow of healing energies. Directive thought energies frequently develop the gift of absent healing.

HEALING INSIGHTS CARRIED OVER FROM THE DREAM STATE TO CONSCIOUSNESS

What recourse is left open to the dreamer if no answers are forthcoming through the medium of dreams? Is one to assume that no solution is available and that the diseased soul must continue to bear the burden of his affliction? Is such a situation justified and attributable to repayment of a karmic debt, or is there perhaps another psychic recourse as yet untapped?

After intensive deliberation and evaluation of a variety of dream methodologies through which vibrant good health may be restored, it became apparent to me that it is not mandatory for individuals to continue to suffer their physical and mental maladies. Even when healing has eluded their grasp with employment of each of the three previously cited dream procedures, there is a fourth curative option available upon request. The formula for achieving a cure is as follows:

1. As with all healing dream requests, formulate and state the health problem concisely, and petition guidance and healing insights for the afflicted soul. If no healing dreams or verbal directives are received after a normally anticipated period of time, employ each succeeding step to realize your goal in the conscious state.

2. Record all "flashes of intuition" that emerge upon your psyche as you involve yourself in daily activities. Switching your focus from one of intensity to "serene faith" can provide the fertile soil necessary for supraliminal thoughts to sprout and grow.

3. Act on unusual hunches. Do you feel a strong urge to call an old friend for no apparent reason? Are you compelled to pay a visit to the newly opened health store although it is a considerable distance from the one you normally frequent? Is there a vitamin book that catches your attention that was not available at the bookstore last week? Act on your intuitive impulses. You may be surprised at just how astute your actions prove to be.

4. Be alert for synchronistic events. Are you invited to a friend's house for lunch and find the subject of conversation centers on the health issue for which you have been actively seeking a solution? Do you turn on the TV set to discover Dr. Lendon Smith lecturing on curative measures for recovery from otitus media? These are not accidental events but rather occur synchronistically in direct response to thought transmissions that arise from the initial dream request and flourish in your active pursuit for succour for the afflicted spirit.

5. Combine all relative information gathered, and assemble a composite healing prescription that can be easily comprehended and understood by the recipient. Presentation of the document should be accomplished in an unassuming and prayerful posture rather than one of ego involvement.

6. Keep in mind that more often than not it is necessary for the individual to schedule an appointment with a practitioner of the healing arts whether it be a chiropractor, a certified masseuse, a psychologist, or a medical doctor. *Do not assume responsibilities beyond your level of competence.*

An example of this process from my own life circumstances is presented in the Alice Green case. Alice requested intuitive evaluation from Jim and me. Upon completion of the evaluation it became obvious from the physical section that a serious muscular disorder had manifested itself. In discussing the results with Alice, I learned that she had lived for several months with the horrible suspicion that she had fallen victim to multiple sclerosis. She was hesitant to seek medical confirmation of this condition fearing the loss of her current employment and ultimately, her livelihood. Now, in light of her confession, we both were ladened with the burden of her dilemma. Upon examination of the reading, I detected no information contained within the suggestions which could possibly result in any type of healing remedy for Alice. (This often happens when it is necessary for the healer to secure trained medical help because of the serious nature of the illness.) Faced with a situation for which I could determine no logical solution, I sought guidance from "The Healing Dream Forces". After a week of recording numerous dreams, none of which afforded me any type of advice concerning Alice's predicament, I was no closer to the answer than I had been before. Pondering matters over in my mind, I decided to research materials and booklets on multiple sclerosis and forward these to Alice in an envelope along with the recommendation that she visit a physician immediately to confirm or deny the diagnosis. However, one thing led to another, and although I held the thought in mind, the project never became a reality.

Three weeks passed, and then synchronicity came into play. One morning JoAnne Squires and I had planned to attend a morning session of an ARE Conference having to do with medicine and healing remedies—a subject dear to both our hearts. Amazingly, just prior to the start of the meeting we encountered Alice Green. This would not have been so surprising if she had been a member of or frequent visitor to ARE—however, not only did she not belong to the Association, but also she had never set foot on the premises until five minutes before our meeting.

"What brings you here?" I gasped.

"Oh," she stated nonchalantly, "I decided to do some research on multiple sclerosis today, and I figured the best place to start was the ARE Library." With that she pulled out several booklets she had already purchased from the ARE Bookstore on the subject.

(These were among those I had intended to send.) Then, she politely inquired about the nature of my visit.

"JoAnne and I are attending a health lecture this morning," I replied.

No sooner had I uttered these words then I recalled having read that the physician addressing the meeting that morning specialized in the treatment of multiple sclerosis. I passed this information on to her, and she promised to make an appointment with him after he completed his speech. Now, how's that for synchronicity, folks?

Prayers and supplications are not always answered through a direct voice experience with God. Occasionally, "short side trips" are required for maximum educational achievement and personal spiritual advancement.

GUIDELINES FOR DREAM HEALING

1. As with all requests for dream guidance state the problem as clearly and concisely as possible. The more specific the inquiry, the more astute the response. You always get exactly what you ask for so *be specific.* You may either write the question in your dream journal or state it silently before entering the sleep state. Always ask with an air of expectancy.

2. It is prudent to ask for a personal item belonging to the individual for whom you are requesting healing. As with psychometry, the item serves as a focus for the channeling of intuitive impressions. Place it beside you or under your pillow, whichever seems more comfortable for you.

3. It is important to seek knowledge regarding the mental origins of the disease as well as its physical manifestation. Without mind healing, the physical cure may be an impossibility.

4. Request information regarding specified modes of treatment for the alleviation of the illness. These might include dietary changes, vitamin therapy, exercise, medical or chiropractic appointments, or even absent healing. If the information is too symbolic, ask for a clarifying dream.

5. Assuming the role of a healer carries with it an innate responsibility for accepting all accompanying duties. Be certain you are willing and able to undertake such a role. If your response is affirmative, then solicit guidance as to practical measures you might personally adopt to increase the chances of an expeditious recovery.

6. *Upon awakening write down all dreams and impressions received.* What you think is nonsense may in reality provide the key to that individual healing. Don't be too quick to judge symbols as meaningless. If the material is largely symbolic, become knowledgeable as to the meaning of your own symbolic associations. A short general list of dream symbols is listed in Appendix D. This will get you started, but a file card system identifying one's personal symbology is by far the best procurer of individualistic dream interpretations.

7. Dreaming as a healing group generates more healing energy and power than solitary dreaming. When two or three people dream together, it is judicious to compare dream themes and content for cross-correspondence. When this phenomenon occurs, you can almost certainly be assured of the validity of the nocturnal wisdom.

8. Healing suggestions sometime require research for validation. After all the proof of the effectiveness of the treatment has been assembled, decide on the best possible method for presentation to the healee.

9. Check with your charge periodically to determine what, if any, progress is being made. If additional dream insights are transmitted as the healing proceeds, be sure to apprise the healee of these alterations.

10. The last rule is simple. Always render thanks for that which is so bountifully given from above.

CHAPTER 6

Shared Dreams

The true reason for helping another is that it is our duty to help others in so far as we can do so wisely, or because it is an expression of love.

Emmet Fox—*The Sermon On The Mount*

As one becomes more sophisticated in dream incubation and self-programming, the ability to cultivate highly specialized nocturnal experiences becomes more and more within the grasp of our subconscious. At some point in the course of this evolutionary dream process, the remarkable phenomenon of reciprocal and shared dreams is discovered.

Shared dreams are precisely what the term implies. Two dreamers share similar if not identical dreams. According to Dr. Stephen LaBerge in Lucid Dreaming: *The Power of Being Awake and Aware in Your Dreams,* "Accounts of 'mutual dreaming' (dreams apparently shared by two or more people) raise the possibility that the dream world may be in some cases just as objectively real as the physical world. This is because the primary criterion of 'objectivity' is that an experience is shared by more than one person—a fact supposedly true of mutual dreams."[1] This may be a once-in-a-lifetime incident or it may be a commonly recurring event depending upon one's receptivity to the concept. "There are suggestions that mutual dreaming abilities have been cultivated to a high level by a number of Sufi Mystics."[2] Various accounts of Sufi Masters being able to appear in the dreams of anyone they choose have been recorded through the centuries.

In my own investigation of advanced dreaming techniques the shared or reciprocal dream ranks high on the list of skills to be desired, refined, and employed as an animating principle for the spiritualization of one's soul. Reciprocation in dreams is also both an invaluable and a mutually informative method of communication between friends and relatives, particularly when times and events of importance are taking place. What type of catalyst serves to ignite an episode of mutual dreaming? Nowhere have I read a more enlightened and illuminating response to this thought-provoking question than that proposed by Ronald Beesley in his *The Emergence of Cosmic Forces.* In a commentary on the power of prayer he wrote, "People often ask how to pray. The best way, of course, is not to pray, just to sit and think. The thoughts of our own deep inner self are better than all the clatter of words read out of a book, or supplications which you think are necessary for your welfare. Thought itself is, or can be, deep prayer because it is communication with our own universe. . . . I was talking once about the power of prayer with a luminous being from the higher life during sleep one night. I asked, 'What is the idea of power within prayer—how does it operate?' He said, 'It is operated by the degree of the individual's own sensitivity to us.' It almost seems as if there has to be a mental-spiritual link to an area of communication which some people are able to develop within themselves, and because of that, when they think of people, talk to them, or ask of them without anything necessarily being said, you can be almost certain that that thing will happen."[3] I am certain the same principles are at work spontaneously when mutual dreaming takes place.

If we accept the proposition that shared dreams are a tenable avenue for a higher level of communication, then the next logical issue for scrutiny would be the conditions that enhance their occurrence. Results of a five-year investigation suggest the following five conditions.

1. Close family members and friends dream together for the fun of shared experience as well as for the acquisition of factual knowledge.

2. Through dream sharing unspoken fears and frustrations can be conveyed from victim to counselor.

3. Mutual dreams can depict positive future events such as a new job, a prospective pregnancy, the seal of approval for a scheduled journey, and heightened creativity. The natural focus of these is to expand current awareness thus increasing the probability of their advent.

4. Shared dreams often bring an element of teaching with one dreamer assuming the role of student and the second a guiding influence.

5. Ultimately, the shared dream may provide the key to previously unresolved problems. This is accomplished with souls dwelling on the Earth Plane or with higher level entities.

The bond of commonality that lies crosscurrent here is the express intent of the soul's intimate desire to explore and release whatever negative or positive emotions are generated by the dreamer in connection with that specific category.

Further insight into shared dreams can be gained by discussing the common dream plots associated with each category of shared dreams.

DREAMING TOGETHER FOR FUN AND KNOWLEDGE

Richard Bach in his best selling novel, *The Bridge Across Forever,* describes how he and his wife, Leslie Parrish, engaged in a joint project whereby they agreed to project themselves out of their bodies while dreaming, and to meet astrally and travel together to worlds unknown. Having read *Journeys Out of the Body, The Practical Guide to Astral Projection* and the like, they began their experiment. It was in no way as easy as they had fantasized. Weeks turned into months with no progress. Five months into the experiment, however, a breakthrough was achieved, and Richard woke up to find himself floating three feet in the air above his sleeping form. Disappointment accompanied success, because the flight was "sans Leslie." Through more concentrated efforts and subsequent refinements of programming, one month hence Bach recorded the following joyous moment—"This time I was sitting in the air when I woke over the bed, and what caught my attention was a radiant form afloat, flawless sparkling silver and gold barely two feet away, equisite living love. 'Oh, my!' I thought. 'The Leslie I've been seeing with my eyes isn't the tiniest part of who she is! She's body within body, life within life; unfolding, unfolding, unfolding—will I ever know all of her?'

"No words required, I knew whatever she wanted me to know.

"Like two warm balloons, we lifted together through the ceiling as if it were cool air.

"The roof of the house sank beneath us, rough wooden shingles covered in fallen pine needles, brick chimney, television antenna pointed toward civilization. Down on the decks, flowers asleep in planters.

"Then we were above the trees, drifting carefully out over the water, on a night of stray wispy clouds in a sky of stars—thin scattered cirrus, visibility unlimited, wind from the south at two knots. There was no temperature.

"If this is life, I thought, it is infinitely beautifuller than anything I have ever—"[4]

The exhilaration of accomplishment in concert with the euphoric release from the body physical render a sense of exhaltation seldom attainable on this plane of existence.

A second example of dreaming together for acquisition of knowledge can be found in this delightful recounting by Elizabeth Hollis of mutual dreams that averted pending disasters on a previously planned trip to the Bahamas. In a letter to me received during the last week in May of 1983 she wrote "Back in February you said that when we went to the Bahamas we should check everything—there was no danger but to check. Well, I tried to get more on this and came up with the fact that the problem would be administrative in some way rather than a physical problem with the plane. John and I racked our brains, checked passports, licenses, and hotel reservations, and everything seemed to be in order. Then we decided to dream together (what do people do who don't have all these resources?). John dreamed about our life jackets being missing and neither one of us had them on our lists. I dreamed that John was on the telephone trying to contact some business that had gone out of business. Today he called the hotel for just one more check on the reservations and found the hotel had no record of us and had rooms for only 2 out of 4 nights! This would have been quite distressing to learn after we had arrived rather than now, when we can scramble to do something about it. We appreciate the tip as well as the resourcefulness of our dream guidance."[5]

DREAMING TOGETHER TO SOLVE PERSONAL FRUSTRATIONS AND ANXIETIES

During late summer of 1985 internal changes at Prentice Hall caused me to become somewhat apprehensive regarding the publication date of my forthcoming book *The Inner Eye.* At times my moods became as black as those quickly forming Virginia Beach thundershowers which, once having amassed themselves, proceeded to drench everything in their path with torrents of rain bringing ground visibility to zero. Having been soaked once too often, my husband Jim came to my rescue and provided me with this uplifting dream. Shades of Richard Bach's *Jonathan Livingston Seagull* provided inspirational credibility due to the fact that I had dreamed of my book at various times as a bird soaring skyward. Note the similarity in symbolism in Jim's dream.

The Beached Gull

> Joan and I are standing on the shore watching a sea gull flying high above our heads. He soars upward toward the heavens and then veers earthward again. At the height of one of his sallies he falters and plummets to earth. He lands nose down in the sand. A group of people nearby laugh at his plight. I shake my head in disbelief. Suddenly, a tall man with dark hair and a beard strides up, and pulling the imprisoned seagull's beak loose, releases him from bondage. The seagull, ecstatic to be free, climbs swiftly skyward again toward the stars.

Immediately upon awaking, he related this dream to me. We both felt assured that the message conveyed was a cosmic communication of hope. Within the next week a member of the production staff of Prentice Hall called to confirm the previously tentative publication date.

The second story revolves around our daughter, Robin, and an episode involving intruders. On the evening in question Jim and I were invited to a friend's house for dinner. Robin and a friend, having decided the movies in town were unappealing, had settled in for a comfortable evening of TV viewing and popcorn consumption. About 10:30 PM the telephone rang. Robin hurried to answer. A gruff male voice on the other end of the line growled, "I'm coming to get you tonight!"

Robin jumped in fear. After several minutes of trembling, she recovered her composure. Then, she and her friend decided to turn out all the lights and retreat to the safety of my bedroom. Huddling under the covers, Robin fell asleep some minutes later and began to dream the intruders had broken down the door and were mounting the stairs to the second floor to my bedroom. At that same instant the telephone rang again. The terror conjured up by her nightmare combined with the frightening anticipation of a second threatening telephone call sent the blood pounding through Robin's veins. She gingerly picked up the receiver.

"Hello?" Her voice was barely audible.

"Hello, yourself!" A jovial voice boomed through the receiver. Robin giggled with relief. The voice was none other than her much-beloved brother Jimmy calling from Richmond to check in on the family as was his custom.

Robin related the events of the evening to him. Jimmy immediately advised her to go down the street to a neighbors' until we returned home. They were preparing to leave as we arrived home at 12:30. Within minutes normalcy returned to our household. We relayed this message to Jimmy in a subsequent telephone call.

On Monday Robin learned that the initial phone call was the work of a jokester classmate of hers. (We failed to see the humor.) The point is this—three days later a letter from Elizabeth arrived describing this dream John had recorded the previous Sunday morning.

The Intruders

> Elizabeth and I visiting you in a different house. You weren't in, but we had the key so we let ourselves in. Robin, who had dark hair (Robin is a golden blonde), came in from another part of the house terrified because she had thought we were intruders.

It is amazing to me how closely the dream coincided with waking reality as well as with what Robin experienced in her dream. Here again the Hollis-Windsor family telepathic connection is at work assuring us that "Uncle John" is also watching Robin in our absence.

DREAMING TOGETHER TO ENHANCE POSITIVE FUTURE REALITIES

The week ending October 20th, 1984, found me in a quandary. Elizabeth and I had airline reservations for our jaunt to California to visit both my sister, Arlene Helmus, and Alan Vaughan. There was one drawback, however. Jim was suffering from periodic spasms of pain from the dislodged kidney stone which made me most reluctant to leave him. I was having second thoughts about the journey and was seriously considering rescheduling the entire trip when this series of dreams encouraged me to remain steadfast in my decision to go.

October 20, 1984
Dream I—The Swerving Car (Joan's Dream)

I am on the way to Virginia Beach and drive through the Hampton Roads Bridge Tunnel. It is wet and slippery and the car swerves to and fro, but I manage to remain on the road.

Then I meet John Schuester, an employee at the ARE Library. He tells me that my sister is on the telephone. I pick up the receiver and notice it is made of gold. She asks if I am coming to California.

Dream II—The Motionless Vehicle (Jim's Dream)

A car is stuck in the mud on the side of the road.

Note that in both dreams my car is either out of my control from vacillation or being completely immobilized. John Schuester's name is a play on words advising me to "shoe stir" and travel to California.

Dream III—The Polluted Pool (Joan's Dream)

A friend has come to dive into our swimming pool. I inform her that she cannot swim because it has not been cleaned for four weeks. (Jim had been ill with his kidney stone for four weeks.)

Dream IV—The Crystal Clear Swimming Pool (Jim's Dream)

I stand beside our swimming pool with several people. The Director of the Mental Health Services in Virginia suddenly jumps in the water. I am going to dive in and rescue him, but before I can, a Nun appears from the depths of the pool and makes the sign of the cross. Immediately the pool water becomes crystal clear. The Director surfaces, his arms loaded with gifts for all present.

In comparing the two dreams one is amazed by the similarity in symbology. Both dreams are concerned with Jim's "polluted kidney water," but mine depicts negativism toward making the journey while his suggests my journey carries with it the possibility of good mental health and the acquisition of newly acquired gifts for all of us.

Interestingly enough, there is also a reference to the regaining of vibrant physical health through divine intervention. One month later Jim was healed by Grace Di Biccari, as discussed earlier, who wore a cross.

This verbal message was given to me as I awoke.

THE PERMISSION
THE TRIP IS NOW POSSIBLE!

The most impressive part about the entire series of our shared dreams is the strong element of reassurance which winds its way through Jim's dreams and finally reaches the point of culmination in *The Permission* message. Thus, armed with blessings from The Higher Realms and a loving kiss from my husband, I light-heartedly packed my bags and boarded the plane for Dallas and San Francisco.

SHARING DREAMS FOR THE EXPRESS PURPOSE OF SPIRITUAL INSTRUCTION

The role of instructor and student are flexible

In this first set of shared dreams I serve as instructor and guide for Elizabeth Hollis. In the second the roles are reversed.

The initial set of shared dreams have as their theme the Windsor-Hollis *Psychical Research Project.* My *Home-Made Teddy Bears* dream was recorded on January 5, 1985 and Elizabeth's *Teddy Bear Twins* on January 21, 1985.

Home-Made Teddy Bears (Joan's Dream)

A close friend and I are looking at a rack of teddy bears that are home-sewn. Many are snatched up as soon as they are

> completed. My friend sees a teddy bear dressed in a blue hat and a uniform. She hugs it and is going to purchase it.

Teddy Bear Twins (Elizabeth's Dream)

> I see a rack of teddy bears. They wear uniforms and blue hats.

The Psychical Research Project idea originated with me. Therefore, I tend to instruct Elizabeth with regard to purpose and format. In my dream the close friend is my partner, Elizabeth. The teddy bear represents security, "baring one's soul"—and a division of emotions. The readings are homemade (home-sewn) and uniform. (There are always 6 sections to a Holistic Life Reading as described in Chapter 3). The blue hat is indicative of spiritual thoughts. Finally, there is a suggestion that they are desirable and beneficial as they are snatched up soon after completion and hugged affectionately. The theme of many is Love Yourself.

There was a time lapse of 16 days between the shared dreams but it is obvious my partner Elizabeth has picked up on the importance of the qualities that are inherent in a Holistic Life Reading for the benefit of both client and sensitive. This was approximately one year after the inception of the Project.

The set of shared dreams in which Elizabeth plays the role of teacher centers upon my disappointment on not being able to go with Jim on a business trip due to work obligations. I recorded a number of dreams in which I was packing, unpacking, and repacking my suit case. These occurred 1–2 weeks before Jim's leaving.

The Unmanageable Suitcase (Joan's Dream)

> I am packing clothes for a trip with Jim. The suitcase is on the packing stand. As I place the last clothes in it, the suitcase falls off the stand dumping my clothes on the floor. This happens repeatedly although I try to secure it several times.

In early May of 1985 Elizabeth wrote the following dream asking for an interpretation. In her wisdom she was asking me to take a look at my own emotions. The UPS Truck is a standing joke between the two of us because we often send things by United Parcel to one another and laugh at our work being parceled out from *UP-per Realms.*

The UPS Truck Journey (Elizabeth's Dream)

> I'm on a UPS truck, going to Williamsburg, which turns a corner too fast and rolls and tips on its front end. It stops short of going down a long steep hill. I'm relieved. I go back to my hotel and realize I have forgotten my suitcase so it's just as well I didn't get there. The driver of the UPS truck says not to worry, as I can sue UPS for whatever I want.[6]

Elizabeth was instructing me to stop worrying about not making the trip. In her estimation if I stopped short regarding the inappropriateness of making the trip, I would not lose ground. Hints of my still desiring to make the trip are in evidence as the bag is left on the UPS truck. Note the driver in control of delivering UPS parcels says not to worry as one can petition (sue) the UPS Company and ask for whatever one wants. This implies visualization for things that will really serve me better. Throughout the entire dream an important lesson is being imparted, and wise Elizabeth requires her student to internalize its message herself.

SHARED DREAMS OFFER THE SOLUTION TO IRRESOLUBLE PROBLEMS

This can be accomplished through shared dreams on this level or through those that emanate from a higher state. Since the majority of examples cited have dealt with mind-to-mind contact on the Earth Plane, it would be judicious to cite an example of communication between cosmic levels.

Ever since giving my first intuitive readings I had been reflecting upon the origin of the material. Whether it originated in my own subconscious or was channeled from spiritual sources was at question. Jim and I had often discussed this issue, particularly in our attempts to refine our reading techniques. Our goal was to achieve a higher level of accuracy with regard to each individual's requests. After three and one half years, The Higher Sources must have finally become fed up with my low level of confidence. Therefore, the evening of March 24, 1984, a High Level Conference was convened and I was invited to attend (in the dream state, of course). The aim of the conclave was to determine once and for all the appropriate demeanour to be assumed as a channel for intuitive readings. The purport of the communiqúe was crystal clear.

The Cosmic Conclave

> My friend comes to invite me to a Board of Directors dinner meeting. We drive to a tall building and take the elevator to the roof garden. He ushers me inside and we seat ourselves at the end of the table. I feel like a klutz because I keep falling off my chair onto the floor, and my friend has to pick me up. Finally, the Board adjourns. We retire to the balcony adjoining the dining room. Then, my friend places his hands on my shoulders and, looking into my eyes, speaks thusly, "Exact percentages do not matter. What is important, however, is how helpful the reading is to an individual. Belief in yourself and our ability to assist is the key to successful readings. *Belief is the Key!*"

No more need be added.

GUIDELINES FOR SHARED DREAM EXPERIMENTS

Dreaming together for fun and knowledge

This should be a lighthearted dream experiment. Begin by mutual agreement on the subject of exploration. Do you want to learn how to develop more refined auric vision? Are you seeking the range and scope of your psychic talents? Is your quest less cosmic such as what your next beau will look like or how to secure the funds for that new outfit for Saturday night? Would it be whether or not you are the designated winner of that coveted sports award? Are you both writers who would benefit from disseminated information regarding expansion of a co-creative work? All these questions might be considered before proceeding further. When the subject for investigation has been determined, decide on a date and time to begin the experiment. Write down in specific terms your inquiry. Mentally repeat your question over and over as you drift off to sleep. Upon awakening, as always, record all dreams and impressions. Now comes the interesting part. Meet with your co-experimenter to share and compare your communications. The results will truly amaze you. Pleasure and fun are often the seedlings of growth which lead to a more joyous and productive life style.

Dreaming together to solve personal frustrations and anxieties

Experiment two is more serious in nature. While the issues are not life threatening, they usually involve some disagreeable frustration or anxiety that has not been or cannot be dealt with on an intellectual level. Consult with your partner to crystallize the issues. Do you suffer from test anxiety? Do you stutter or stammer when you are asked to speak before an audience? Do you drive six days from Washington to Los Angeles rather than setting foot on an airplane for the six-hour cross-country trip? Are you so shy that you become tongue-tied when being introduced to strangers? Do shopping malls, tunnels, and high places cause you to break out in a cold sweat? Once the problem has been delineated, follow the same procedure as with Experiment one. Once all the dream material is recorded, pool your insights. It has been my experience that verbally shared dream insights give rise to expanded resolutions. Eventually, more ideas are channeled than those solely received through dreams. *One more comment*—Don't discount counseling as an option. A competent counselor can often accomplish more in several hours than you can personally achieve in months of fruitless individual self-seeking.

Dreaming together to enhance positive future realities

As with Experiment one, Experiment three contains an element of joy. The question to be asked here is, "Can you change your reality by refocusing your thought patterns?" The answer is "Absolutely!" And the key that opens the lock is *visual imagery.* How does this work? First, decide on the goal to be achieved. Have you seen the house of your dreams, but the price tag is too high? Visualize an affordable price. Are you in competition with a co-worker for a job promotion? You are more competent, but he is more aggressively pursuing the opportunity. See yourself already occupying the new office. Are you an undiscovered artist trying to market your new paintings? Envision several buyers writing you substantial checks for your creations. Whatever the desired circumstances, new realities can be created faster by the thought patterns of several minds than by a single mentality. Have your partners write down their enhancements and then *dream, dream, dream* and *visualize, visualize, visualize.* Your shared dream knowledge will undoubtedly provide action-oriented plans to be carried out after careful deliberations regarding their outcomes. The Power of the Mind is the greatest transforming resource in the Universe. Use it!

Shared dreams for the express purpose of spiritual instruction. The role of instructor and student are flexible.

Experiment four is a more advanced type of experiment. It should be done with an intimate or spiritually developed personality. The core of the experiment is to seek self-understanding and beyond that, self-growth. One of the partners chooses the role of the student and the other the instructor. The student should feel secure that the instructor will provide the lessons in an atmosphere of unconditional acceptance and love. Within this context, gigantic personal strides can be affected. Questions to be posed in this experiment might be, "What are my best and worst character traits?" "What does the chronic health condition I suffer from symbolize?" "What is my soul's purpose?" The role of the student is to be receptive. The challenge to the teacher is to present in love. Dream teaching in exercises such as this provide invaluable lessons in self-examination.

Shared dreams offer solutions to irresoluble problems

Experiment five is the most sophisticated. The dream partners should be actual participants in the complaint or dilemma. If this is not possible, close intimates can serve as telepathic partners. Personal guides or higher entities can fulfill this role also. Clarification of the issues is the first step. (Formulation of the major life question should be stated. They might focus on: Why is there such intense jealousy between my siblings, and how can it be resolved? What are the major issues in our marital conflicts? Can these tensions be reduced or eliminated? Why did my mother choose to die in this manner and at this time? Why do I constantly treat my father-in-law so negatively? And the last and greatest question of all—What is my personal relationship to the universe and God? When dreams on these inquiries have been received, a time for *discussion* and *open communication* needs to be scheduled. Open-mindedness, acceptance of self-responsibility, and forgiveness are the ingredients of self- and family healing. Outlining of short- and long-range goals and plans can then serve as a life map to follow on the road to soul-actualization. Praying together at the end of these sessions seals the bonds of friendship and love and acknowledges the Christ-consciousness within each of us. Within this Partnership failure is not possible.

CHAPTER 7

Serial Dreams

Just as your attitudes and behavior in relation to a particular issue may change over time, so a dream series will reflect and parallel the patterns of your waking life.

Phyllis R. Koch-Sheras—
Dream On

For four years or more during our childhood my sister, Arlene, and I attended Saturday afternoon matinees at our local movie theatre on a regular basis. Serial movies were often featured. Week after week the fade-out found the heroine dangling by a rope from a lofty precipice. The villain was poised above her, knife in hand, and an evil smirk on his lips. How would she escape from the clutches of this depraved scoundrel? This burning question motivated us to lay aside nickles and dimes that would have otherwise been spent for ice cream or candy until we could amass another 40 cents—the price of admission to next Saturday's movie—and learn the answer. Once having successfully extricated herself from one perilous situation, it required only thirty short minutes for this adventuresome lass to permit herself to be recaptured by her foul arch enemy. Once again Arlene and I perched on the edge of our seats as a speeding engine bore down on her at 90 mph. Alas, we left the movie in dismay realizing that another 40 cents out of our allowances would have to be laid aside to discover the outcome of this latest episode. Eventually, with enough money, patience, and time invested the serial would end happily with the heroine gazing soulfully into the eyes of her beloved as they rode off into the sunset.

What does all of this have to do with dreams? Simply this: Week after week, as the dreamer records innumerable dreams in a journal, patterns begin to emerge each having a central focus or core theme. Each theme delineates an issue currently prominent in waking reality. Further, these dream patterns progress in serial form so that forward momentum is more pronounced as the dreaming mind becomes more attuned to the issue at hand. As with my serial movie, a satisfying conclusion is achieved only in direct proportion to the personal time, patience, and effort expended.

After five years of investigating serial dreams, I have concluded that there are seven important characteristics to be considered regarding serial dreams. These characteristics should be thoroughly examined and internalized before attempting to immerse oneself in these nocturnal serializations.

SEVEN BASIC RULES FOR MASTERY OF SERIAL DREAMS

Serial dreams are clearly recognizable, because of the recurrence of identical symbology. Dreaming continuously of stopped up toilets suggests that the dreamer should perhaps begin a program of freer elimination and internal cleansing. A gift of precious jewels carries with it the message of receiving gems of wisdom or it could indeed mean a literal presentation. One of the symbols for my books is a baby who grows into a toddler as the publication date draws near. "After you have kept your dream journal for some time, you will find that certain themes and symbols recur. Usually, these have the same, or a similar, meaning for the various dreams in which they appear. Dreams that seem nonsensical or baffling may make perfect sense later when the same theme or symbol appears again in a dream where its meaning is clear."[1]

A series of three dreams recorded in January of 1984 presents the same symbol several times in order to alert me to the danger of a potential infection.

A Future Ear Infection (January 4, 1985)

There is a large quantity of hard wax in my left ear. This needs to be cleared. It will take two attempts to procure it. (Two attempts meant 2 more dreams in the series to secure my undivided attention.)

The Toppling Audi (January 16, 1985)

It is snowing out. I find myself in our Shellbank home. The small Audi (Aud-I) has toppled over on its *left* side. Someone straightens it up. (Aud-I means hearing as I associate this with *audio* testing.)

Advice for a Healthy Left Ear (January 16, 1985)

There is a tube which is full of hot water and a metal pan. I am getting all the wax cleaned out of my left ear. The red appearance disappears.

Note in all three dreams the symbology is the same or similar—the *left ear* is in danger of becoming infected because of impacted wax. The third dream prompted me to call for an immediate appointment with Dr. Bell, at which time the measures suggested were implemented and a possible infection was fended off.

A definitive step-by-step progression involving a central theme is evident upon examination of a set of serial dreams. When a series of dreams centering around a particular issue is received, an advancing pattern of action begins to emerge offering a commentary upon the intensity of emotion or energy the dreamer is expending to resolve or ignore the problem situation with which he or she is confronted. The frequency or recurrence of serial dreams is in direct proportion to the attention of dream focuses on the issue as well as to the enormity of the impact exerted in waking reality.

A delightful sequence of dreams related to me by Grace Fogg, Reference Librarian for the ARE Library, provides us with an excellent example of progressive dreaming. The dream series in question unfolded when Grace was a mere child of ten, but the lesson for the psyche imparted by the serialization remains etched upon her mind to this day. The series is entitled *The Treasure House.*

Dream I—The Tunnel

> I (Grace) am standing at the entrance to a long tunnel. The way is well-lighted and I begin to cautiously make my way down the corridor toward a closed door at the end of the passageway. An air of mystery pervades.

Here the dream ended. As a girl of ten Grace had become an avid reader of Carolyn Keene's Nancy Drew mystery books. Thus, her natural curiosity and love of detective stories led her to wonder throughout the day what might lie behind that closed door. Tantalized by the pending mystery she retired slightly earlier the following evening. *The dream continued.*

Dream II—The Key

> I find myself again in the same tunnel, but on this occasion I have arrived before the locked wooden door. A thought crosses my mind that if I possessed the key, I would be privy to what lies beyond. I reach in my pocket and retrieve *a key!* I place it in the lock.

Again the dream terminates! With this turn of events Grace was truly hooked! All day she waited impatiently for the arrival of evening and the eventual solution to *The Mystery Behind The Locked Door.* She retired an hour earlier than usual in order to attend "The Early Bird Matinee." *The dream continued.*

Dream III—The Treasure

> Again I stand before the locked door. I turn the key and hear the latch click. Slowly, the door creaks open. Behind it I catch glimpses of shining treasure.

The alarm sounded. 7:00 AM. "Impossible!" cried Grace. "I was almost there!" That day she mustered up all of her mental resouces and determined to secure the treasure by the end of the next dream. *She retired at 6:00 PM. She awoke at 4:00 AM to the same situation. With the coming of dawn, the treasure behind the door still eluded her.* With the passage of time the dream never reappeared and as little girls will reason, she thought the treasure was forever lost. As Grace and I have become friends over the past several years, and I have learned so much by assimilating her philosophy of life, it is my unwavering belief that Grace did procure the treasure she so diligently sought. It is exemplified in her love of dancing, her work with educationally handicapped children, her broad scope of knowledge which enables her to select just the right books for fledgling intuitive students, and the acts of kindness she delves out unselfishly—*all these characteristics* interwoven within her personality attest to the fact that she did indeed solve *The Mystery Behind the Locked Door.*

Serial dreams progress slowly if there is a lack of emotional intensity or sense of urgency. Simply put—Without a strong emotional impetus these dream progressions are enjoyable but are not capable of the high level of instructional quality essential for training the dreaming mind to meet and accept the challenge of life's most important lessons.

Three simple dreams that can be categorized under this heading are concerned with my son Jimmy's future employment prospects. As these are reviewed, note the languid air that surrounds them.

Jimmy's Virginia Beach House (November 10, 1984)

There is a third house we own halfway between Virginia Beach and Williamsburg. The storage area is not complete. There is a second story.

At this point in time Jimmy was beginning to consider jobs in the Tidewater area, but had made no definite decisions on jobs or places of residence.

A Potential Job (December 10, 1984)

> A lady calls me from a Newport News law firm. I have tested the child of one of the lawyers there. She says, "We would be very partial to your son if he would apply for a position that is open."

I advised Jimmy concerning the possible position and he called for an interview. He found, however, the date of the opening was considerably later than his targeted date for employment.

The Norfolk Job (January 4, 1985)

> Jimmy says, "I am glad I live in Virginia Beach so I can commute home from my job. I have met with several officials who like me. Several officials have left this group. I am comfortable working here."

In March Jimmy eventually secured a position with a prominent law firm in Norfolk that appeared tailor-made for his particular training and unique qualifications—*and he decided to take up residence in our Virginia Beach home.*

Vital life issues in conjunction with intensification of emotional focus are causal factors for rapid progression of serial dreams. One of the most vital areas of our life pattern is the question of whether or not we enjoy excellent health. It would therefore seem logical that not only would there be intense emotional overtones experienced in connection with health dreams thus providing the ignition to increase their rapidity of succession, but further—since almost all other aspects of one's existence are directly affected by one's state of health, there should then be a preponderance of physical dreams for harmonious maintenance of a perfect state of physical equilibrium. My five-year study of dreams suggests that these statements have merit. Apropos to these ideas is a hypothesis set forth by Stephen La Berge in *Lucid Dreaming.* "A frequently described part of the techniques commonly used by so-called 'paranormal healers' consists in imaging the patient to be in a state of perfect health. Since while dreaming we generate body images in the form of our dream bodies, why shouldn't we be able to initiate self-healing processes during lucid dreams by consciously envisioning our dream bodies as perfectly healthy? Further, if our dream bodies do not appear in a state of perfect health, we can heal them symbolically in the same manner. . . . if we heal the dream body, to what extent will we also heal the physical body?"[2]

During the three-month period when Jim suffered excruciating pain from being unable to pass his kidney stone, I not only recorded his suffering in my dreams, but received guidance concerning the direction that should be taken for his healing. One suggestion, discussed previously, was drinking rosemary tea. The main one, however, was to visit a healer. A dream recorded on September 9, 1984, provided initial hints, but I did not seek clarification about the details until two weeks later. These dreams occured after having dinner with our friend, John.

Introduction to Grace N' Vessels (September 9, 1984)

I am in a concert at Chrysler Hall. A lady wears a long white evening gown with bows in the back. Her hair is tied in pink ribbons. She leads all the singers in a concert. (Chrysler Hall suggests *cars* which are bodies to be healed.)

By September 28th Jim was in considerable pain as depicted in this dream.

A Ring of Pain (September 28, 1984)

I am feeling a ring of intense pain all around me.

During this period we had acted on the suggestion to have Jim ingest rosemary tea, but in spite of a clarification dream received on September 26th, our plans to travel to Connecticut were only tentative. My dream of October 8, 1984 was instrumental in finalizing our decision.

Jim's Three-Minute Surgery **(October 8, 1984)**

> Jim is taken to the hospital for emergency surgery because of a stoppage. He is operated on in *three* minutes.

We traveled to Connecticut and sought healing from Grace Di Biccari on November 30, 1984, as described earlier. *The Tombstones in Brooklyn* dream that night attests to the success of Grace's healing energies through the symbology of the fuel truck empowering the moving of the stones.

Tombstones in Brooklyn **(November 30, 1984)**

> We drive into Dad's relative's cemetery in Brooklyn. I see tombstones on a hill. I see a fuel truck fueling vehicles in the cemetery so they can move.

Guidance transmitted through serial dreams is often reinforced by synchronistic events in reality. As one becomes more attuned to the Universal Mind and the intuitive energies flow continuously, synchronistic events tend to occur at a higher level of frequency. These types of incidents are designed to reaffirm advice already imparted in the dream state. This extra exertion of synchronism oft times furnishes the essential impetus to launch the dreamer into carrying out a goal-oriented plan of action. Without this component a person might mentally weigh the bit of information and find it fascinating, but never advance beyond the contemplative state. As dream students become more and more focused on using their dream creativity, they are astounded at how the phenomenon of synchronicity adds to the richness of their daily lives.

Earlier I mentioned the use of rosemary tea to alleviate Jim's pain spasms, as well as for improved circulation. This dream is also cited in Chapter Five to re-emphasize the importance of taking correct action with regard to dream material. It provides a superior exercise in synchronistic concurrences.

The Analgestic Quality of Rosemary Tea (September 28, 1984)

> It is raining, and a man is ill. I read a book that discusses the healing quality of rosemary. I think I should use it in hot water.

Upon researching the healing properties of the herb rosemary we did indeed find it to prove beneficial and intended to pick some up later in the day. On the way home from Virginia Beach to Williamsburg we stopped at the Heritage Store to pick up some castor oil for Jim's castor oil pack. To our amazement and delight there on the second shelf near the rear of the store we discovered a package of rosemary tea ready to be brewed. There was no doubt in my mind that the Forces had place it auspiciously on the shelf to assure that the purchase would be made that day.

Occasionally, serial dreams are conveyed with a lack of clarity. A request for additional clarification is then necessitated. Serial dreams are more prone to lack of clarity then singular dreams because the purpose of repetition is due to the fact that the dreamer is not attuned to the message being channeled or has taken no literal action on the contents. With enough reviews the attention of the inner eye is ultimately captured and the psyche prepares to decipher the symbolic code. If, however, the dreams are not completely clear, it is reasonable and perhaps even mandatory to seek further clarification by requesting another dream in the series.

Let me exemplify this point by returning to my *Introduction to Grace N' Vessels.* Although I had been made aware of healing ability of Grace Di Biccari, I was only vaguely familiar with laying-on-of-hands healers in general and even less knowledgable when it came to the lady herself. Therefore, a request for additional information following the introductory dream seemed a prudent course to pursue. A lengthy response to my inquiry was received 17 days later.

The Healing Ministry of Grace Di Biccari

> Jim, Jimmy, Sylvia Hunt, someone else, and I have traveled to visit Grace N' Vessels. Grace is dressed in a lovely white dress on the stage. There are chairs marked for our party.
>
> One healing session has already taken place. Grace is now singing. I read her mind—she died and at that point she realized that all her body parts were in conflict. When she returned to her body, she determined that she and her organization would work together for healing.
>
> Several people come to watch as great "rays of energy" emanate from her fingertips. Two of the people fall down from the impact of her healing. The third is healed standing there.
>
> Jim goes up to talk to her. I notice her eyes are huge voids as if she has absented herself and serves as a channel for the Energies to pass through.
>
> There is one man at the service who can't be healed. He has conflicts in his life philosophy and is unwilling to give these up. All others who begin to live in harmony are healed.

I awoke with a start from this illuminating vision at 3:00 AM. The Creative Forces had affirmed their confidence in the healing ministry of Grace N' Vessels and had given her their Heavenly Stamp of Approval.

Without mental or physical action serial dreams may terminate with a lack of resolution. Conversely, serial completion is more often achieved through appropriate acts and behaviors resulting in a reward dream. Irresolution can be attributed to crippling emotions, a lack of concern, or a stubborn opposition to practical change. In all cases the results are highly undesirable and, at times, border on the catastrophic. Spiritually oriented souls would do well to avoid these fathomless pitfalls.

Serial dreams that culminate with a direct mental or physical act by the dreamer invariably result in significant gains in soul growth. An added benefit is the reward dream which portrays the spiritual harvest that has been sown and is about to be reaped. This is the course most frequently elected by advancing souls with a New Age orientation.

From August 30 to September 25, 1984, I was plagued with a serious local infection. The focus of my dreams during that period centered upon its expeditious removal. Over the course of 27 days the infection was cured. The series of dreams recorded during that time traces the course of the infection from inception to healing.

Draining The Infection **(August 30, 1984)**

A female physician tells me an infection needs to be drained.

Moving Closer to the Light **(August 30, 1984)**

I am in a class taking a test. Everyone else is finished, and I am left crying because I can't see to finish the last four problems. A lady comes to assist. She whispers, "Move closer to the Light."

The First Healing Treatment **(September 1, 1984)**

A lady makes an appointment with a physician because she has a health problem. I accompany her. The physician says she does not have a serious disorder. He encourages her by saying, "Be patient. You have just had the first treatment." She goes dancing out of the office and leaps in the air. She feels she may now regain her health.

Epilepsy **(September 2, 1984)**

I find myself shaking for no reason and fear that I have epilepsy.

Healing through the Light **(September 25, 1984)**

I am in a library where the lights are off and there is no service. Suddenly, the lights go on again.

On August 30th the suggestion is given to open the infected area physically. On a higher level the recommended treatment for passing "the test" is to edge near to the Light. (The Christ Source of Energy). Following this one week hence I saw Dr. Bell who lanced the infection. Thus, the precognitive dream of September 1 was fulfilled. A side effect of the lancing was a shaking reaction which resembled the physical malady depicted in the dream entitled *Epilepsy.* Unfortunately, the infection continued to rage until finally on September 26 as I was about to submit to surgery, it broke open again of its own accord and the poisons emptied out of my system. The night before I had apparently taken the advice of August 30 and moved closer to the Light.

In concluding this section on serial dreams I am prompted to recount a story related to me by Erik Jensen, Chairman of the ARE Board of Trustees, regarding immediate positive action in response to direct Guidance.

Erik came to this country from Denmark in the capacity of a young business executive. He held various positions as a representative of Danish firms in the United States and eventually served as Danish Counsel to the Danish Embassy in Washington D.C. There was one particular period in his life, however, that was somewhat unsettled due to the changing of positions. He eventually secured interviews from two Danish exporting companies and determined that if he accepted both their offers, their combined salaries would be sufficient to meet his needs. His first interview proved successful and he was about to embark on the second when he learned that the first offer was withdrawn due to internal problems with the company itself. It was with this discouraging news in mind that he now entered the office of a prospective employer.

The man facing him was a pleasant enough individual, but he questioned him at length about his background, work experience, and philosophy of life. After an unnerving 45 minutes, he posed the final question.

"Well, young man," he inquired, interrogating him with a note of admonishment in his voice, "just what do you think you are worth?"

Erik was about to respond with a figure he had originally determined to be equitable, given the existence of a second employment situation, when within himself he heard a loud voice bellow—"Double!" Needless to say, he was rather shocked by this turn of events. He was even more stunned, however, to hear his own voice stammer a salary request for *twice* the amount he had originally determined to seek.

"Hired!" The voice of his prospective employer boomed resoundingly accepting his bold offer without a moment's hesitation.

"I wouldn't have done it for less myself!"

Why study shared and serial dreams and engage in dream creativity? In seeking guidance through the dream process as well as altered states of consciousness it is probable that, like Erik Jensen, we will ultimately learn that the value of our own true worth is far greater than we initially deemed it to be.

GUIDELINES FOR WORKING EFFECTIVELY WITH SERIAL DREAMS

Symbology

1. When the same symbol appears again and again in a series of dreams, locate other dreams with the identical symbol. What do you associate with that symbol?
2. Review the content of other dreams containing that symbol. Do similar threads run throughout, or is there progressive action?
3. Does the symbol change slightly as the dreams evolve? Is that change negative or positive?

Progressive Themes

1. Once a theme has been identified, review dreams that have been recorded for the last several weeks to assemble a step-by-step progression in the action of the dreams.

2. If you cannot find enough evidence of this step-by-step progression, it may be necessary to return to dreams in a longer time span. Dreams written down three to six months prior may contain the theme and progression desired.

3. Note the frequency with which the dreams occur. The higher the rate of frequency, the more urgent the lesson to be taught.

4. Analyze the emotional impact in relation to reality. The greater the intensity, the more importance attached to facing the issues squarely.

Serial Dreams—Slow Progression

1. Some serial dreams are transmitted for enjoyment. These make light impressions upon the mind and may not involve any form of action at all. If this is the case, then merely enjoy them.

2. The slowness of the pace may be allowing you more time to understand the situation while pressing for a solution. Examine slowly evolving themes in this light.

Serial Dreams—Rapid Progression

1. Serial dreams with vital life issues unfold rapidly and oft times announce their presence through powerful accompanying emotions. Dreams of this type need intensive study and interpretation to avoid future calamities. Some identifying characteristics are:

a. A feeling of tremendous fear upon awakening.
b. A marvelous feeling of joy or a sense of great peace with regard to the disturbing issue discussed.
c. Dreaming in vibrant positive colors.
d. Dreaming in stark black and white.
e. Witnessing a dramatic climax.
f. Experiencing a feeling of precognition.

2. It is vital to determine whether this is symbolic or an actual event. The course of action is often dependent on this decision.

Synchronicity in Reality

1. When objects or events previewed in dreams make their appearance in daily life, the dreamer should determine whether there is a negative or a positive relationship and then elect the appropriate action.
2. If the synchronistic event or object is noted on three separate occasions, it demands *immediate attention.*
3. When action is taken, look for synchronistic nods from objects or reality events to say that you have followed the correct course. You can almost count on such confirmation.

Clarification of Nebulous Serial Dreams

1. When dream transmissions are not understood or their message is garbled, always ask for more information. Look for the answer not only in the dream state but in meditation and in daily life. The spring never runs dry.
2. Research may be required for clarification. If this is the case, perform it willingly. Spiritual growth demands a cooperative effort and co-creativity.

Termination of Serial Dreams

1. Lack of action may lead to the termination of serial dreams. This is not a desirable outcome, however, as it may result in one of three situations:

   a. No life progress.
   b. Regression in life.

c. Catastrophic disaster.

Wisdom dictates decisiveness in action directed toward goal achievements.

2. When decisive actions are completed, note the harmony and balance in all phases of your existence. Positive signposts in dreams and daily living provide recognition of astuteness of resolution.

3. Rewards will be rendered in accordance with personal life energies expended. Bonuses in the form of prosperity gifts are often received as recognition of a job well done. These might be considered merit pay.

4. The formula to remember for serial dreams:

A + C = B

ACTION + COMMITMENT = BLESSINGS

Commit this simple formula to memory, and as with serial dreams, *success* will follow you step-by-step.

CHAPTER 8

Dream Creativity in Daily Living

Developing awareness of your life's events, then, begins with attempts to analyze their meaning, in the same way you analyze a dream's meaning. Symbols are the language of dreams; so let us assume they are also the language of life—that synchronistic events, coincidental happenings of every day, have symbolic meaning when they refer to the star of a life.

Alan Vaughan—*Incredible Coincidence*

Dreams are one of the primary tools for efficiency in our daily lives. It is through the medium of dreams that each soul is spiritually taught and ultimately evolves. Dream sponsored higher education courses impart lessons concerning life issues such as: how effectively past challenges have been met; the validity of plans for resolving current life issues; and future realities likely to be encountered by the soul in its journey upward in the infinite quest for Unity with the Father.

This nocturnal instruction is essentially of little value to the dream student if he or she views these dramatizations in a detached manner and fails to accept the wisdom communicated. If steps are not taken to incorporate the new-found wisdom into one's life any possibility of spiritual progression is nullified. Further, if one continues to fail to act in response to these dreams this pattern may culminate in a spiritual void, or regression, thus negating previous gains.

In *The Inner Eye* a twelve-dream classification was proposed in order to identify dreams according to the type of material involved. (Dreams of Healing and Health—Guidance and Creative Dreams for Self and Others—Business Dreams—Telepathic Dreams—Clairvoyant Dreams—Precognitive and Retrocognitive Dreams—Dreams of Local and World Events—Dreams of Death and the Departed—Past Life Dreams—Lucid Dreams—Message Dreams—Visionary Dreams.) With this method, an organizational framework which facilitated the process of dream interpretation was provided. The ideas promoted in this chapter are intended to expand this procedure one step further and activate the process of *dream creativity.* The term *dream creativity* as used in this book implies *inspired* mental or physical action taken as a result of intensive analysis and interpretation of the concepts, symbols, themes, and guidance received in dreams. The process of dream creativity empowers goal realizations and forward spiritual momentum in one's life which would otherwise be literally impossible without its incorporation and usage. With the adoption of dream creativity into the routine of one's daily existence, dreams become the focal point of a transformation which enables the spiritual pilgrim to achieve a mastery of major life issues which had previously appeared to be colorful fantasies of chaos and confusion.

This leads us to a consideration of the following question: *How can we employ dream creativity in daily living so that we may be assured of incorporating into our life pattern the maximum spiritual truths imparted?*

Dream creativity's prime goal is behavioral change in the individual's life. This can be an alteration in attitude or as the result of decisive action. Keeping this goal in mind, let us examine the process of dream creativity. The following three points should serve as guidelines for proper utilization of the material contained in the remainder of this chapter.

1. Begin by reviewing the *Twelve Dream Classification System: How to Use It More Effectively in the Process of Dream Creativity* in order to determine to which of the particular categories your dream belongs. A series of pertinent questions accompany each category. Personal responses to each may stimulate novel ideas and courses of action that can then be utilized to effect positive changes in one's world of reality.

2. When reading *The Twelve Dream Classification System* you will note I have included personal and non-personal dreams which are prime examples of the successes and failures of the process of dream creativity in action. The failures are also included as it is one of my fondest hopes that you might avoid some of the "psychic quagmires" to which my fellow compatriots and I fell victim to during our own spiritual quests.

3. The second section of this chapter, *Guidelines for Creative Dreaming,* contains a set of thirteen suggestions for enhancing the likelihood of receiving accurate self-knowledge and insightful guidance through a practical step-by-step procedure. *Employ these wisely and daily.*

THE TWELVE-DREAM CLASSIFICATION SYSTEM: HOW TO USE IT MORE EFFECTIVELY IN THE PROCESS OF DREAM CREATIVITY

In combining the process of dream creativity with the Twelve-Dream Classification System, one has the advantage of establishing a firm base from which to launch inspirational endeavors. After the proper classification has been ascertained, the dream-creativity process can be utilized. It is my firm conviction that through ardent pursuit of dream creativity, it becomes the primal force in attaining spiritual truths and in the progress of the soul.

Dreams of Healing and Physical Health

Dreams of healing and physical health contain information regarding the disease with which the patient is afflicted, the organ involved, the severity of the illness with accompanying reasons for its appearance, and more often than not, a prescriptive treatment for alleviation of the condition. Health dreams are easily identifiable by the following symbolic associations: Cars in need of repair, poor plumbing, houses on fire or damaged (note the room; Ex: *Living room* = problems with daily activities; *kitchen* = problems with food, *bathroom* = problems with elimination; *bedroom* = problems with relationships), hospitals, drug stores, medical treatment, and physician-oriented, or herbal prescriptive remedies. Recommendations for dietary changes and for exercises to improve one's bodily health frequently show up, particularly if the dreamer has become lax in his general health habits. A dream of this sort should be taken as a signal that health problems may be imminent, and some preventative or curative action should be taken immediately. The process of dream creativity can be of invaluable assistance in deciding upon a course of action. Upon receiving the health warning or suggestion review the following set of questions. These can help you determine the most practical healing solutions for the problem portrayed. Then, implement your course of action based on this information.

Questions Posed in Connection with Dreams of Healing and Physical Health

1. Is this a dietary or exercise suggestion for current usage?

2. Does the dream describe a future personal health problem that can be avoided or minimized?

3. Is it a current health issue that's under consideration?

4. If the dream appears to have no particular meaning for you, does it pertain to the health of a friend? Would it be possible, and/or beneficial, to advise the friend of the condition foreseen? (See guidelines on this topic on page 137 of chapter 4 regarding the concept of *balanced introspection.*)

5. Are specific healing prescriptions or techniques discussed?

6. If healing prescriptions are given, can the ingredients be located easily, or will it involve some research?

7. Does the dream identify any known physician, or are unfamiliar names supplied requiring identification?

8. Since holistic health encompasses the physical, mental, and spiritual states of being, are clues provided that define the mental or spiritual cause of the physical problem?

9. Could additional health or prescriptive data be acquired through the incubation of future dreams?

The following three dreams are excellent examples of how the process of dream creativity can work for or against you depending on how carefully you heed the proffered advice.

Ten months before the infection of my Bartholin gland, I received a preventative prescription.

Hot Oil Rubs Shrink Bartholin Gland Infection **(October 18, 1983)**

> I see an infection in my Bartholin gland. I begin to rub hot oil on the area. It becomes smaller and smaller.

Leading the busy life that all the Windsors do, I applied *cold* castor oil to it infrequently, and as time passed, I neglected the treatment altogether. Thus, ten months later the previewed problem became reality. I frantically researched my library in a desperate effort to relieve my misery. I finally located a treatment for infections in Dr. William McGarey's book *Physician's Reference Notebook.* Along with some internal recommendations for stimulating glandular activity, *the prime method of treatment was rubbing the area with warmed dissolved cocoa butter and olive oil.*

An example of spiritual humor in the face of blatant self-ignorance can be observed in a dream recorded February 4, 1985. The flu season was upon us, and I was extremely perturbed because neither my husband nor children seemed to be taking the health precautions I deemed necessary to avoid catching the bug. Indeed, I was sure each would fall victim to the illness as people were dropping like flies all around us. Thus, I began giving daily lectures on *How to Avoid the 1985 Flu in Six Easy Lessons.* About the fifth day of my lecture series I began to note a raspiness in the tone of my voice and soon the remainder of my lecture series was cancelled as my throat became extremely inflamed, and I took to my bed. A plea for relief from my affliction fell on deaf ears. (What ye sow, ye reap!) Instead the necessity for an immediate change of attitude was graphically depicted in no uncertain terms:

"A Rotten Yoke" **(February 4, 1985)**

I am being served a hard boiled egg that is 5/6 rotten. Jim and I complain to the waitress that this is bad food.
This was truly a "Bad Yoke" on me.

However, healing dreams can pay positive dividends when heeded. During the last week of October of 1984, Elizabeth and I journeyed west to San Francisco to visit my sister, Arlene. An auto trip from San Francisco to Los Angeles was interrupted with frequent pit stops to refuel the auto with gasoline and ourselves with ice cream and soft drinks—I was definitely avoiding orange juice, which is so necessary to control hypoglycemia. At supper Arlene and Elizabeth indulged themselves in cheesecake and strawberries and I eagerly ordered up a piece of apple pie a la mode. With tummy full, I crawled into my bed contentedly and immediately fell asleep. Having just barely drifted off, I found myself in my chiropractic physician's office. Although Dr. Haller was smiling, I felt I was definitely in trouble. The dream unfolded:

Paying Dr. Haller's Bill

I have kept an appointment with Dr. Haller and sit in her office. She smiles and hands me some papers she wants me to review.

> I find they are patients' statements and *I am checking to see who has to pay her bills.*

The next day it was back to orange juice, avocados, and a high protein diet. I was rewarded for the rest of the trip with considerably more energy, and I undoubtedly avoided the addition of several extra pounds. In accordance with the Edgar Cayce philosophy, "Prevention is better than Cure."[1]

Healing dreams can also be sent for the benefit of others closely connected to us. An intimate associate of mine, Dr. JoAnne Squires, has served as an invaluable consultant to Personal Development Services, Inc. for over fifteen years. Late in December of 1984 she began experiencing back spasms which increased in severity with each passing day. During a conversation about her problem, I recounted a mixture of myrrh, wintergreen, and rosewater a friend of ours had used to cure leg cramps. This remedy seemed plausible to her as her daughter, Anne knew of another remedy called Tiger Balm which possessed similar healing properties. No more was said on the matter until after January 16, 1985, when I had a healing dream for JoAnne.

The Chinese Healer's Prescription (January 16, 1985)

> I feel a robber had invaded a house.
> I see an old Chinese Physician with a beard entering the Williamsburg Professional Pharmacy. JoAnne and I follow him. When we return, JoAnne shows me her brand new golden Cadillac she has just purchased.

On January 17 JoAnne came to visit us. At dinner she began to relate how well her back was healing since she had purchased Tiger Balm. Upon comparing the directions for usage that accompanied the Tiger Balm with the ingredients of my friend's prescription I saw before me on the top of the page a picture of an old Chinese gentleman with a long beard.

The following dream encapsulates in one sentence the entire message I wish to convey in this book.

The Healing Gifts

Margit Nassi, a spiritual healer, lectures to our Parapsychology class. She concludes with this affirmation. "Know that dream interpretation, counseling, teaching, psychic readings, laying-on-of-hands—*All are healing!*"

Guidance and Creative Dreams for the Self and Others

The basic premise underlying guidance and creative dreams is the assumption that all subconscious minds are in contact with one another. Therefore, a genuine concern for the welfare of others should enhance one's intuitive receptivity to the point where inspirational guidance and creativity are experienced constantly, thus producing a better world for all concerned.

The questions listed below offer guidelines by which the maximum benefit can be gotten from these dreams.

Questions Posed in Connection with Guidance and Creative Dreams for the Self and Others

1. Does the dream offer new inspirational ideas or a fresh perspective in resolving a problem for which one has been fruitlessly searching for a solution?

2. Does the guidance apply to a current project in progress?

3. Are persons who would benefit this project introduced? Are they known entities or future associates?

4. Does the dream contain organizational suggestions for streamlining the project?

5. Are there specific recommendations that apply to oneself that can be implemented?

6. Can the advice imparted be of ultimate service to others in your circle of friends and co-workers?

In my exuberance to eagerly embrace all aspects of spirituality, I had decided to study astrology. After consistently ignoring the inner promptings that insisted this was not a subject in which I should engage and after reading three books on the subject, I began to realize that I was as much in the dark as when I had begun. The following dream depicted my current situation.

The Perfume Dream

> I have Cholê lotion on my hands. The lady next to me looks like a southern belle. (Emma Belle Donath was teaching an Astrology class in which I had enrolled several weeks hence). She wears Chantilly perfume. This makes me sneeze as I am allergic to it. I feel I had better stick to my own scent.

This did make some impression upon me, since it clearly stated I was definitely *allergic to astrology* and needed to stick to my own brand of intuitive essence. Little by little, however, I began again to read snatches of astrology here and there—to expand my meager knowledge.

A second dream arrived, which I had extreme difficulty interpreting (especially since I was mentally blocking its meaning.)

Astrology Conference Canceled

> The first two days of the Astrology Conference are canceled.

I thought that the conference I had planned to attend had probably lost a speaker and went on my merry way. However, when the week of the Astrology Conference arrived, *my* first two days of it were canceled! *I was so sick with an infection I could hardly walk let alone sit in a conference all day long.* It was then I made a firm commitment to myself to cancel all Astrology pursuits.

Dreams of inspiration and encouragement often occur when one is devoid of hope and spiritual energies run at a low ebb. Such was the case for me in January of 1984 before I received notification that my first book was to be published. I had sent my manuscript to several publishers in November of 1983, and by January of 1984 had heard nothing. It seemed to me that all the work and energy I had poured into "my third child" was for naught. I was extremely depressed to say the least. As if to lift me from the depths of despair to the heights of jubilation, a message of hope was transmitted in the dream state:

The Book Will Be Published **(January 26, 1984)**

Word has come from the higher realms that you have succeeded!

This provided the incentive I needed to avoid the negative thinking, which so often thwarts all of our fondest hopes and desires. Then, on March 21, 1984, a letter arrived from Prentice Hall expressing considerable interest in publishing *The Inner Eye,* if I would make the changes recommended. I find it of extreme interest that of all the publishers to whom I submitted my manuscript, Prentice Hall was my first choice. My fondest hopes had materialized. I recalled Richard Bach's statement in *The Bridge Across Forever* regarding wishes—"You are never given a wish without also being given the power to make it true."[2]

The final two examples of inspirational guidance were two simple directives received while in the hypnogogic state. This is a time of peace and complete serenity for me. It is probably because I am so open in this state of mind that messages of spiritual import slip easily into my consciousness. The first directive concerns the use of prayer. It states:

In preparation for all things you should pray.

The second message instructs one as to the position to be assumed with regard to personal or financial difficulties that arise.

Look upon these things as opportunities.

These two statements appear to me to be connected to a more general statement I once read in *The Sermon on the Mount,* by Emmet Fox. He theorizes that each time a problem is surmounted through prayer, the entire human race is improved in a general fashion and that particular difficulty is more easily met and resolved by others who encounter it again in the future.

Business Dreams

Business dreams contain suggestions for profitable business management. As with most things the person who focuses the most energies in the practice of a specialty derives its maximum rewards. Therefore, business entrepreneurs are the souls most likely to dream prolifically about business affairs. This does not, however, preclude those of us who have elected to pursue other professions from occasionally receiving insights into business transactions, or hot stock tips.

When your dreams appear to center around current business dealings, or personal finances, use the following questions to guide your exploration of the situation:

Questions Posed in Connection with Business Dreams

1. Does the dream portray business conditions at work, or does it involve personal business investigations?

2. Are favorable future trends for expansion and/or new ventures forecasted, or does the dream contain a warning to avoid probable financial pitfalls?

3. What specific courses of action are indicated?

- **a.** Checking the stock index.
- **b.** Developing an awareness for attitudes or deceptive behaviors among current business associates or clients.
- **c.** "Going with the flow" in present business trends.
- **d.** Research into new sources of financial wellsprings, thus providing an ever-widening horizon for future expansive trends.
- **e.** Insights provided for new, more rewarding job opportunities.

An intriguing intuitive adventure centered around a series of stocks left me by my father after his death. Jim awoke one morning and asked me if my father ever played basketball. I was unaware of any such interest and replied in the negative, asking why he had such an inquiry.

"Well," he said. "I dreamed your father and I were walking down a road. He kept skipping along, throwing a wad of paper into a basket, and then pulling it out again." Neither of us could make any sense out of the dream, but it was so vivid in my husband's mind that I made a note of it and filed it away mentally.

Several weeks later I received another uninterpretable message.

Look to the pine tree. Don't look to Oakland.
Don't sell!

The only sense I could make of it was that it had something to do with my sister Arlene who lived near Oakland, California. As far as I could tell, I wasn't planning to sell anything.

The morning mail contained several letters from friends and an envelope from one of the stock companies in which my father had invested money. I opened it, and saw it appeared to contain information concerning reinvestment. Uninterested, I tossed it in the basket. The Inner Voice said, "Pull it out." I retrieved it, intending to reread it in depth later in the day. At that moment the telephone rang. It was Arlene.

"Have you received the news about the stock split?" she inquired.

"What are you talking about?" I replied.

"The company split their stock, so now you own double the amount of shares Dad left you. Unfortunately, I put some of mine up for sale last week," she added in a disgruntled fashion, "but you have all of yours."

Frantically, I searched for the retrieved letter and examined its contents. There, buried among several pages of business information was the notification of the stock split. Now, I realized why my father was so joyfully engaging in a game of basketball. I finally understood the admonition at the end of the message—Don't sell!

Our close friends and co-workers in the world of intuitive exploration, John and Elizabeth Hollis, moved to Carrollton, Texas, in August of 1984 for a brief period of time. This was the result of a promotion John had received. His new position was as an instructor for new groups of trainees joining his company, which specializes in computers. In this capacity John reported two instances in which the process of dream creativity could have been, or was, beneficial to him. The advice from the following dream was ignored.

The Offensive Co-Pilot

> I (John) am flying my airplane with a co-worker. The co-worker is engaged in a radio conversation with the control tower. The choice of words he uses is offensive to the traffic controller. The traffic controller warns him that they are flying in an area where everyone tuned into the same frequency can monitor their exchange and this requires more prudence in his choice of words.

During this time John had been in the process of evaluating his students in their performance and, in retrospect, felt he had been extremely critical of one particular trainee. This proved to be an accurate assessment of John's part for at a later date he, in turn, was evaluated negatively by his students.

John, being the intelligent fellow that he is, does not make the same mistake twice. John used the information from his next creative dream experience to maximum advantage. The situation also involved his class of trainees.

The Disruptive Employee

> I (John) am instructing a class of employees. I serve as class manager. In looking over my students I observe that one particular fellow is being disruptive. I immediately ask him to leave. I am sorry for this action later, as the employee turns out to be extremely helpful.

The following day this exact series of events occurred, but John, acting on the instructions from his dream, refrained from evicting the individual from his class. *Result*—The disruptor was later transformed into one of the star pupils in the program based on his contributions, and *best of all, through the process of dream creativity, John had learned patience.*

God is not absent from the world of business. Indeed, he is a living force. This statement expresses the concept quite astutely. "God's aid to man—is not a vague, abstract assistance, but as concrete and immediate as the daily work, or daily prayer."[3]

Telepathic Dreams

Telepathic communication between minds is the direct result of close emotional ties that bond the dreamers together. The process requires both a transmitter and a receiver. The transmitting mind dispatches information concerning current life issues. The receptive mind reaches out to procure and process these transmissions.

Telepathic communication is *especially important* in the process of dream creativity because the slumbering subconscious mind will often willingly convey messages of spiritual import that the conscious mind in the waking state would never dare imply. If you are the recipient of these mind-to-mind communiqués, it is in your best interest, even your spiritual duty, to initiate a specific plan of thought, or action, which allows the psychic stream of energy to circulate freely and accomplish the utmost good for both participants.

The following questions should help you in your review of telepathic dreams and out-of-body experiences.

Questions Posed in Connection with Telepathic Dreams

1. Does the message transmitted contain information that needs to be acted on, or does it require a change in attitude?

2. Are the ideas relevant to making constructive changes in your own existence?
3. What do you think is the basic reason you were the recipient of the communication?
4. Is there an ultimate solution contained in the dream?
5. Is there just one short message, or can you detect a continuing pattern of communication in subsequent dreams?
6. Are dreams involving out-of-body experiences given in order to alert one to surrounding conditions from which it is necessary to escape, or are these engaged in for the pure pleasure of the "visit"?

Earlier (page 21) I described the ordeal a close friend underwent while anticipating her hysterectomy. During this period, Margit Nassi, a healer, and I were busily engaged in applying many healing techniques, and continuously lecturing our patient on how to rid herself of the unwanted disease. I fear we did not often truly listen well. Instructions from On High were funneled down in this fashion. (Our friend had received the news from her physician on March 8 that her operation was scheduled for April 8.)

The Verdict

My ill friend calls to tell me the verdict of her examination. As I try to talk to her, I notice there are two men in white physicians jackets who stand next to us. They talk so loudly I cannot understand what my close associate is trying to convey.

The admonition is to close one's mouth long enough to comprehend and experience empathetically the feelings of the other person involved—good advice for all!

On a lighter note, mind-to-mind communication transpired between Kay Gentry, the daughter of a former parapsychology student of ours, and me regarding whether or not she should engage in lessons to awaken her dormant intuition.

I had met Kay Gentry several times over a period of fifteen years and had always enjoyed conversing with her, but we had always remained nothing more than nodding acquaintances. However, when Jim and I issued invitations to the former members of our parapsychology class to attend a picnic at Shellbank in May of 1984, Kay asked if she could accompany her mother to the festivities. I was delighted to see her again. As the evening wore on, I felt she became more comfortable, and although I perceived she was intensely interested in the events of the evening, I sensed that many questions remained unspoken. The dream I recorded the next morning clearly portrayed her sentiments.

The Reluctant Ski Student

> Kay Gentry stands beside me just beyond our patio. A new ski jump has just been constructed with a connecting conveyor belt that leads into our house. I encourage Kay to learn how to ski and ride the conveyor belt. She refuses to climb up the steps to the top of the jump.

I had no further contact with Kay until mid-February of 1985 when I met her at a Mental Health dinner. As our conversation progressed during this chance meeting, it became evident that she was more intent than ever on understanding life from a more spiritual stance. I made an appointment for her to come to my office where we began by discussing several of her recent dreams. One of them sounded extremely familiar.

The Eager Ski Student

> I (Kay) am at home where I am about to ski. I get up on a platform and notice a small child who is afraid to learn. I tell her mother and father I will accompany her down the slope and onto the conveyor belt so she will feel secure. The trip begins.

The similarity of our dreams is striking. The first clearly depicts her reluctance, in May 1984, to engage in spiritual activities. Yet by

February of 1985, she has overcome her inhibitions sufficiently to climb up on the platform and go for it. Her journey has truly begun!

Clairvoyant Dreams

Clairvoyance is a word which has its root in a French derivation meaning "clear seeing, or clear vision." Thus, when we discuss clairvoyance in dreams, we are referring to a type of dream in which a person views an actual event which may be occurring (now or in the future) hundreds of miles away. The individual experiences it as if he were an on-site participant.

Creative visualization is closely related to clairvoyance, for what our subconscious mind selects to concentrate upon usually transpires in direct proportion to the strength of the emotional impact our thoughts focus on the matter. *This, then, is the key:* Your thoughts create your present and future realities and therefore are the real causitive force in life. Since this is the case, it logically follows that if one changes his mental diet, a transformation of outer conditions must ensue shortly thereafter.

It is my opinion that clairvoyant dreams occur for three different reasons. The questions one should ask of oneself are these:

1. Is the event being viewed to intensify future pleasure when it actually occurs?

2. Does the incident contain negative elements that could be diminished or negated by action taken on the dreamer's part?

3. Could creative visualization be employed to change future circumstances?

Illustrations for each of the three questions will provide us with the necessary insights required to master the dream creativity process in relation to clairvoyance.

Elizabeth's Book-Like Letter

> I am standing over Elizabeth's shoulder reading a letter she is writing which contains so many pages it appears almost like a book. She is writing it on her beige paper. What fun to read it!

I felt this dream was one of clairvoyance. Therefore I eagerly anticipated the arrival of the epistle she was so joyfully composing—reading it was double the pleasure, double the fun—when it arrived several days hence.

Illustration two is concerned with a tardiness on my part in mailing a test report for a recent client of mine.

***The Tardy Report* (February 18, 1985)**

> I am engaged in conversation with *Jane Smith.* She glares at me and asks why her child's report is so late in arriving.

There was little doubt in my mind as to the meaning conveyed by the dream. To avoid more anger and future repercussions, I rushed to the Post Office early the next morning and mailed the report.

The third example illustrates precisely how to combine the process of dream creativity and revisualization when the current situation portends negative consequences.

Jim and I decided to spend our twenty-sixth wedding anniversary at the Hotel Roanoke. As the time grew closer, I realized that neither Jim nor I had made reservations. On the night of June 20, my apprehension regarding the hotel room was confirmed.

***No Room at the Hotel Roanoke* (June 20, 1983)**

> We have lost our house and have to build a new one. We shall. There is a big line waiting for new houses.

Upon awaking I made the dreaded call. To my dismay (but not surprise), I learned all rooms were occupied due to a Ministerial

Association Convention. A spark of hope was ignited in my breast. "Surely," I thought, "one kind Christian soul will be willing to give us his room because it is our anniversary." Then, I began visualizing in earnest our checking in and the hotel clerk smiling and handing us a key to a room that had just become available. For the next day and night I continuously focused all the positive energies I could muster on bringing this event into reality.

Since our plans were already made, Jim decided that we would make the drive anyhow and eat at the Hotel Roanoke even if we could not spend the night there. (My subconscious kept x-ing out all alternative maneuvers.) We stopped once on the way to phone the hotel, which was still a two-hour drive away only to receive the disconcerting news that the Hotel Roanoke was still completely booked.

The moment of truth was upon me as we parked our car and made our way through the Hotel Roanoke lobby and to the front desk. All around us were men in black ministerial suits with white clerical collars already having secured their rooms.

Jim took a deep breath and then framed the fateful question—"I'm Dr. James Windsor. I called earlier concerning a room for this evening. Have any become available yet?"

A smile of pleasure replaced the frown that had furrowed the hotel clerk's brow.

"Oh, Dr. Windsor," he exclaimed. "How fortunate you are!" I have been turning away people all day, but just ten minutes ago Reverend Johnson called and canceled his reservations. Would you like the bellboy to take your bags to Room 332?"

"Yes, indeed!" I chuckled inwardly. Thanks to dream creativity and the visualization process, I could already taste the Shrimp Scampi.

A thought entered my mind as Jim and I took the elevator to our room. I recalled Dr. Emmet Fox's idea from *Find and Use Your Inner Power*—"True wishes have wings and will bear you to your heart's desire."[4]

Precognition and Retrocognition in Dreams

Precognition refers to a foreknowledge of future events. Retrocognition is the reviewing of past events, many of which may be completely unknown to the mind that is experiencing the dream. Logical minds wonder how such processes are possible. The explanation lies in the interrelationship of all minds. That is, each individual soul is psychically linked with all other souls and this vast compository is eternally expanding through creative and novel activities. Further, this reservoir of activities is forever engrained within the Universal Mind which is the basis of All Creation. If this theory is correct, then activating the precognitive and retrocognitive processes is as simple as making a telephone call to a nearby neighbor, or a long-lost companion of by-gone days. Thus, it is possible to tune in on past incidents or probable futures for oneself or one's friends.

Questions Posed for Precognitive and Retrocognitive Dreams

1. Is there a similar past situation, or an exact episode that appears to be connected to the circumstances portrayed in the dream?

2. Does the dream provide a warning and/or advice regarding a future problem? Do negative behaviors need to be halted. Is positive action needed?

3. Is it possible that no action can be taken at all and the dream is one of preparation?

4. Are there other recent dreams recorded that will add additional insights, or credence to the prediction?

5. If the dream portends prosperity and future blessings, besides focusing mental energies, what practical steps can one take to assure passage into reality?

The first example of these types of dreams falls into the category of blessings bestowed for the pure enjoyment of the gift.

During my cooking career I had continuously used a hand mixer given to me as a wedding gift by my aunt, Mrs. Pearl Morton. I had always desired a larger Sunbeam Mixmaster and would frequently stop to admire them in various department stores. On April 20, 1983, I recorded the following in my dream journal.

The Sunbeam Mixmaster

> A friend of mine demonstrates a Mixmaster to me. The Mixmaster is a blender, a cake mixer, and a beater. The brand is Sunbeam. She shows it to her family across the street also.

Sixteen months later, a mysterious parcel was brought to my door by United Parcel Service. Upon opening the package, I squealed with delight. Elizabeth and John had sent their Sunbeam Mixmaster as she had purchased a new one. *The point is, however, that Elizabeth had never been aware of my strong desire for a Sunbeam Mixmaster, as I had never discussed it with her.*

The Locksmith Dream contains within it elements of retrocognition along with a reminder to halt a negative behavior, while *The Dropping shelf* issues a warning of a future disaster if there is no further action.

***The Locksmith Dream* (November 6, 1984)**

> A locksmith arrives in a black truck to help clean a new room in the attic for Robin. He is of great assistance in cleaning it up.

One of my continuing bad habits involves locking myself out of my car. Since the acquisition of our new Cutlass in January of 1984, I had promised myself I would have a second key made to carry in my wallet to avoid future lock-outs. I never acted upon the inclination. Habits are hard to break. In early December when I found myself gazing forlornly at my keys safely in the ignition behind a carefully locked door, I determined to clean up at least one mess that had too long caught dust in the corner of my attic. The locksmith's bill provided additional impetus for the purchase of an additional key within a matter of hours.

Example two reinforces the wisdom of taking preventative action to forestall, or eliminate, future problems.

***The Dropping Shelf* (September 29, 1984)**

> I see my plants situated on the shelf in our Virginia Beach home becoming unbalanced.

"I must adjust those shelves soon," I thought and immediately plunged into a dozen other activities that needed my undivided attention. *Crash!* Within three days my plants were spread all over the kitchen floor, and three pots were broken in the process.

A dream about an unknown black dog foretold an event that seemed predestined.

***The Black Dog's Demise* (November 3, 1984)**

> A lady asks me to hold a jeweled leash with a small dog on the end. He runs into the road. I pull on the leash to hold him back, but cannot. He is run over by first one truck and then another. I think he is still alive, but then see the leash with no dog on the end.

Although I frantically searched my memory for clues to the identities of both parties, I found I had no recollection of either knowing or seeing either of them at anytime past or present. Within a matter of weeks, a lovely dog who had been out for a walk with his mistress broke away, and upon dashing into the oncoming traffic in front of me was instantaneously killed. It seemed to me that on this occasion I was powerless to act in any constructive fashion. Therefore, I considered this a *preparation dream.*

I cannot close this section without relating this message.

A High Percentage of Precognition

> My students, my husband, and I dream dreams. Each feels he or she has a high number of precognitive dreams. Someone tells me mine approach a figure of 75%.

The impact of this dream in combination with precognitive episodes experienced almost daily have had a profound effect on heightening my cosmic awareness. I am now considerably more prone to search my dream journal for the impartation of sage advice and then *heed it!*

Dreams of Local and World Events

Both positve and negative thoughts comprise our overall attitude and create our unique pattern of life. If a broader view of this concept is taken, all individual thought patterns should then form a composite. That composite is then the expression of the group consciousness. Logically, reshaping the group consciousness of society could begin with the simple act of refocusing one's own thoughts toward more spiritual ideals as one engages in personal activities connected with family, work, and community. By activating the process of dream creativity, in combination with local, national, and international information received while in the dream state, there is a distinct possibility to be entertained that one's ideas might literally "change the world."

Questions Posed in Connection With Dreams of Local and World Events:

1. Does the information received pertain to a local happening? Is the issue a major or minor one? Is an attitude change or physical action required?

2. Is there an international issue involved that offers the challenge of change by one's personal actions?

3. Is a disaster previewed? Is there any way you can prevent the calamity?

4. Is the dream one of epic proportions forcasting a probable future for the world? Would personal prayer or direction action divert such an event?

During the months of January and February 1984, the communities of Williamsburg and Newport News were terrorized by a maniacal killer who indiscriminately killed innocent women by shooting each in the head. One of those cruelly murdered was a lady in her eighties who worked as a hotel manager. Another was a clerk at a convenience store. The body of a third woman was discovered in a church parking lot. The law enforcement agencies of each community banded together to apprehend the killer and bring him to justice. Eventually, an unemployed drifter who had a history of frequent skirmishes with the law was arrested, convicted, and sentenced to death. These crimes were so abhorrent to me that, although I could do little to assist in arresting the killer, my subconscious demanded an explanation for such purposeless killings.

On the night of February 3, 1984, I received a message revealing the personality characteristic that led him to commit such atrocities.

The Flaw in the Criminal Personality
(February 3, 1984)

> He hated to be admonished. (He could not stand authority.) Therefore, he shot authority figures in the head.

The head, of course, was symbolically appropriate as it represents authority.

The final dream presented in this section has reverberations of epic proportion if one believes in the likelihood of a future Armageddon. The question to ponder is, "Can this catastrophe be averted?"

The Shift Dream (July 13, 1984)

> Jim and I are taking our parapsychology class to the top of the RCA Building. I stand in the doorway and lecture. I feel all of us are safe here. The students look over the side of the building. I am afraid to look down. Eventually, I summon up enough courage to peer over the edge and expect to see New York City as others are seeing it. Instead, I see red and yellow clay adobe abodes and almost total devastation. I am seeing things differently from the others. I blink my eyes and look again. All I see is a beach. I leave the building and go to Christopher Newport College. A new course is being added in nutrition. I decide to retreat to a quiet place and write a new lecture for it.

Being an eternal optimist, I am convinced, as others also are, that a future Armageddon may be averted by positive thoughts and constructive actions on the part of all spiritually minded and peace-loving individuals. The new nutrition course represents a new "mental diet" that contains the essential ingredients to regenerate the future of all mankind.

Will a world recreation come about through destruction and devastation, or can a refocusing of our purpose and ideals achieve the same ends through peaceful methods? Will you join me in prayerfully envisioning the latter? The choice is yours!

Dreams of Death and the Departed

As a general rule dreams of death do not portend one's immediate demise, or the passing of loved ones. Usually, this theme symbolizes the death of outmoded patterns of thought accompanied by a rebirth of new ideals, and changes in spiritual direction that will eventually result in the advancement of the soul.

There are, of course, other reasons for dreaming about death, or for contacting those who have departed *this* life. Among them would be social visitation, the impartations of Universal Truths essential for proper progress in life, emotional support provided in times of duress, and the issuing of warnings for avoidance of future calamities. A minority of death dreams do, in fact, forsee the end of one's human existence and herald the rebirth of the soul into a higher dimension. All of the above possibilities should be considered when examining dreams of such import.

Common symbols that accompany this category are a hearse, black clothing, birds at a window, the ace of spades, a spray of flowers, a stopped clock, crossing a river, or being present at a funeral.

Questions Posed in Connection with Dreams of Death and the Departed:

1. Is one of your departed loved ones contacting you for a social visitation?
2. Has contact been established for the express purpose of delivering an important piece of information? If so, check on its validity.
3. Does the discarnate require personal support himself? What specific measures can be taken to aid him?
4. If the dream revolves around a famous personality, are you really dreaming about that person, or do her characteristics merely reflect a portion of your own personality augmented or de-emphasized?
5. Is this a death of a portion of your own life? How well are you prepared to handle it?
6. Might the dream truly pose a warning of the death of an individual close to you? Will your attitude be one of avoidance or preparation?
7. Does the dream comment on the inherent qualities of death which ultimately lead to maximized spiritual understanding of the true nature of reality?

A lecture centering on the concept of soulmates, contained in the dream that follows, was delivered to me by Robert Stephens who had been one of my father's closest friends. He preceeded my father in death by only six months. His wife, Lillian Stephens, still resides in their home at Elm Avenue. There is little doubt in my mind that these two dear friends of ours serve as the ultimate personification of twin flame soulmates.

Butterflies and Soulmates **(March 1, 1984)**

> Lillian Stephens writes us a note and invites us to dinner. Bob Stephens sits next to me with my sister, Arlene, and my Dad on my right. Bob has on a dark blue bathrobe like Jim owns. I talk aloud saying "I know I am here in the land of the dead, but I also know I am alive."
>
> Bob replies, "I want to show you something." I see a large butterfly perched on a brick, and a smaller one lights nearby.
>
> Bob says, "This represents Lillian and our soulmate relationship. Even though we are apart, we are together."

Butterflies often symbolize the immortality of the soul.

One of the finest examples of death dreams and the joyous donning of the mantle of a new phase of one's being was related to me by my neighbor and dear friend, Sylvia Hunt. The message was communicated two weeks before her youngest child, Roger Hunt, was to leave for college. With his departure Bob and Sylvia were the sole occupants of their home.

Sylvia's Happy Funeral

> I (Sylvia) am gravely (pun) ill and have been transported to the Williamsburg Community Hospital. The Physician in charge tells me not to worry as the staff has already made a diagnosis in my case, and formulated a prognosis. Then he throws back his head and, laughing gleefully, informs me that my death is momentary. "And," he adds with a twinkle in his eye, "Wait until you see the funeral we have planned for you!"

The elements of the dream imply that what might appear to be a painful death and separation could evolve into joyful transformation freeing Sylvia to explore limitless possibilities. These doors had been closed to her in the past because of her full-time duties as a mother. The dream did indeed signify this was a time of fruitful new beginnings. The pink rays I viewed in her aura as she humorously finished the recounting further served to intensify the positive possibilities.

Past Life Dreams

The fallacy connected with past life dreams is that most reincarnational detectives assume the posture that past life dreams are only valid if the setting is one of antiquity, and the characters are garbed in dated apparel. This may, or may not be the case. I believe that many past life episodes have been modernized so that only the past life *theme* is brought to bear. Whether you were Sarah Harrison, wife of a local Williamsburg politician in 1789, or Rose Adams nursing wounded soldiers during the Civil War is not nearly as consequential as the utilizing of the soul knowledge gleaned from "reincarnational film clips" to further inspire and promote spiritual growth. The importance of developing a latent ability, conquering a negative personality trait, or employing one's specialized talent for the advancement of mankind, comprise the true demands and objectives in all reincarnational dream lessons. It is essential here to reiterate the directive from *The Inner Eye.* **"Decisive actions taken in response to the theme of the dream, whether past or present, should be the prime focus of all dreaming."[5]** And this is where the creative dreaming process comes in.

Questions Posed in Connection with Past-Life Dreams:

1. Does the dream contain clues as to the origins of current day fears or phobias? Could they have evolved from a past-life trauma? Can the information be useful in alleviating the conditions?

2. Can unfamiliar names, dates, and settings be checked for accuracy? If so, the verification of such personalities and environments could tremendously increase one's personal understanding of present-day issues and circumstances.

3. Does the central theme of the dream lend itself to provide answers to previously unresolved life issues?
4. Does the personnage portrayed in the dream gain or lose in spirituality? Does this apply to you?
5. Is this dream of serious import, or is it perhaps just given as a form of entertainment? (The latter is seldom the case.)
6. Are there references to past-life ties with current family, friends, and associates? Karmic associations need to be carefully reviewed for the purpose of either clearing away "bad karma," or for promoting mutually beneficial and creative relationships.
7. *Most important of all*—Is there a depiction of malignant personality characteristics that place insurmountable barriers before you, thus prohibiting your soul from realizing maximum spiritual progress?

In my previous book *The Inner Eye* I mentioned the fact that I have experienced numerous dreams of an ancient French monastery or a colonial life in eighteenth-century Virginia. Dreams involving these themes continue to the present. Therefore, in light of the aforementioned criteria for achieving self-understanding and self-improvement, let me recount two of my *Sister Marie Dreams.*

Climb Every Mountain (January 16, 1983)

I see myself dressed in a nun's costume in *The Sound of Music.* I sing *Climb Every Mountain.* There are lovely stained-glass windows here. I sense I have a bad case of stage fright, but I continue singing anyhow.

Sister Marie's Elevated Post (October 25, 1983)

I am in my thirties, and see myself being installed as a nun of high rank in a French Nunnery. My inner voice asks, 'Sister Marie, are you worthy to do justice to this elevated post?'

Both dreams clearly define some inner conflicts I struggle with today. My intellectual side says, "You have the capabilities to do a good job with the project." Then, a small voice interjects, "But what if you fail?" Thus, I often engage in a continuing battle to overcome "stage fright," to perform well. Being aware of this makes me more determined than ever to accomplish my task. The question is: Do some of my insecurities with positions of importance have their roots in a past life as the nun—Sister Marie? *But more important, can I deal with them effectively and continue to evolve into a truly productive, and secure individual?* This is one of the issues I am apparently working on in this lifetime.

One of John Hollis's favorite pastimes is piloting his plane. Elizabeth and I have often wondered what hidden impulses propelled him to unrelentingly immerse himself in this avocation. He also has a passion for vintage aircraft.

A dream of John's recorded in the summer of 1983 offers a logical explanation for his avid interest in flying, and activities related to it.

Henry Emerson—World War II Pilot **(John's Dream)**

> My name is Henry Emerson. I am flying a Spitfire in the Royal Air Force during World War II. It is late 1943. There is a lot of flack on today's mission. I am about to engage a German plane in combat when there is an explosion. My Spitfire catches a round of flack and I feel the engine lose power. Then, everything goes black.

A channeling personality in England, without knowing of this dream, informed John that he had been involved in an air battle during the second World War and had experienced "death by fire in the air." (Of course, it is possible that he could have been reading John's mind.) In any case, this is just one of a series of lives wherein John has been a pilot.

A message I received offers a bit of sage advise to all of us: **The ardent study of relevant past lives carries with it the distinct possibility of increasing one's future happiness.**

Lucid Dreaming

Lucid dreaming refers to that state of mind in which the dreamer is consciously aware that he is dreaming, and thereafter actively participates in the ongoing dream. Lucid dreaming is a relatively rare phenomenon, but with concerted effort this skill may be developed to the point that it becomes a standard part of one's spiritual repertoire of tools. When lucidity is achieved, the awakened mind has the opportunity to objectively review the events and to respond in the most beneficial way. The goals achieved through lucid dreaming are well worth the efforts required to gain that skill. When one becomes a lucid dreamer, he is already deeply immersed in the dream creativity process.

Questions Posed in Connection with Lucid Dreaming:

1. What circumstances or attitudes are touched upon in the lucid dream? Can you note any actual changes in the waking state?

2. Are your lucid dreams ever like attending a class? Do the lectures contain information that is unfamiliar to you, but that turns out to be essential at some point in your future reality?

3. Is the dream one of preparation designed to crystallize or refine any of your current activities?

Since August of 1981 when I initially began working with my dreams, I have recorded numerous instances of visits to educational institutions. The lectures encompass health remedies, dream interpretation methods, recommendations for expansion of intuitive awareness, as well as discourses on religion and philosophy. More often than not, the ideas contain concepts and knowledge to which I had never been exposed. In discussing these visitations with Elizabeth I was intrigued to learn that she recalled often having identical experiences. Soon after our discussion, during the course of continually reading books pertaining to development of intuition, I stumbled across the same phenomenon in *Breakthrough to Crea-*

tivity by Shasica Karagulla. It would seem a logical assumption therefore that ardent students of spirituality receive continuing instruction while in the sleep state. Furthermore, the subjects of the lectures are geared to the particular specialities and talents exhibited by the student.

A Health Lecture For Us (July 2, 1983)

> There is a He/She Person (Balanced Soul) giving a health lecture. He/She states the causes of lower intestinal problems, and gives me a list of changes in diet. He/She says, "Get Swiss Chard." He/She also comments on how it lowers blood pressure. The lecture is over, and class is dismissed.

A lucid dream experience I had on September 11, 1984, enabled me to teach my Parapsychology Class at Christopher Newport College more effectively the following evening than I would have if the nocturnal instructions had not been issued. (The dream will be interpreted as it unfolds.)

Advice For An Effective Christopher Newport College Dream Lecture (September 11, 1984)

> I am about to lecture to our Christopher Newport College Parapsychology Class on dreams. I am uncertain regarding my notes. I draw a moon on the blackboard and begin to lecture on astrology and become stymied.

(Point one) *Do not talk about subjects on which you have no expertise!*

> I speak with a lack of enthusiasm and read my notes.

(Point two) *Lecture with enthusiasm, and add your own personal ideas as you proceed.* DO NOT READ LECTURES.

> A student questions me from the rear of the room and asks me why I have not mentioned certain names in psychology. I state

> strongly that I am speaking only from my point of view and about persons I know connected with the subject of dreams. He withdraws the question, and the class applauds me.

(Point three) *Stand firmly on issues and ideas about which you are certain.*

> A student gets up and draws a five-pointed star on the left side of the blackboard. He fills it in with chalk. His comments and illustrations add to the lecture.

(Point four) *Permit others to share their ideas in class to further expand class consciousness.*

> I am all alone in the classroom and feel isolated. Then, I find I am not alone at all, but I am speaking to Caroline Parrish, the younger sister of my "big sister" in my sorority.

(Point five) *There are others in the class who are on the same path as you. You are not among strangers.*

> Jim announces there will be no test tonight. I am glad to hear this.

The lecture proved not only to be "no test," but was one of the most rewarding speaking engagements of my career.

In retrospect, the lucidity of the dream was such that I was certain I was physically delivering the dream lecture one night before I was scheduled to appear. *Was the lucid dream a practice session?*

Message Dreams

Message dreams are almost always received in the same fashion—*through clairaudience.* Spiritual directives are frequently transmitted when the receiver is in a semi-conscious state between waking and sleeping, or these dreams may be perceived equally well in trance. The ideas, or ideals intrinsic within these transmissions, vary in degree of weight. A few carry with them an air of frivolity having no other purpose than to bring a smile to the lips or a hearty laugh aloud. Others contain advice for the proper use of one's specific talents and abilities. The majority of these spiritual mandates are concerned with the communication of inspirational maxims and Universal Truths. Such messages should be translated into attitude adjustments or personal acts of love and service, toward one's fellowman. Rewards for such actions are accrued far beyond the limits of man's narrow perceptions.

Questions Posed in Connection with Message Dreams:

1. Is the message provided for the dreamer's entertainment?

2. Are the ideas focused on the expansion of psychic awareness?

3. Was the directive prompted by a personal act of dietary overindulgence or some negative behavior in which the dreamer persists? Is a cessation or change of course necessary?

4. Is a little gem of wisdom communicated for personal edification?

5. Is this a commentary on Universal Laws?

6. Is the wisdom contained of such magnitude that it is truly designed to touch the very ideals that comprise the core of our beings?

During a January visit to the Hollis residence John, Elizabeth, Jim, and I had indulged ourselves in a delicious meal the evening before I received the following admonition.

If you eat or drink too much, *meditate all day,* and you will find this solves the difficulty.

Since I am not in the habit of consuming alcohol, the reference to drinking seemed out of place, until Elizabeth and I recalled that too much sugar turns to alcohol thus intoxicating the body in a similar fashion. Our indulgence being great, we determined that our absolution was in direct proportion to the amount of physical damage was had inflicted on our bodies—and in this case, length of the sentence was *all day!*

Several mornings per month I am privileged to receive messages which serve as inspirational guideposts providing me with direction and with a means for gauging my spiritual progress. Skeptics will undoubtedly ponder the source, but it has been my philosophy that the origin is not as important as the sagacity of the maxim or of the action evoked by it. Each precept has touched the core of my being, and it is my fondest hope that one or two of them will prove equally as inspiring for you.

Preparation for Life **(April 3, 1984)**

In preparation for all things you should pray.

Abounding Love **(May 21, 1984)**

You should not measure love, for those who need it most often do not get it in abundance.

Faith Gives Answers **(June 23, 1984)**

Those who seek in faith will always find answers.

The Four Bes **(June 11, 1984)**

Be still. Be aware. Be perceptive. Be assured.

Truth (My Favorite) **(January 21, 1984)**

Meditation, manifestation, and faith bring truth.

Visionary Dreams

Visionary dreams are a rarity, but when experienced their resonance is forever with us. Evolving from the superconscious they bequeath visions and dream elucidations revolving around our personal relationship with God, the workings of Universal Laws, the power of love, and, most important of all, the imparting of lessons and guidance that provide us with enlightenment for our raison d'etre. If, through singularity of focus and intensity of study, we are able to discover the true purpose of our soul's incarnation, how much greater then would be the joy and creativity expressed in our mode of daily living. The magnanimity of such evocations is awe-inspiring to ponder.

Questions Posed In Connection With Visionary Dreams:

1. Is there a central figure or religious personage depicted in the dream? Can you identify the personality as someone of world renown, a master teacher, a celestial being, or perhaps even Jesus of Nazareth himself?

2. What lies within the heart of his message?

3. Is the visionary dream strictly a mental communiqué, or is it experiential in nature to be revered and revelled in?

4. Does the mandate apply solely to you, include family or friends, or provide inspiration and healing for humanity as a whole?

5. Is this an actual contact with God the Father, resulting in renewed life energies or more rarely, a complete Transfiguration of the Soul Identity itself?

Virginia Light, Executive Director of the Advanced Healing Research Foundation in Great Falls, Virginia, recounted a visionary dream she experienced several years ago during the initial phases of the development of her healership. The Spiritual Comminqué left no doubt in her mind regarding the purpose of her current incarnation. The dream is entitled *The Healer.*

The Healer (Virginia Light)

> I (Virginia) stand in a temple among many learned souls. As we converse on a platform, I am aware of a multitude of people surging toward us with hands outstretched. There are piteous cries and wailing. 'Help me! Help me!' Each cries out in anguish. I shake my head in bewilderment not knowing in what way I can relieve their pain.
>
> The teacher beside me beckons me to follow him. We leave through an entrance on the left and walk down some stairs. He motions toward an open pit. I lean my head over to view its contents and draw back in horror. In the pit reside the Demons of Hell. I begin to pray the Lord's Prayer, but realize that the words I utter are in a language completely unintelligible to me. The teacher opens my hand, and in the center of my palm is a Silver Cross. I now realize how I can personally help the crowd with pleading hands. The teacher says, "Go! Heal!"

Taking the advice to heart, Virginia transformed herself into a spiritual healer of the highest order and truly exhibits all of the qualities one would expect in a soul who has dedicated her life to the alleviation of mankind's ills.

The final dream chosen to exemplify the category of visionary dreams contains an element of actual contact and possesses transforming attributes.

The Being of Light (January 26, 1985)

> There is a tall man who is aglow with Light. He, and two other men, are about to enter a plane and go on a trip. I would like to wish him good-bye but realize that the Light is so powerful that if I touch him, I will be burned. I reach up, and he reaches down to touch my finger. There is a spark between us, and my finger is ignited for an instant. I now see a small mark on the top.

When I awoke, the tip of my right finger was darkened. This faded in time, but returned again as I finished writing this dream. It has now faded into nothingness, but the love transmitted from the contact remains with me always.

In closing this section I would like to share a quotation with you by Emmet Fox from *Power through Positive Thinking.* It has always provided inspiration and inner joy to me. I trust it will be so with you.

"Always the best is yet to be. Always the future will be better than the present, or the past, because I am ever growing and progressing, and I am an immortal soul. I am the master of my fate. I greet the unknown with a cheer and press forward joyously, exulting in the Great Adventure.

Armed with this philosophy, and really understanding its power, you have nothing to fear in life, or death—because God is All, and God is Good."[6]

GUIDELINES FOR CREATIVE DREAMING

1. Just before falling asleep at night ask a predetermined question, or in your mind's eye review a puzzling dilemma which up to that point has proved insolvable. If there are no critical issues to be dealt with at the moment, merely request inner guidance with regard to major focal points to your current life situation.

2. Upon awakening write down all dreams, messages, thoughts, feelings, and impressions that flood your consciousness. Oft times a revelation may present itself in the dead of night so don't hesitate to jump out of bed to record your impressions even if it is 3:00 AM.

3. Determine which, if any, of the dreams contain pertinent information and/or a viable solution to the problem in question. There is a possibility that all dreams may be involved or none. If it is the latter, information may appear later in meditation or be received in dreams experienced on future nights.

4. Review the twelve-dream classification system (see page 157) and categorize the dream, or dreams, according to the rationale set forth in that system. Determining the classification

enables one to achieve a clearer vantage point from which to perceive and design a promising course of action.

5. Determine primary and secondary goals to be attained. Then proceed to list suitable and realistic courses of action which incorporate the highest probability of success. Be sure to include the optimum resources at your disposal to assure the realization of your plan.

6. Make an effort to preview the ultimate outcome of your plan. What are the most realistic probabilities of its success? If the plan fails, have you formulated a secondary course of procedure?

7. Allow an adequate length of time for your plan to materialize. Remember time limits are a veritable menace to the psychic realization of one's desires. Continue to monitor current dreams for signs of progress.

8. Seek guidance through daily meditation and sudden flashes of intuitive insights. These contain signposts indicating whether or not you are proceeding correctly.

9. Once a positive outcome is achieved from the goal-oriented plan, evaluate the determining factors and circumstances that were responsible for its success. List them in order of significance so that subsequently, a viable formula can be devised that will supply you with creative options which are keyed to a high level of goal realization on a continuing basis.

10. If your plans fail to materialize, return to square one and reprogram adopting your secondary course of action. Examine the pitfalls and flaws concealed in your primary design so that you will be immediately aware of the fallacies when formulating future creative dream projects.

11. *Important!* Allow one morning per week to sleep later than normal. This will provide an additional opportunity for a broader spectrum of spiritual insights to be previewed by the dreaming mind.

12. Keep a journal of creative dream efforts and successes. This will not only increase your own level of confidence, but encourage others within your circle of friends to adopt similar methods. *Nothing succeeds like someone else's unqualified successes, especially where dreams are concerned.*

13. It might seem wise to have others evaluate your creative dream plans and objectives, but in the final analysis, the most sagacious wisdom of all belongs to the promptings of the Still Small Voice Within. Be attentive, act judiciously, and radiate confidence that you are on the course that will lead to the best of all possible solutions, and then merely *allow.* When the synchronistic circumstances become reality (and they will), gratefully offer prayers of appreciation and thanksgiving to your Creator for the boundless blessings continuously bestowed upon you from His Storehouse of Infinite Goodness.

Expanding Transpersonal Consciousness through Intuition, Spiritual Healing and Intuitive Counseling

CHAPTER 9

Advanced Techniques for the Enhancement of Intuitive and Healing Abilities

If you truly live this life, then it does not in the least matter what your present circumstances may be, or what difficulties you may have to struggle against, you will triumph over them all—you wil be, and in a very positve and literal sense, a healing and illuminating influence on all around you, and a blessing to the whole human race.

Emmet Fox—*The Sermon on the Mount*

One of the primary avenues for the advancement of spiritual development is the expansion of one's intuition. There are specific methodologies and techniques, the practice of which have proven highly successful over time. Although many of these methods of enhancement trace their origin to antiquity, these practices are not without merit. Therefore, students who are seriously engaged in the study of healing and in the pursuit of heightened awareness of intuitive absolutes would do well to appraise themselves of these spiritually advanced techniques and, after an initial period of trial and error, avail themselves of those regimes that provide them with the highest degree of psychical progress.

Chapter nine is divided into two sections. Section One presents a synopsis of five practical enhancers for raising one's consciousness to a higher level of awareness. Four are of a physical nature, and the fifth leans more toward mental expansion. The enhancers discussed are fasting, cleansing, breathing, gems and stones, and visualization. The second portion of the chapter deals strictly with mental processes through which one's personal intuition may be expanded. These include Past Life memories, How to Give a Holistic Life Reading, Questions Regarding Intuitive Readings, and Suggestions For Successful Readings. Having outlined the procedures to be followed, let us now turn our attention to the tasks at hand.

INTUITIVE ENHANCERS

Fasting

"Fasting involves complete abstinence from food, or the use of diets wherein partial exclusion of food substances is practiced. Throughout the ages, fasting has been seen as a means of spiritual growth in the practices of many religions. . . . In the context of the Cayce readings . . . it becomes a setting aside of our own concepts of what or how something should be done. It serves as an opportunity for an individual to allow himself to become *a channel through which God may work.* It is a supplying of energy to the body that promotes the coordination of organs and systems and enhances assimilation and elimination. Thus, in purifying a mind that is in a condition of mental confusion, fasting accompanied by prayer is a mechanism of the mind, not of the body or of the diet."[1]

What is the underlying rationale behind the theory of fasting? The first is the worsening reality of air pollution. Inhabitants of large metropolitan areas are far more susceptible to heart trouble or deadly lung diseases than their country cousins. The country cousins are not exempt by any means, however, as soot and smoke from factories, incinerators, and the exhaust fumes of cars and other vehicles of transportation continually spew their noxious poisons into the atmosphere and spread throughout the surrounding countryside. Polluted air is a true health hazard. Periodic fasting offers an answer to eliminating these accumulated poisons from our systems.

A second premise in support of fasting is dietary pollution. The majority of our population regularly ingests a diet consisting of fried foods, ham, bacon, heavy cream, pies, cakes, and white bread. These are washed down with alcohol, coffee, tea, soft drinks, and tranquilizers. Eventually, the bloodstream becomes poisoned due to the toxic residues which collect throughout the body and a condition known as acidosis occurs. Since the bloodstream should be alkaline, the primary source of the illness we contact (along with negative thinking) arise from this condition. Reversing this process is simple—alkaline the bloodstream. According to Paul Bragg, Life Extension Specialist, "On the first sign of auto-intoxication you should go on a three-to-four-day water fast, and after the fast, switch to an alkaline-forming diet, and at all times you should avoid acid-forming foods. "But what are alkaline-forming foods?" you ask. Generally speaking, raw fruits and vegetables—made into salads—along with leafy, green, cooked vegetables. Three-fifths of your diet should be composed of fruits and vegetables—both raw and cooked. *Always eat a raw vegetable salad or fresh fruit before you eat any meal.*"[2]

How does one undertake fasting? *In my opinion no one should fast unless he has first seen a physician for a complete physical examination.* Then, and only then, can you be sure there is no undetected health problem which would be aggravated by long-term fasting. If the examination reveals a generally good physical state of being, then the following program might be undertaken:

- Either eat absolutely no food, fruit, or vegetable juices and drink only distilled water or, as I have found in my own practice to serve a similar purpose, try a three-day diet of apples or a four-day diet of grapes accompanied by ingestion of the same type of fruit juice.

- It would seem that a long fast sounds good theoretically, but in actual practice this is not the case. Greater benefits are achieved with short fasting periods. Paul Bragg states "Starting with a 24 to 36 hour fast weekly, I find that the faster can really give himself a splendid internal house cleaning. With a no breakfast plan except fruit—along with a program of eating only whole natural foods, the person who really wishes to attain vitality supreme and agelessness can prepare himself for a fast of 3 to 4 days in several months."[3] *Longer fasts should be done only under medical supervision.*

- "At the end of the 24-hour fast, the very first food that reaches your taste buds should be a raw variety vegetable salad with a base of grated carrots and cabbage. (Use either juice of lemon or orange over salad as dressing.) This will act as a broom in the 30 feet of intestines. This will give the muscles along the gastrointestinal tract something to work with. You can follow this salad with one or two cooked vegetables."[4]
- Once you fast for 24 or 36 hours or longer periods as your body becomes accustomed to the process, the healing power in your body is energized. This power that would ordinarily be used to digest and eliminate your food is now used to purify your body and ultimately your mind.
- To maintain the benefits of fasting a natural diet is essential. "The ideal diet is made up of 3/5 raw fruits and vegetables, and 1/5 protein. This protein can be in the form of meat, fish, eggs, natural cheese, or it can be in vegetarian form such as nuts, nut-butters, seeds, or seed meal such as sunflower seeds, sesame seeds, or pumpkin seeds. Brewer's yeast and wheat germ also form an important part of your protein. The last fifth is divided into three. One-third of one-fifth is natural starches, such as whole-grains, in the form of bread or cereals, brown rice, dried legumes, such as lentils, all kinds of dried beans, garbanzos, dried lima beans, and dried lentils. The next one-third of one-fifth is devoted to natural sugars, found in sun-dried fruits such as dates, figs, raisins, honey, maple syrup, unsulphured molasses and black-

> strap molasses. The last one-third of one-fifth of food is devoted to natural unsaturated oils, such as safflower oil, soya oil, olive oil, walnut oil and any unsaturated natural oil."[5]

On the mental plane fasting has been employed by spiritual leaders of all religious sects as a method of intensifying prayer and contacting the Creative Force. David, Elijah, the apostle Paul, and even Jesus himself all realized the value of its use. More recent advocates include John Calvin, Martin Luther, and John Wesley. Abstinence from food opened up spiritual avenues of perception and enlightenment unavailable to them otherwise. Through the deliberate disciplining of the body, God provided them with clarity of purpose and direction.

In my own experience the once-a-week grape, apple, or orange fast seems to prove very beneficial. It gives the body a rest, a well-earned chance to cleanse itself. It also seems to assist clarifying my mental perceptions and provides me with a higher energy level. The philosophy of current day nutritionists advocating just fruit for breakfast for promotion of a higher energy level seems to be consistent with these practices.

Cleansing by Water

From ancient to modern times water has been associated with spiritual activities such as baptism, miracle healing, and divine cleansing. Water is essential for the continuation of life. People can survive five times as long without food as without water.

"Hydrotherapy is the science of the application of waters to the human body for the cure or prevention of disease, correction of physical or mental disorders, and maintenance and improvement of general health. Water can be used in three different forms; as a liquid, as a solid, or ice; or as a gas, that is, steam or vapor.

"The application of water may be external or internal. It can be used for simple cleansing; for internal cleansing, orally or rectally; for stimulation of the circulation by alternate hot and cold water; for relaxation in a tepid bath; for massage by pressure or percussion; for healing action by various combinations of various hydrotherapeutic modalities; and to relieve pain with heat or extreme cold (as ice)."[6]

I have found in my continuing search toward refining the accuracy of the intuitive reading process that immersion in a warm bath intensifies the visualization process as well as transports healing energies over long distances. The bath should be 90–101 degrees with perhaps oil of balsam or pine added. Immersion should be 10–15 minutes with an option of a cross-legged position being assumed as in yoga if this feels comfortable to the body. This procedure lowers blood pressure and relaxes the nerves. *(Caution: This should never be done alone for fear of over-relaxation and loss of consciousness.)*

To energize the body if sluggishness is present, the opposite process is recommended. The temperature for a cold bath ranges from 40–55 degrees for a cool bath from 65–85 degrees. The immersion period should be short—one to one and a half minutes initially extending to two to three minutes with acclimation of the body. This stimulates the heart, increases respiration and circulation, and energizes the nervous system.

An alternate method would be showering as a cleansing procedure. The advantage here is that the body does not bathe in all the bacteria and negative vibrations that have been washed away, but rather these are flushed downward and eliminated through the drain and the body is then cleansed and purified by pure clean water. Shower as a preliminary cleansing process before each intuitive reading. This is without exception in order to eliminate all negative influences from the physical body.

A final word regarding the healing, energizing, and cleansing power of water. The most common use of water is for drinking. We are fortunate to have good well water at Shellbank. However, in some localities it may be wise to purchase spring water to avoid any chemical impurities that may be present. The purer the water, the more physical benefits accrued. With regard to intuitive development the consumption of 8 to 10 glasses of water a day is a physical necessity. It is my personal belief that engaging in psychic activities and healing for *extended periods of time* depletes the body's water supply. The immediate replacement of such vast expenditures of psychic energies is therefore mandatory. This is readily accomplished by continually ingesting water at regulated intervals throughout the waking hours.

Breathing Techniques

Rhythmic or patterned breathing is one of the most widely accepted methods of promoting total relaxation. A side benefit is oxygenation of the blood and energizement of the body.

Rhythmic breathing is an integral part of healing also. Personal energies may be employed both for healing the self as well as the transport of bio-energy to others not present. Energy healing for oneself is discussed by William Last, M.Sc. in his publication, *Heal Yourself.* He recommends an 8-2 rhythm; that is, inhale for a count of eight, hold for two, exhale for eight, hold for two. This pattern lends itself to about three full breaths per minute. To direct the healing energies to a bodily part under stress, simply consciously direct the flow of prana to this part and use imagination to experience a warm, tingling sensation. This can be done upon awaking or prior to retiring for 10 to 30 minutes. An innovative thrust to this method is to visualize, upon inhaling, a suitable healing color bathing the afflicted portion of the body.

It is possible to transfer healing energies to a person not physically present. The healing energies are sent through a personal possession, a photograph, via telephone, or merely by mentioning the person's name.

There are three channels which need to be activated to accomplish long-distance healing. They are the release channel, the healing channel, and the focal channel.

- "The *release channel* is a passageway that allows extra body energy, that cannot be drained through extremities, to leave your body. If you feel energy buildup, needless worry, anxiety, depression, confusion, or overstimulation, you can expend this energy through your *release channel.* . . . If you are right-handed, envision a pathway leading outward from your right temple area. If you are left-handed, the pathway is located at your left temple area. This pathway is your *release channel*."[7] Place your hand palm downward a few inches from your temple and ask that all excess energies be released. Keep your hand there for a few minutes, and then remove your hand and place it on an inanimate object to drain any excess energy. Continue releasing any excess energy periodically throughout the day.

- "The channel located at the temple opposite your *release channel* is your *healing channel*. It is located at your left temple if you are right-handed; your right temple if you are left-handed. . . . When you are healing another person or if you want to heal yourself, open your *healing channel* inward to allow more energy to aid the healing process."[8]
- "Another body channel that is useful in the healing process also is located in your head. It is called the *focal center* and is centered in the middle of your forehead, equal distance from your eyebrows. This space, often referred to as your *third eye*, is where you send out your healing energy."[9] The focal center is capable of channeling healing energy to any area on the body of another person. Moreover, distance is not a barrier. The opening of the focal center activates the healing energies received from your healing channel. These are then transferred without physical limitations to any chosen spot on the globe. They increase the effectiveness of the healee's personal healing energies.
- Long distance healing may be accomplished in the following manner. Place yourself in a relaxed state. Open your release center and drain off all excess energies. Then activate your healing and focal centers. Hold in your left (or right) hand a photograph or personal possession of the person desiring the healing. If this is not feasible, just visualize the person's face in your mind's eye. Focus on the object, photograph, or person's face and direct the healing energies there. You may

want to move your hands over the item as if you were doing an aura healing with the person present. If no item is used, transmit the healing energies through your focal center. Continue this procedure until you feel the healing is complete. At a later date you may want to contact the healee to determine the effectiveness of the treatment and to decide if additional healings are necessary.

In my own experiments with long distance healing I have experienced considerable success using two innovative techniques based on the same principles.

a. Long distance healing energies possess additional power if transmitted while the healer is immersed in water. Therefore, I often send out healing energies during meditation in the bath. I employ a 4, 12, 8 breathing technique with the transmission of each healing thought.
b. I am often awakened between 2:00 and 3:00 AM for long distance healings. It would seem logical to me that with the healee's mind at rest, he is more open to the healing process. This method of healing has proven most successful on a personal level as well as when working in healing partnerships.

Gems and Stones

There are large bodies of literature dealing with the properties and energies of gems and stones. In the interest of space and brevity, however, it would seem prudent to focus on gems whose primary vibrations are highly attuned to the intensification of meditation and healing. Apropos to this statement I cite specific types of crystals and lapis lazuli.

CRYSTALS When selecting crystals for specific physical problems, consult a book such as *The Spiritual Value of Gem Stones* by Wally and Jenny Richardson and Lenora Huett. A general guide is as follows:

a. *Clear Quartz*—This is a stone that is a total body energizer.

b. *Smoky Quartz*—Smoky quartz tends to focus straying attention when worn.
c. *Green Quartz*—The endocrine glands are balanced by this particular stone.
d. *Light orange to brown citrine Quartz*—The natural citrine balances the energies of the groin, spleen, and the solar plexus.
e. *Rose Quartz*—This gemstone harmonizes the love emotions of the four upper centers—the heart, throat, forehead, and crown chakras.
f. *Purple Amethyst*—The purple amethyst is steeped in spirituality and transforms lower energies into higher spiritual level vibrations.

How does one go about selecting the crystal that is most appropriate for his or her personal needs? As you examine a large number of crystals, the ones most valuable for your unique vibrational attunement will begin to transmit signals to your sensitive psychic centers. The more you remain in their vicinity, the stronger the attraction grows. This is why all that is really important, after determining the uses you intend for your crystals, is to sense the ones to which you are spiritually drawn. These are truly the ones most suitable for your personality.

A major usage for crystals is the expansion of awareness. When held in the hand or worn around the neck during meditation, crystals tend to focus energies so that you are more attuned to your own divinity and spiral toward higher and higher levels of consciousness.

In healing, energy flows in the left hand and exits from the right. Therefore, to alleviate personal pain hold your crystal in your left hand while placing the right one over the pain area.

When healing others the Aura Scan provides the healer with a viable form of healing treatment. "Have the client lie down on his back, hands beside him. Hold your crystal lightly between the thumb and the first three fingers. Start at the top of the head and hold the crystal about an inch away from the body at all times during this procedure. When you feel heat or a tingling sensation, begin to move the crystal slowly over the body. As you move, be aware of any changes in the feel of the crystal or of the body.

The change may be a resistance to your movement, a sense of heat, a tingling sensation, coolness, or simply a feeling that something is there even if you have no sensation. When you come to such a change, stop and begin making a circular counterclockwise motion around the center of the disturbance. Keep making this motion until you feel the crystal get heavier, pulling your hand down toward the body. Stop the circular motion, and touch the tip of the crystal to the body in the center of the circle.

Continue to move the crystal down over the front and sides of the body. Whenever you find a difference, make a correction using the circular counter-clockwise motion.

When you reach the feet and have finished, go back to the top of the head and move the crystal from the head to the feet in a sweeping motion. Turn the client over and to the back side using the same procedure. You have the chakras very open, now. Close them down to normal by imagining a zipper at the feet. Reach down and grasp the zipper and pull it all the way to the top of the head.[10] The healee should now feel balanced and exhibit a sense of heightened well-being.

For indepth exploration of the properties of crystals, I recommend *The Crystal Book by Dael and Cosmic Crystals* by Ra Bonewitz.

LAPIS LAZULI The lapis lazuli in its pure form is deep blue in color but is often intermixed with white calcite. Flecks of gold or purite are frequently intermingled.

The lapis lazuli is one of the greatest spiritual stones, although in the mundane world it commands little monetary value.

"Lapis lazuli has the qualities of fineness, of high intensity, and yet etheric in quality. It is a stone which enables a wearer to tune his own etheric body to the particular vibration of that stone and in doing so, it facilitates the opening of many of the chakra centers. For one that is contemplating the opening of his centers using the stone, it is wise that he do this only with love in his heart, comprehension in his mind, and with wisdom in his soul, for as this is done, he will find that new avenues are open to that particular life. It should be done with caution and not in a matter of curiosity."[11]

To open the kundalini centers wear the stone close to the throat chakra which is aligned with the will and the energies will always seek the highest center.

It has been my personal experience as well as the experience of several of my most advanced student sensitives that the wearing of a lapis lazuli seems to intensify and clarify the incoming visual imagery. The employment of the lapis should be done on a trial basis, as what works for one student does not necessarily succeed for another. I do not recommend wearing a lapis lazuli for extended periods of time because of its powerful energizing effects.

To use the lapis for healing hold it in the left hand and work with the right.

Visualization

Visualization is among the most powerful tools one possesses to influence reality.

In my work with creative visualization and imaging over the last five years I have become firmly convinced that each of us is in a unique position to create or reshape our own futures. Not all techniques which I have studied, however, can effectively metamorphose the future with equal potency. As I have worked with and developed a variety of methodologies over the past several years, the refinement process "weeded out" less promising methods. I was eventually left with three sets of intuitive enhancers that continually demonstrated a high degree of success. These were formulating affirmations, ways to use affirmations, and concrete expression of visual images. All these were utilized in conjunction with intensive visualization in meditation and while in the conscious state. They can be employed to energize and empower the probable futures that you have elected to become part of your destiny. Futures received with a negativistic result can be x'ed out and replaced with more desirable and rewarding sets of circumstances. The three psychic enhancers are reviewed below thus enabling you to reprogram and revitalize your future as you choose.

Formulating Affirmations

"Affirmations are one of the most important elements of creative visualization. To affirm means to 'make firm.' An affirmation is a strong, positive statement that something is *already* so. It is a way of 'making firm' that which you are imagining."[12] Examples of positive affirmations to accompany a pictured visualization are:

A. *Businessman*—I am successful in my work and am amply rewarded monetarily and creatively.

B. *Writer*—Each day through my writing I am being of service to mankind.

C. *Mother*—In working with my children I am enabling them to evolve into enlightened and happy human beings.

D. *Composer*—My music creates harmony and revitalization to all who hear the melody. The songs are universally popular.

E. *Physician*—I am a mental, physical, and spiritual healer in the finest sense of the words.

Formulate each affirmation according to the life fulfillment you desire and use it in conjunction with your visualizations during meditation. Shakti Gawain in her book *Creative Visualization* offers these guidelines:

"**1.** Always phrase affirmations in the present tense not the future. It is important to create it as if it *already exists.*

2. Always phrase affirmations in the most positive way you can. Affirm what you *do* want, not what you *don't* want.

3. In general, the shorter and simpler the affirmation, the more effective.

4. Always choose affirmations that feel totally right for you. . . . Try changing the words until it feels right.

5. Always remember when doing affirmations that you are creating something new and fresh. *You are not trying to redo or change what already exists.*

6. Affirmations are not meant to *contradict* or *try to change* your feelings or emotions . . . Affirmations can help you create a new point of view about life which will enable you to have more and more satisfying experiences from now on. . . .

7. When using affirmations, try as much as possible to create a feeling of belief, an experience that they can be true."[13]

Creative Ways To Use Affirmations

The use of affirmations are not only limited to meditation periods, but may be employed periodically throughout the day. Two of the most beneficial times are just before going to sleep at night and upon awaking. The affirmation chosen should be spoken silently, but with absolute conviction as the envisioned event is programmed on the screen of the mind. The subconscious is more likely to be accepting of the suggestion at these times because of the existence of a "trance-like state."

Affirmations may be written on a small card and repeated before the mirror as you are dressing. The card may be carried in your wallet and removed at convenient times throughout the day when you are alone. It is wise to remove the card and read the affirmation three times while visualizing the desired outcome.

An alternative way to use written affirmations is to purchase a notebook and record your affirmations and desires on the blank page, again employing creative visualization as a catalyst. This may be done one, three, or ten times depending on the number that is intuitively correct for you.

The third and most powerful way for the usage of affirmations is through the spoken word. Why is the spoken word the most powerful tool? Because of the dynamics of sound. Every word that is uttered exerts tremendous vibratory power. Therefore, it logically follows that specific sequences of words produce efficacious vibrations sufficiently powerful to affirm and vitalize the probable futures we desire. *There is one prerequisite however. The choice of words must be succinctly definitive in meaning.* It is then and only then that the vibratory force of the selected words begins to attract the necessary ingredients to create the exact set of circumstances visualized. Dr. Catherine Ponder in her book, *Open Your Mind to Prosperity*, feels that the spoken word method can increase the rate at which prosperity events are realized by 80 percent.

Concrete Expressions of Visual Images

A final method for re-creating in reality the mind-pictures envisioned is through *tangible representations* of these mental events. Their physical replication increases the likelihood of manifestation a hundredfold. Again, we pose the question as to why? Imagination is one of our strongest abilities. Therefore, by transferring this power into concrete form *we are physically affirming our mental and spiritual intention.* Since body, mind, and spirit work as a triune, you have captured on paper what the ancients might have termed "pyramid power." Dr. Catherine Ponder terms these picture representations as your "Wheel of Fortune" and provides us with several suggestions.

1. Use large poster board to construct these pictures.
2. Select specific colors for precise results.
   - **a.** *Green or gold* for prosperity in job or career.
   - **b.** *Yellow or white* to promote spiritual understanding.
   - **c.** *Blue* for developing intellectual areas of your life.
   - **d.** *Orange* for health and energy.
   - **e.** *Pink, rose, or warm red* for harmony in all relationships.
3. Cut out colored pictures and provide plenty of space on each selected board.
4. Always place a spiritual symbol on each board for protection and as an energizing force (eg. Christ, The Bible).
5. Tell no one of your pictures, but view your wheel every day before retiring. This provides the subconscious with additional creativity to grant you your heart's desires.

You have just read one of the most important sections in this entire publication. Reread this again and again, for within these several pages lies the power of life mastery. Formulate, visualize, and believe. *Your life will never be the same.*

METHODOLOGIES FOR THE REFINEMENT OF INTUITIVE AND HEALING ABILITIES

Past Life Memories

Elizabeth Hollis is well-versed on the subjects of reincarnation and past life memories. I have asked her to contribute to this section in order that my readers may have access to the depth and breadth of the knowledge she has accrued. Learn then from her own words how therapeutically valuable this concept truly is.

Reincarnation, the idea that our souls return to the earth to inhabit different bodies in our search for perfection, is potentially a source of great help to those on the spiritual quest. Although many people pursue past life knowledge out of curiosity, there are several ways in which an understanding of our past experiences can lead to growth and self-awareness.

1. Knowledge of past lives can show the original causes of phobias, anxieties, and problems which are surfacing in the present time and provide a starting point for treatment.
2. Sometimes reliving a past experience through hypnosis can alleviate the existing problem.
3. Past life information can reveal themes throughout different lifetimes which are helpful in working on soul goals.
4. The law of karma is frequently illustrated for us in a personal way when we examine past life information. We learn that life proceeds in an orderly way, and that cause and effect is indeed working to help us learn our lessons.

There are numerous avenues to take in trying to retrieve past life information. Some of these are hidden from the conscious level. Some are directly sought after. We may have feelings, intuitions, and emotions about things that seem to have no connection with our actual experiences in this life. This may take the form of an attraction (or a distaste) for a particular country or culture. Through our dreams we may view ourselves in another place and time. Oft times this helps us see the connection between the past and present. We don't need to wait for glimpses of the past to come to us however. Through hypnosis, we are allowed access to the Higher Self. Retrieving past life memories can be accomplished through self-hypnosis or past life regression by a responsible hypnotherapist.

The hypnotist induces a state of relaxation in the client, frequently by suggesting that each part of the body is relaxed and at ease. He then suggests that the mind can let go of its conscious thoughts. Visualization might be used as a relaxing and focusing device, so that the client begins to use visual images as a resource in receiving information. In vividly imagining an ocean scene, perhaps, the mind lets go of current thoughts and leaves itself receptive to incoming impressions.

When the client is in hypnosis, a relaxed yet aware state, the hypnotist might suggest that the client relive events that took place at an earlier time in his or her life. The final stage is to suggest that the client find herself in a situation that took place prior to her birth in the present incarnation. This can be a suggestion for a lifetime which pertains to the problem at hand, or simply an open suggestion, trusting that what information comes is what is needed at that time. Finally, the conductor suggests that the subject return to the present place and time. The subject is allowed to come to a fully conscious state at her own pace.

In self-hypnosis the procedure is the same, with suggestions coming from the individual rather than from a conductor. We may also receive past life information from spiritual sources and then are able to pursue it further through our own efforts. Both methods are desirable.

An intuitive who works with past life vibrations follows a routine which might include these elements:

1. A prayer or invocation for protection and guidance while in an "open" state.
2. Centering, also known as focusing, going into trance, achieving an alpha state.
3. Asking for the information desired, and allowing that information to flow with as little interference as possible.

Past life information can be of enormous benefit in helping us discover ourselves, our motivations, our lessons, and our avenues of soul growth. What it cannot do is provide an excuse for our present life situations and problems. What we are today is surely related to what we were, but we must begin today to evolve and to grow toward God, regardless of what we have done before. Each incarnation is a specially designed opportunity to rise above ourselves and should be used as such.

How To Give A Holistic Life Reading

Each intuitive has his or her own mode for giving a reading. Therefore, the information contained in this section is presented to offer a set of guidelines rather than to aggressively direct the process. Feel free to elect whatever portions of the Holistic Life Reading feel comfortable to you. Then file the remainder away for future use.

Exercises for Training Your Inner Eye

Focusing Attention through Relaxation

For all beginning students, attaining a receptive meditative state is the initial step taken when embarking on a program to develop one's intuitive abilities. A successful formula for achieving this altered state of consciousness would be the following:

"**1.** Find a location where you are not likely to be disturbed. Make yourself as comfortable as possible whether it be reclining in your favorite chair or lying down on a couch or bed. Place your hands at your sides and your legs and feet flat on the floor or straight out on the bed.

2. Close your eyes and begin a pattern of rhythmic breathing, taking a series of deep breaths through the nostrils. As the pattern progresses, you will become more and more aware of a sense of increased relaxation flowing through your mind and body. When this occurs, begin to focus your attention on your feet and legs and, working up to the top of your head, instruct each part of your body to relax in turn. Examples of self-suggestive commands would be: 'I feel my feet. All tension has vanished, leaving them free and light. I notice all tension is being released in my legs and a sensation of complete freedom now exists.' Do not hurry to complete this exercise; the slower pace will enhance the desired results. Continue in this fashion until you reach the top of the head. At this point you should feel energized and buoyant, having reached a peak of mental and physical relaxation.

3. Becoming a highly attuned intuitive channel carries with it the requirement of divorcing oneself from preconceived notions and ideas and being absolutely open to the flow of information received. In this manner one truly becomes 'a channel of blessings for others.' A prayer of attunement can be initiated through the use of an affirmation such as *'May the protection and knowledge of the Lord so fill me physically, mentally and spiritually that I become a healing channel in his name.'*

4. Psychic work often involves the need for protection against harmful or negative influences that may intrude upon our subconscious when we open ourselves up psychically. Therefore, it is mandatory to invoke spiritual protection against these unwholesome forces. To do this, imagine that you are surrounded by a cocoon of brillant white light that acts as a divine shield, neutralizing all negativity that may enter into your auric field. An affirmation such as 'I am protected by the love of God' serves a similar purpose.

5. Psychic states can vary from a light trance to a deep hypnotic state of meditative silence. Once having arrived at a state of complete relaxation, the next procedure revolves around a gradual psychic 'turning inward.' This is accomplished by counting backward slowly from ten to one while simultaneously visualizing yourself walking down a flight of steps. The count should be synchronized with each descending step. At the end of this flight of stairs you will enter into a room and seat yourself in front of a screen. A feeling of reverence should be all-pervasive. You are now ready to view the awe-inspiring presentations of the inner eye."[14]

Obtaining Holistic Life Information

1. When you have achieved a state of intense relaxation, you are ready to use psychometry as a centralizing focus for the retrieval of holistic life information. All objects carry with them a vibrational record of their history. Psychometry allows the intuitive to attune his or her own subconscious to that of the subconscious vibrational pattern that the owner of the object has impressed upon it. When contact is established, the holistic life information begins to flow.

2. To facilitate that flow, hold the object in your left hand, in both hands, or to your forehead. As you become more accustomed to doing intuitive readings, your personal experience will tell you which placement offers you the optimum clarity for the inner eye.

3. Now, in your state of intense concentration sense or see what pictures, feelings, symbols, or verbal messages are transmitted. Be receptive, and report whatever "intuits" appear. *Guard against intellectualizing through your own interpretations.* If this format is adhered to, your rate of accuracy should rise with each psychic reading session.

4. There are six separate sections which comprise a Holistic Life Reading. These are Physical Symbology, Current Issues, Future Trends, Character Analysis, Past Lives, and Soul's Purpose. Specific questions should be asked as each portion of the Holistic Life Reading is accomplished.

5. Physical Symbology—As you view the body as a whole, do you notice any darkened portions? Where are they located?

What organs are affected? What does the condition mean symbolically? Continue with this procedure until the entire physical body is covered. *Do not consider these impressions the diagnosis of an illness.*

6. **Current Issues**—These consist of important issues of immediacy in your client's life that may be either a source of joy or trouble depending upon the attitude adopted. Does he feel competent in his chosen job, or is he bored and ready to consider a change of careers? Are there financial problems? What is his marital status? Is he single, is he happily married, or is this an area of emotional turmoil? Are there children? Is the personal relationship healthy in regard to each? Does he enjoy his current place of residence? What are his best and worst abilities? Eventually, the information will cease to flow and you can move on to Future Trends.

7. **Future Trends**—This is one of the most difficult sections on which to achieve a high degree of accuracy because of the existence of free will. However, there will be future events connected or not connected to current issues. Merely, read what is presented. Will your client get the new job he is seeking? Will his daughter win that scholarship to college? Is an exotic vacation in the offing? This section should contain positive events to give your readee hope for a better life to focus his attention upon in the future.

8. **Character Assessment**—This portion is an analysis of both the positive and negative character traits of the individual. This must be presented very tactfully or else you will infuriate your client by sounding too judgemental. Is he an introvert or an extrovert? Is he generous, honest, pleasure-seeking, service oriented, loving? Negative mind set patterns include laziness, selfishness, jealousy, arrogance, maliciousness, anger, envy, etc. *Tiptoe through this section.*

9. **Past Lives**—The importance of this section is not in whether the readee really existed as such a person, but in how the

information can be used to solve present-day dilemmas or to heighten current abilities. One or two prominent lives should be previewed which are closely associated with personal issues of today. Is there a latent artistic talent noted that can be explored and realized? Could the current marital problems stem from a past mother-son relationship? What past life fears are responsible for existing phobias? Note the individual's native origin. This will provide evidence for present life natural tastes and inclinations. Do not try to read ten lives at once. This will prove fruitless and non-educational.

10. **Soul's Purpose**—As you read through the variety of information contained in the Holistic Life Reading, you will note a theme throughout. This is the individual's true purpose or chosen reincarnational lesson. Is he here to learn generosity, service to others, the proper use of financial wealth, honesty, patience, self-worth? Or is this perhaps a life of sheer enjoyment to be shared with loved ones from the past. This is one of the most crucial sections of the reading because of its teaching value. *Read carefully!*

11. After you have completed all divisions of the Holistic Life Reading, ask if the reading is complete. If no additional information is forthcoming, then the reading is finished. Bless the client for whom you have served as a channel. Request that the reading be of the highest value to him as he continues his life progression.

12. You may now reverse the procedure given in the relaxation section, utter a prayer of thanks to the All Loving and Generous Creator with whom you have been communing.

Questions Regarding Holistic Life Readings

Throughout my training as a sensitive I have been blessed with several gifted teachers. No one has proved to be a better instructor, however, than Alan Vaughan. His logical and viable approach to the mysterious world of metaphysics is unequalled when compared with other courses which purport to offer mastery in intuitive readings. Therefore, I would be remiss if I did not offer him my heartfelt thanks for his invaluable contributions to my own ongoing philosophy. An intermingling of our ideas is expected here due to the parallel-thinking.

1. What constitutes a good intuitive reading? The best readings occur when people really need them. They ask very specific questions which demonstrate their needs. This type of person is open and interesting and evokes a sympathetic attitude. You can sense at a distance or face-to-face that he or she is easy to read.

2. When do the worst intuitive readings take place? Generally, readings tend to be inaccurate for curiosity seekers or individuals who try to test your abilities. These types usually lead a dull life and want to hear that something wonderful is going to happen to them when, in fact, there is no chance of this due to their negativism.

3. What is the proper procedure when unpleasant events are foreseen? It is prudent to program your subconscious to view events that will contribute to the highest good of the recipient. If, however, during the course of the reading, an unpleasant scenario is reviewed, it might be dealt with by stating, "I feel there is a possibility that an incident such as this might occur. Can you take steps to prevent this?" In reality, each person has to take responsibility for his or her own life. All the intuitive can do is pick up on life images.

4. Why are names, dates, and places so difficult to read accurately? Usually, the person being read already knows this information. In addition, abstract ideas are of an intellectual, not an intuitive nature. It is more important to focus on current issues that are troubling your client at the moment and illuminate several possibilities that might guide him or her in making positive future decisions.

5. What method is suggested to visualize time frames accurately? Visualize the months of the year as a clock and request to see the particular month the event might transpire. Continually working with this visualization will increase your level of accuracy.

6. Why is it important to read past lives? When a past life is encountered during the course of a reading, it is because there is a parallel or counterpart to the current existence. Whether it is true is not as important as whether the client is capable of internalizing the lessons learned from the material channeled.

7. Are future patterns set? No. The intuitive usually views probable futures for his or her client. The future is pliable and usually subject to change. Which future materializes depends entirely upon the person's free will the majority of the time, although at times some patterns are set because of pre-life selections. Therefore, it behooves each of us to focus upon our best possible future and work toward that end.

If we run into future patterns which seem to occur again and again, we are experiencing "practice sessions" until we learn well the lesson intended.

8. What is the value of overlapping information if readings are done by two intuitives? If there is a consensus of opinion on issues, the information received should then be viewed as highly trustworthy because of the "blindfold effect." This effect is present when two intuitives read for the same entity and do not consult beforehand. Crosscurrent events forseen should then be taken into serious consideration.

9. Why should you charge for an intuitive reading? Just as with other professionals there should be some remuneration for the intuitive's talent and time. A reasonable fee commands respect and enhances your reputation in terms of the value of your work.

10. Is there a reliable measure for evaluating your intuitive abilities? If you find it easy to do intuitive work and are comfortable doing it, you are probably balanced and well-endowed psychically. A good intuitive also learns to sense the truth of incoming material by gauging the energy levels of the Third Eye and Solar Plexus Psychic Centers. *One of the joys connected with intuitive work is watching other people discover their own individualized talents.*

According to Alan Vaughan people have no idea of the incredible power available to them for transforming their lives. It is just a matter of asking your consciousness and you can have anything you want.

Suggestions for Successful Readings

1. Always assume an attitude of helpfulness and love when beginning a reading for your client.
2. Give readings at the time you are at your best physically and mentally. You court disaster otherwise.
3. Don't read to meet the client's expectations. Read positively but objectively.
4. Don't block or edit material. You just might miss the key focus of the entire reading.
5. Ask for further clarification if issues remain unclear.
6. Always program the very best and most positive events for your clients.
7. Remember, there are times when you will misinterpret, or be completely wrong. Don't be discouraged. Pick up the pieces and try again. Practice makes perfect (almost!).
8. There will be some clients for whom it will be impossible to read. When this situation unfolds, apologize and return their money. *Forget pride and don't fake it!* This would be an injustice to both you and your client.
9. Always sum up the essence of the reading in your final statement. This is most likely what the client will carry away with him or her. *Therefore, it is mandatory to summarize the main issues succinctly.*

The opportunities for advancing your intuitive abilities and healing potential are unlimited. These should be numbered among the most valuable assets of soul creativity, and the proper use of them considered synonymous with one's soul growth.

An inspirational treatise channeled through me perhaps states the case more concisely.

On Proper Utilization of The Creative Process

Then, it is these Forces that are primarily responsible for the major events of life. The pulsation of their positive and negative vibratory influences promulgates the likelihood of occurrence.

The Forces of which we speak are neutral in initial form, their energies without substance or aim. The thought process of an individual activates their electrical field, thus charging their atomic structure either positively or negatively. These then assume substantive direction to accomplish the individual goal, or end, for which they were set in motion.

The Power of the vibratory flow is literally limitless, though few demonstrate a sufficient awareness to engage the Source currents, and continually master and monitor their amplification. There are those among us, however, who through intensification and expansion of spiritual aptitudes achieve unity with The Creative Forces. Then understanding of the universality and applicability of spiritual laws enables them in effect to accept the role of an attuned instrument for the proper and efficient utilization of these Forces. Once having firmly in hand the reins, these individuals not only channel the electrical flow toward the accomplishment of ideals, but moreover, also magnify the Power to such a degree that the process is truly one of co-creativity at the highest vibratory level.

It is through the method just described that miracle healings, great literary works, masterpieces of art, medical advancements, and the like are made available for the edification of mankind.

Therefore, give thanks for the process of co-creativity, and work diligently towards its perfection. The rewards for the realization of one's goals are truly worth the price exacted. Success in the venture brings humankind ever in closer contact with our Creator.

CHAPTER 10

Healers and the Healing Process

I bandaged the wound—God healed it.

Ambrose Pare, French Surgeon
George W. Meek—*Healers and The Healing Process*

A THEORETICAL APPROACH TO SPIRITUAL HEALING

Dreams, intuition, and healing are so closely interwoven that it is oft times difficult to determine their boundaries. One's intuition signals when a bodily illness is about to appear. Dreams frequently supply the healing recommendations for the removal of the malady. Eventually, the healee passes this newly acquired knowledge on to others of us who are unfortunate enough to experience similar plights. This is a form of spiritual healing in the broadest sense.

The purpose of this chapter, however, is to examine spiritual healing more definitively. From a more scientific standpoint, the verification of concepts involved in spiritual healing are readily accessible for inquiring minds to acknowledge if the veils of illusion are drawn aside and the most expedient questions posed. From this vantage point it is possible to gather a sufficient amount of scientifically oriented evidence and examples to lend some degree of credence to a subject which has too long been steeped in emotionality.

The initial subject for consideration when investigating spiritual healing is: What are the postulates and theories that undergird this process?

According to Harry Edwards, all spiritual healing is basically achieved through the medium of thought. This is especially true in absentee healing where there is no physical contact between the healer and the patient. Through the power of thought, the "healing forces are able to create chemical changes through the application of one given form of energy to another. Beneficial chemical changes are also induced through the bodily intelligence. The healing forces possess individual, particularized characteristics to effect beneficial change through introducing new factors that alter or disperse the harmful conditions."[1]

Spiritual healing is not a modern phenomenon, but rather a form of treating illness that dates back to Biblical times. The New Testament contains evidence of 26 individual and 27 group healings by The Master Physician, Jesus. These were accomplished through ingestion of medicinal preparations, touch, words, faith, exorcism, and prayers. Therefore, the practices that produced successful results almost 2000 years ago serve as the foundation of spiritual healing as it is conceived in modern times.

In spiritual healing as well as in other forms of healing, each person has the God-given right to choose between a perfected state of health and a continuously debilitating state of illness. If the former is elected, there is no necessity for a spiritual intercessor. If, however, the latter conditions have persisted for a considerable term, then one essential must be met before any healing is extended into the realm of possibility—*the cause must first be overcome.* "If the primary causation lies within disharmony, frustration, anguish, etc. of the inner mind, then that must first be erased and removed. This can come only within the sphere of influence of Spirit—it cannot be overcome by taking medicine. With its overcoming, then the symptoms of the disease are soon mastered, provided the bodily state is not too weak to respond."[2]

Although it has become fashionable to make appointments for absent spiritual healing, the truth of the matter is that from the moment the healing process is instituted, these powerful energies are directed to the sick at a constant and continuous rate. In some cases conditions are optimum for restoring health and vitality when the patient lies in the sleep state with his mind freed from stress and daily toil, but in the final analysis, time is not a constant in reality; therefore, its limitations should not be imposed on the healing forces.

Another issue of inestimable importance with regard to this form of healing is what are the basic personality characteristics exhibited by a healer. George Meek in his publication, *Healers and the Healing Process,* provides us with an excellent profile typical of those currently found in the United States, England, and Brazil.

According to Mr. Meek healers may be male or female and of any race or color. Belief in an organized system of religion is not a prerequisite. Nor is formal education. In fact, the reverse seems to be true.

The level of healing ability varies greatly between practitioners although success appears to depend upon native ability, desire for service (love), attunement with the universe, and understanding human nature. The majority of healers exhibit specialities with specific types of ailments. A profound intuitive knowledge of human nature on the part of the healer is the key to helping patients who would otherwise remain ill.

With regard to the healing act itself, the healer may not find it necessary to have physical contact with the patient, nor does the patient need strong faith in the healer. It would seem that faith in his own belief system is of more importance. A healing can take place instantly, but more often it requires days or even weeks or months for the results to be evident.

Healers who become obsessed with ego or money often suffer a decline in healing potency. In general, however, healers exhibit a very balanced personality and superior mental health as healing demands a positive and trusting attitude toward humanity and the cosmos.

An absolute in spiritual healing is that *the healer does not cure diseases, but is rather the instrument of healing.* This being the case, "is the healing process facilitated by the actual transfer of energy from the healer to the patient, or is it facilitated by the powerful influence of the patient's own mind?

"This is a very difficult distinction to make and perhaps in the last analysis it does not matter—*at least to the patient.* All healing ultimately occurs from within. The surgeon's knife, the internist's drugs do not heal the body. At best they give the body's defenses and homeostasis mechanism a chance to rally; at worst, they cause further stress and suppression of natural defenses and homeostasis mechanisms. Perhaps in paranormal healing it is the energy transfer which arrests the disease process long enough to allow natural body defenses to get back on their feet."[3]

If the subject of spiritual healing is to be approached from a scientific standpoint, then of necessity, laboratory experiments must be designed which provide incontrovertible proof of its authenticity. Has any such stringently controlled research been undertaken? The answer is unequivocally *Yes!* Dr. Bernard Grad, a geriatrics researcher at McGill University's Allen Memorial Institute, conducted a rigorously designed experiment directed toward solving the question. . . . *Is the healing that is achieved through the laying-on-of-hands method attributable to the power of suggestion or a more objective source?*

Dr. Grad selected mice as his experimental targets. Forty-eight female mice were divided into three groups, each group having small amounts of skin removed from their backs. The sizes of the wounds were measured and recorded. As the subject of the experiment, Dr. Grad placed his confidence in Colonel Oskar Estebany, a healer who initially used his abilities with cavalry horses and later treated people during the Hungarian Revolution when physicians were almost non-existent. "The first was treated by Colonel Estebany in a cage resting on his left palm with his right hand held above the wire mesh—not touching the animals. The second group was cared for in identical ways, but was not treated by the healer. The third group was given identical routine without treatment but was heated to the same degree as those heated slightly by the healer's hands. This was to test whether heat alone would accelerate wound healing.

The skin wounds were measured periodically up to 20 days and the rates of healing analyzed."[4] The results were amazing! The table below reports them in weight (mg) of Paper Projections of Wounds.

The wounds treated by the healer were far smaller than those in the control groups. Artificial heating demonstrated no advantage in speeding up the healing process.

Of current interest is the parapsychological research reported by Ted and Virginia Light, Co-founders of The Advanced Healing Research Foundation. Among the diseases for which they claim successful healings have been achieved are arthritis, deafness, epilepsy, multiple sclerosis, ruptured discs, and visual traumas. During the early phases of their research about one-half of the patients showed significant improvement. As their healing programs became more refined and new procedures were adopted, the healing rate accelerated to 90 percent. The Lights work in conjunction with medical doctors. Therefore, their spiritually oriented cures are often authenticated by physicians. With numerous documented cases currently in their files, Ted invites all interested researchers to examine their healing methodologies as long as confidentiality is maintained.

	On Day Of Wounding		**Fourteen Days After Wounding**	
	(#)	(#)(#)	(#)	(#)(#)
Group I (Mr. Estebany)	8.051 ±	.234	.562 ±	.146
Group II (No Treatment)	7.547 ±	.211	2.043 ±	.379
Group III (Heat)	7.711 ±	.284	2.323 ±	.442

(#) Mean
(#)(#) Standard Error

One cannot become involved in the study of spiritual healers and healing for any extended length of time without formulating strong personal convictions. Three such axioms have emerged for me in this regard.

1. The primary healing achieved through miracle healing or a laying-on-of-hands technique appears to afford only temporary relief unless it is accompanied by an acknowledgement of the causative factor.

2. A major change in life orientation is an incurred obligation for the permanent restoration and maintenance of an optimum state of physical well-being and mental balance. This may include a change of diet, vitamin therapy, meditation, a positive attitudinal posture, and love of self and others. Whatever the requirement may be, meet it, for herein lies the key to a joyful and productive future.

3. Personal experience always offers the best lessons for self-growth and self-renewal. Therefore, be open to generously sharing your newly acquired "healing expertise" with others. Bestowed blessings always revert to their original source.

MEETING THE HEALERS

Now that we have reviewed the theological aspects of spiritual healing, you are in an excellent position to elect the type of healer and healing methods which are most suited to your needs.

So let me introduce you to five of the most extraordinarily talented healers with whom it has been my privilege to become acquainted. Review their healing philosophies and, then through both analytical and intuitive determination, choose those healing alternatives that appeal most to your own personal psyche.

Dr. Norman Shealy

Dr. Norman Shealy is a medical doctor by profession. He is trained as a neurosurgeon and has also earned a Ph.D. in Psychology using the latter training with considerable competence in reprogramming patients afflicted with severe eposodic pain disorders. He is the founder of Shealy Institute for Comprehensive Pain and Health Care in Springfield, Missouri, where he employs biofeedback, autogenic training, and self hypnosis techniques to retrain the suffering soul's thoughts and feelings.

Under Dr. Shealy's care the majority of patients improve dramatically after several days in residency. His basic premise is that all healing involves the harmonious use of what he terms *love energy.* This force combined with proper manipulation of diet, exercise, and emotional components identified as the causal factors for the onset of the disease promulgates physical and spiritual healing in the finest sense of the word.

Dr. Shealy expresses his theories concerning the healing process in this presentation.

Self-Healing through Love Energy—
C. Norman Shealy, M.D., Ph.D.

During the past 15 years, I have worked with 4,000 chronic pain patients, given workshops to many thousands of health professionals, and counseled countless acquaintances along the way. Each year I gain more personal insight into basic causes of illness and suffering. This insight increasingly supports my belief that the root of human suffering is a feeling of poor self-esteem derived from actual or imagined love-deficiency in early life. This leads to greater stress than any other problem.

Most parents probably initiate child bearing with totally naive, bright-eyed, bushy-tailed enthusiasm. Too little planning and logic are involved in conception, pregnancy, and child rearing. Thus, the inherent immaturity of most individuals pervades their consciousness during those critical development periods for each new generation, not because of a conscious, purposeful meanness or badness on the part of parents, but because they lack the wisdom of mature spiritual development. Dr. Robert Leichtman, an outstanding clairvoyant, has told me that he thinks no one should become clairvoyant before age 30 as people are too immature to handle the responsibility. Parenting is another aspect of life in which maturity comes much later than is desirable.

In my own case, I am certain I would have been a far superior parent if I'd begun at age 45! Fortunately, my wife matured earlier and provided a superior milieu for our children who would otherwise have suffered more from my earlier erratic inconsistencies and relatively typical American male minimal involvement. Quality time with both parents is crucial and ideal, especially when done with love.

The immaturity of parents leads them to live their own "fight or flight" existence on a moment to moment basis. They are captured by their feelings of insecurity, loneliness, stress, unresolved anger, etc. This is conveyed in varying dosages to each child so that different children with the same parents may wind up with markedly different personalities.

Each child then reaches adulthood with varying ego strengths, fears, and unresolved anger. It is important to recognize that the root of all human suffering is fear of loss. There are only five possible losses; there is fear of loss of:

life (death)
health (illness)
love (acceptance, approval)
money (security)
moral values

Threats, real or imagined, lead to reactions:

Outright fear—terror, worry.
Anger—How dare you threaten me.
Guilt—I've not lived up to my moral values, responsibilities, etc.
Depression—I can't win; the threat is stronger than I.

Anxiety—I don't want to admit it's fear, so I use a less awesome word.

Emotions are messages from our body to our mind, telling us that an event inside or outside is in harmony or in conflict with our ideals. They lead us to actions.

When one is threatened with loss, there are only four possible actions:

1. *Worry, fears,* etc.—which, if continued, is committing suicide in a socially acceptable way, perpetuating the "fight or flight" stress reaction.
2. *Assertion*—to correct the threat—is desirable if feasible. This may be accomplished in four ways:
   a. Write a letter.
   b. Have a discussion or argument.
   c. Have a fight ("war" when between nations).
   d. File a law suit.
   If the situation is not correctable, then one should make a written list of the good and bad, grading each aspect. Then, one may be able to decide *logically* to:
3. *Divorce the intolerable situation with joy* ("Whee, I don't have to put up with that anymore") or
4. *Accept and forgive the individual threatening us* (go for sainthood).

Once the "logical" decision is made, then one needs to work with the options in a deep state of relaxed detachment to determine which potential solution *feels* best. We need to recognize that life is a series of gives and takes, compromises, and opportunities to grow, first in forgiveness, later in other human attributes.

Ultimately, I believe the purpose in life is to move beyond forgiveness to pure love. There are many steps along the way. These include:

Tolerance—an acceptance of widely differing beliefs.
Serenity—being able to be at peace in the face of relative chaos.
Motivation—determination to succeed.
Confidence—in one's ability.

Charity—sharing with those less fortunate.
Compassion—for those less fortunate.
Courage—to face whatever life offers.
Hope—that tomorrow will be better.
Faith—that the purpose in life is good.
Joy—in the beauty of life.
Will—to pursue attunement with soul, God, or divine.
Wisdom—to make the right decisions.
Reason—to make logical decisions.
Love—for all aspects of life and the universe; unconditional, agape love.

Working toward optimal expression of these attributes is a lifelong responsibility. Progress may be slow, with occasional skips into less mature behavior. Success in accomplishing the ultimate goal comes more easily to those willing to study, to think, to plan, to practice on a regular basis. Practice sessions require both self-analysis and detached deep relaxation with creative visualization.

Actually, all thought is ultimately visual, for words are but substitute symbols for images. We learn early in life to associate words with images. For instance, "my hand" provides a clear-cut image as well as inner sensing. To one speaking English, the French "Ma main" has no meaning. When we hear words, our magnificent mind-computer automatically converts the words into stored images, memories.

More abstract concepts such as forgiveness, tolerance, serenity, love, etc., require a much more complex mental process. These involve abstract universal symbols, perhaps primordial in all human beings. But, they are enhanced by conscious creative mental experiences. One can, for instance, examine consciously one's memories and beliefs related to such abstract concepts. This should be done in a state of quiet, personal reflection. Later it may help to discuss the concept with a friend or counselor.

Further progress can be made by creating a variety of personal scenarios in which one plays the role of a student practicing forgiveness under a variety of circumstances. A first step requires identifying all individuals who have offended, threatened, or wronged one. When the list is as comprehensive as possible, then in a state of relaxed detachment, one visualizes the individual who has left one upset and sees oneself saying, "I forgive you for the problem between us." Be as specific as possible in identifying the problem. Practice until you *mean* it.

Next make a list of all the persons *you* have threatened, offended, or mistreated, and see yourself asking those individuals one at a time to forgive you! Sometimes it is worth practicing this until you feel comfortable doing it in writing or in person.

The final test of your forgiveness is testing your inner feelings when you actually encounter the individual(s) in question. It doesn't count until you feel at peace in their presence! In general, until forgiveness is fairly advanced, it is unlikely that you can make great progress in other attributes. Each of the great human potentials requires progressive work. You might find the *Human Potential Attitude Inventory* helpful in stimulating your thoughts concerning various spiritual values *(Appendix B).* Once you've pondered these questions, then grade yourself on the *Human Potential Development Scale* (Appendix C).

These evaluations of human potential offer you an opportunity to compare your conscious and subconscious reactions to these broad categories of characteristics. Ultimately, only *you* can truly evaluate your progress. The goal is to achieve steady growth. If you were perfect, it is unlikely that you would be here! The goal is a score of 100 on all 15 scales. You may achieve high performance scores on some attributes, under some circumstances but not under others. Only when you achieve a score of 100 of all others is it possible to achieve a score of 100 on the love scale. A true score of 100 on love requires a score of 100 on all 15 scales.

The question: Is it worth it? Of course! The answer you find will provide meaning. As Victor Frankl indicated in *Man's Search for Meaning,* nothing is more important than meaning. When that meaning results in perfect love, one has truly achieved sainthood. In developing that love, you can experience healing at all levels of Being, for love is the ultimate antidote for stress.

Dr. Genevieve Haller

Healing is a common occurrance in Dr. Haller's office. It is achieved in an understated manner without the fanfare and "razzle-dazzle" that often accompany the more dramatic hands-on type of healing which often renders people immobile because of the sheer force of energy transference. In Dr. Haller's line of work the force is frequently felt in the releasing of a stiff neck or in the vigorous massage of a poisoned lymph gland. Mechanical cures are coupled with nutritional counseling, vitamin recommendation, and subtle psychological probing of one's psyche so that in the final analysis all aspects of one's personality are eventually brought into harmonious balance.

Dr. Haller has been engaged in chiropractic healing in Virginia Beach for the past 19 years. She served as Director of The Chiropractic Research Division of The Edgar Cayce Foundation and, in that capacity, trained neophyte practitioners around the United States in innovative manipulations and nutritional therapies that are a direct outgrowth of her own experiences.

Anyone desirous of internalizing the core of knowledge of spiritual healing would do well to internalize her ideas.

A Philosophy of Health—Dr. Genevieve M. Haller

When it comes to body mechanics, even Hippocrates, the father of medicine, recognized the importance of the spine and nervous system as they relate to health and disease. The prevention of disease is now recognized in the medical field, although chiropractors have been involved with preventative health care from the inception of Chiropractic because of the nature of their philosophy.

Chiropractic is a branch of the healing arts relating to the normal function of the nervous system, composed of the cerebrospinal and autonomic nervous system, which is housed in the spinal column and the cranium. Normal function of the physical body is dependent on normal structure.

We expect our houses, automobiles, airplanes, etc., to have a balanced structure, yet have not applied the law of gravity very seriously to our own body mechanics. As I measure patients during examination in relation to the plumb line, I frequently have to admit to the patient that if he were an airplane, I'd have to ground him. I wouldn't care to fly in a plane with one wing slightly off balance. Yet many patients think nothing of walking around with one shoulder higher than another, or a hip, or one leg shorter than another . . . to say nothing of one ear slightly lower than the other.

A postural examination starts from the ground up . . . which means examining the feet. A weak arch or cuboid bone can be responsible for symptoms above this . . . such as a knee, hip, or shoulder problem. Even the coccyx bone (tail bone) plays a vital part in the body mechanics. If a patient has fallen backward and landed on this part of the anatomy, the injury may affect the ganglion of impar, which is a part of the nervous system that lies anterior to the coccyx. The jolt then can reflexly affect almost any part of the spinal cord.

The body mechanics of the lower back (lumbars) are also influenced by the neck (cervicals) or vice versa. If a patient has experienced a whiplash accident, the *lower* back needs to be examined too for it may be out of alignment. The old song about the hipbone being connected to the leg bone has a lot of truth, and a force from an injury can easily ricochet from one area to another of the spine.

The chiropractor then has the role of being a body mechanic and helps to realign the spine and cranium in order to remove any physical blocks that could affect the transmission of energy in the nervous system . . . or even in the acupuncture meridians since they tie into the nervous system. The lymph and circulatory systems are also tied in with this approach, and many reflexes on the body can be used to improve these systems (through Kinesiology techniques).

The skull has eight cranial bones which move with the cranial respiratory mechanism involving the cranium and tailbone (sacrum and coccyx). The spinal fluid bathes the brain and nervous system as it moves about 8 to 12 times a minute from the skull down to the base of the sacrum, then returning again to the cranial area. Blows from head injuries, for example, can jam cranial sutures—not allowing the normal skull movement to be properly activated. The cerebrospinal fluid surrounds the brain and spinal cord and is responsible for many functions in the central nervous system. Some of the more common symptomatic signs of this imbalanced flow include headaches, sinus, loss of balance, neck problems, or visual problems. Doctor John Upledger, D.O., has found quite a number of dyslexia patients have an internally rotated temporal bone.

All of the systems of the body need to be in communication with each other. The proper alignment of the spine then, aids the communion of the various nervous, circulatory, and lymph systems. Where there is an abberant condition, there is established then the ability to accept and communicate with this area of the body. We need to love, rather than to reject, this area where there has been trouble. Through spinal manipulations, the chiropractor aids in aligning the coordination of these forces, and also helps align the conscious activity of the mind toward the idea. For example . . . occasionally a patient will admit to me that his or her small daughter said, "You are getting grumpy . . . it's time for you to see your chiropractor." When a patient is willing to have the spine realigned and released, the spiritual forces can work and make straighter the pathway to the light itself. So by "setting straight" . . . or correcting the spinal misalignments, there is definite spiritual healing. The central nervous system corresponds to the conscious mind; the sympathetic nervous system to the unconscious mind; the parasympathetic to the super-conscious mind. Manipulations help the coordination of these forces and the chiropractor is helping to align the conscious activity of the mind with the ideal.

When you correct the position of the spine, you are setting the potential for a greater channeling of the spiritual forces in the body, even if the individual is not aware of it. The skeletal structure upholds the very physical existence of the spiritual forces which are traveling through the vertebrae, including those fused together in the lower region of the spine . . . so you have a total of 33 vertebrae there. These are equivalent to the number of years Jesus lived on the earth. It is the spiritual number and pathway of man's progress to oneness with the source of love and light.

The energy field which surrounds all physical bodies is often referred to as the astral or etheric body, perceived as the "halo" which is the electro-magnetic field. This bubble of energy that surrounds each of us is influenced by our thought patterns . . . positively or negatively. A negative emotion (such as fear, resentment, hate) can upset the magnetic balance in the field resulting in less energy flowing into the physical body.

Thus, our state of good health depends on happy/joyful emotions. At the level of the 3rd cervical, the 9th dorsal and the 4th lumbar, the Kundalini energies enter into the spine. Chiropractors and osteopaths should coordinate these three areas of the spine whenever they give an adjustment; thus, you have preventative health care of the spine with periodic check-ups.

The second area of balance in the philosophy of health relates to bio-chemical and to cleansing. If we could balance our assimilations with our eliminations, we could live as long as we desired. The anabolic (building up) and catabolic (tearing down) metabolism needs to be balanced. It's easy to overload our plates when going through a cafeteria line, for our eyes are sometimes bigger than our stomachs. To balance this over-eating, we need to consider a cleansing period, even if it's only one day a week, of water and light fruits or vegetables and purifying herbal teas.

Although we eat a balanced diet, many of us find symptoms of pain in our body, and we cannot understand why. Frequently, it is not *what* the body takes in that is at fault, but *how* it is digested and absored. When the body is under stress, the digestive system doesn't make sufficient hydrochloric acid, pepsin, pancreatic enzymes, bile, etc. to handle foods properly and as a result, the foods become toxic wastes to our body. We become allergic to these toxins with resulting painful symptoms. One alternative is to take digestive enzymes to offset this problem.

Tests show that by the time a person is 65 years old, only 15 percent of the hydrochloric acid is present in the stomach to help prepare the proteins for digestion, or properly utilize the calcium, magnesium, iron, etc. This may be one of the reasons for osteoporosis appearing later in life . . . even though a person has used calcium foods or supplements. The body has *not* been able to use them. We also need Vitamin D to help absorb the calcium, and this leads us to another lack of balance . . . which we find in our environment.

With depleted soils, impure air, poisons in our water, clouds covering our bright sunlight . . . is it any wonder that man is becoming allergic to his surroundings? Mineral analysis from hair tests are indicating many patients are accumulating *toxic* minerals in their systems such as lead, cadmium, copper, mercury, nickel, and aluminum, which upset their metabolism and hormonal system. Even aluminum is being linked to Alzheimer's disease . . . and what could be more pathetic than to lose one's memory in old age . . . not recognizing loved ones . . . existing trapped in a physical body for several years? And yet, our soft drinks are all in aluminum cans; many cooking pots are aluminum; antacids and underarm deodorants contain aluminum . . . so we have found a long list of ways to contaminate our bodies . . . insideously, over the years. There are some foods and supplements that can help remove aluminum, and probably the chelation therapy removes it quicker than most methods. Then, there is a seven-year cycle that gives us hope . . . for every seven years the body renews itself. If we are serious about our health, then we need to plan to work on a program for that time span.

The most important of the three areas of health (#1 Biomechanics; #2 Bio-chemical) is #3, Emotional and Spiritual health. This is where the *will* to be healthy is necessary so that we can have a *change* in consciousness. All great seekers of truth will tell you in no uncertain terms that healing comes from *within* to without . . . and not from without to within. This means *we* have to take the initiative for health and healing and cannot transport our bodies to the doctor's and say, "heal me." The responsibility lies within each individual.

The first step then to health is accepting that responsibility. We must learn to keep our energy high with meditation and let go of our fear and negative programming. The second step is to exercise and maintain our spinal balance with chiropractic or osteopathic care. Third, investigate our eating habits, balance our assimilations and eliminations. Lastly, we should do what we can to pray and to legislate for a healthier environment in which to live. And let *love* restore *peace* on earth.

Margit Nassi

Margit is a native of Germany but has resided in Virginia Beach for the past three years. She is married to Joseph Nassi, a businessman who is an international distributor of gems. Both husband and wife are deeply dedicated to spiritual ideals. Each has been certified as a healer through the College of Psycho-Therapeutics in White Lodge, England. Margit has also received instruction from Dr. Harold Reilly in therapeutic massage.

Although a novice in this field in comparison with the extensive careers of the other healers, she is nevertheless adroit at obtaining optimum results through the integration of manual manipulation and energy transfer. Chakra healing is a specialty of Margit's and, if one is open enough to perceive auras, continuous pulsations of white light can be observed between healer and healee as the healing progresses. Margit Nassi is one who bears watching.

Massage Therapy—Margit Nassi

''Are there energies, forces and vibrations involved that are normally not taught?'' Almost all books and articles on massage mention that this healing art is probably one of the oldest forms of treatment applied today. Intuitively humans rub, touch, and stroke injured or painful areas of the body. Recent research shows that there is an energy ''flowing'' through the hands and body. The ancient Hindu and Chinese therapists had knowledge of this energy as their literature about the Chakra-system and the Meridians indicates. With

children it is also probably more than just the longing for comforting words and hugs from a loving mother when they run and ask that a paining part of their body be touched and rubbed. Caring mothers stroke the heads and backs of their crying babies.

Massage given with the hands (but in some instances and countries with elbows, and feet) is defined as systematic therapeutical friction, stroking, and kneading of the body. It affects the skin, connective tissues, muscles, ligaments, tendons, blood circulation, blood vessels, lymph, joints, and nervous system and thus brings about the following beneficial results:

> Relieving tension, relief in fatigue and loss of sleep, emotional release, relieving pain, restoring a sense of well-being, stimulating circulation, removal of waste products, improving digestion, and cramping in muscles.

The question to be answered here is: *Is there another force involved which is responsible for some masseurs/therapists being more successful in healing and helping people than others?*

In George Meek's book *The Reality of Healing Energies* the results of tests suggest that the *immediate* rather than usual state of mind is the one that is the most influential. The question raised in this section is whether the healing method of laying-on-of-hands (with a general massage the complete body of a person is touched from top to toe) produces results in a psychological way or by some more objective means.

A Canadian Scientist, Dr. B. Grad, did research with the famous healer Col. Estebany. The experiment was performed with barley seeds. The group of seeds was watered from a bottle that had been held in Estebany's hand for 15 minutes. The seed growth showed remarkable results: more plants and more height. There must have been some unseen force at work. Dr. Grad knew that healers go into a peaceful or often even prayerful, meditative state of mind before attempting to heal. Therefore, in another experiment he investigated whether really disturbed people could even inhibit the healing process. He experimented with a 26-year-old depressive neurotic woman, a 37-year-old man with psychotic depression and a normal person, J. B., who had a "green thumb." J. B. produced greater stimulation to plant growth. An inhibition in plant growth was visible in the group that was given water that had been held in a bottle by the psychotic man when anxious, agitated, and depressed. The depressive-neurotic woman was told of the nature of the experiment, her mood cheered up, and she cradled the bottle like a baby. The result was better than with the untreated controls.

Does this indicate that in the future a massage student, nurse, or other therapist involved in touching people should be trained much more thoroughly in mental disciplines apart from merely a solid technical training? Since there is strong evidence to support this assumption, new standards and devices must then be applied to select students carefully—the motivation to heal and to be of help being of utmost importance.

Personal experience has taught me that therapists handling patients must have a clean touch and understand what purity means both physically and mentally. They must also understand the oneness of body, mind, and spirit. Could it be that some masseurs—who do not have what we call a good character, good physical health, and a balanced mind, actually dirty their patients all over the body through touch?

When I studied chakra-treatment in England in 1975, Ronald Beesley had already used terms like electro-magnetic field and gravity field to describe the body energies. After a treatment from him, the patient looked so different that it was visible to all of us. His eyes sparkled again where before the expression had been dull. The skin seemed to take on a new lustre. People felt much lighter on their feet after the gravity field had been restored. In Mr. Beesley's book about the human aura he mentions that the body itself also produces a lot of electrical impulses and uses these for its communication system. I have seen chakra-treatments successfully performed on people who were very depleted of energy. They had a leakage in one of the chakras which can happen because of shock when the thermal field collapses. The chakras are invisible energy centers and are linked to the glandular system of the physical body. A treatment looks like a laying-on-of-hands on various parts of the body with one hand always on or over a chakra but not touching the physical body.

Massage as taught by Dr. Harold J. Reilly is so thorough that people who are familiar with healing marvel at the composition of movements. Dr. Reilly's knowledge of the human body and how to manipulate is such that no part of the human body remains untouched. His general massage includes all movements that a normal massage consists of: touching, stroking, kneading, friction, rolling, wringing, nerve compression, percussion, and some manipulation. His general massage now called "Cayce-Reilly-massage" is started with the left arm of the patient while the patient lies in a supine position on a massage table. Is there a reason for this? Energy is released on the left side. This part of the body has to be freed from blockages first so that the energy can flow more freely. Some of the foot movements feel like foot-reflexology. After the neck, the face gets a treatment. The sinus area and the pineal area between the eye brow are tapped as a stimulation. The thyroid is vibrated with the fingertips or even slightly beaten with the hand to stimulate the immune system.

The finishing strokes on the back of the patient, while he is in the prone position, are very important. The hands are outspread over the sides of the back with the thumbs on the spine. The stroking is started at the base of the neck down with pressure to the end of the spine at the sacrum. The hands are returned to the neck by trailing the fingers lightly along the sides of the back. The degree of relaxation is achieved by the amount or strength of pressure. The last two movements on the back can be performed so lightly that the hands hardly touch the skin. These movements remind me of the smoothing and soothing of the electro-magnetic field and the restoring of the gravity field of the body by chakra-treatment as taught by Ronald Beesley.

George Meek mentions that all the precise mechanisms by which the attitude and emotions of the healer/therapist help the patient to re-energize the weakened or diseased cells of his body are not yet understood by science but there can be no doubt that love and compassion are the very cornerstones of health, healing, and wholeness. Dr. Reilly also expresses the belief that when the help of experts is required, it is just as important and perhaps more so that there be a great will on the part of the healer to effect the improvement. Results are best when the doctor/healer/therapist treats the patient with his soul, his mind, and his physical energy.

Even if people are skeptical concerning the theory of different energies and fields and forces, it can still be proven that massages when performed by a good therapist can have a relaxing and/or stimulating effect on the central nervous system and physical body. They also release tension and start or speed up the healing process. In the Encyclopedia Americana it is stated that, in addition to the purely physical effects, massage may exert a beneficial effect on the nervous system of the body through a variety of complicated nerve reflexes whose nature is not too well understood at the present time and may also exert a most desirable though temporary psychotherapeutic value. Massage for this purpose has come to be quite widely employed.

Andrew Weil reports in the 'Placebo Response' that some patients are told in so many words that the pills they are taking contain nothing but sugar. Satisfactory placebo responses still occurred. This finding suggests that what a doctor tells a patient may be less important than what the doctor feels and expresses non-verbally. That belief, communicated in some way, may be a crucial determinant of therapeutic outcome. I recall my own personal experience massaging a patient who saw red when angry thoughts momentarily went through my mind. This phenomena took place simultaneously with my touching of her head. In the case of massage I believe that much more is taking place than the placebo response or purely physical effects because of the body to body contacts for about one hour or longer. The transfer of energies and forces seems to be an important factor demonstrating that massage and manipulation can perform miracles if carried out by the right person.

Ted and Virginia Light

The name here is synonymous with the level of spirituality attained by this husband and wife team. Hailing from Great Falls, Virginia, Ted and Virginia Light are co-founders of the Advanced Healing Research Foundation, an organization designed to train, promote, protect, and support healing practitioners and research the noetic sciences and spiritual work in the broadest sense possible. Virginia, Executive Director of the Foundation, has been an intuitive and a healer throughout her entire lifetime. She possesses the ability to review the body physically and determine the sites of diseased organs as well as the origins of the illness. After determining the nature of the dysfunction, she offers healing in the form of holistic measures and laying-on-of-hands. If the client is unable to be physically present, absentee healing is the elected alternative. In these cases healing energies are transmitted from Virginia to her patient without benefit of personal contact.

Ted Light possesses healing skills also, but prefers to act as orchestrator for the various requests and demands their vigorous schedule places upon them. Virginia and Ted are both members of the National Federation of Spiritual Healers. The Advanced Healing Research Foundation sponsors a program of healer certification for individuals who demonstrate talents in this direction.

The Process of Spiritual Healing: Its Essential Components for Success and Failure—Virginia Light

Personality Qualities Exhibited by Advanced Healers There are literally thousands of healers jumping out from behind every bush throughout the world today. There are very few extraordinary healers just as there are very few Beethovens, Shakespeares, and Chagalls. The public needs to realize the wide spectrum of healing levels within the healing community and be able to determine the quality of a healer before seeking assistance. What makes an extraordinary and powerful healer? What qualities do these advanced healers have in common that they do not share with healers of less developed ability and how have they arrived at this high level?

The most overlooked element in the making of a healer is that he has *earned* this ability. It does not strike from the heavens, nor is it a result of some accident. We need to purge the bizarre from the healing act and from the public's concept of healers. This is a natural, painless, quiet, and comforting event which can result in the disappearance of large cancerous tumors, the regrowth of healthy tissue, bone, muscle, and can return the mentally ill to a functioning life, to list only a few.

The first element in healing is a deep caring for other life forms which we refer to as Love and which the healer shares with God and its limitless quality and its understanding. Knowing about life forms comes at an early age and increases steadily if truth is adhered to religiously. This requires first that the healer love self and realize his sacred quality and his unity with God which, in turn, commits the healer to a life wherein he is pure in heart and mind. In turn, the healer will be provided with high sacred sources after he has proven himself. If not, he may find himself healing with his own body energy, psychic sources such as spirit doctors, or by using the energy of emotional audiences as faith healers practice. Desire to be a healer is only a small step. The quantum leaps occur through a profound ability to love since no healer can heal another unless the vibratory levels are brought into harmony. This cannot happen if there is bigotry, disapproval, or egotism. Negative attitudes by a healer toward a healee will entrain the healee's vibratory levels on the same level and no healing can occur where there is negativity.

The recognition of changing vibratory levels in healing as well as in other intuitive or spiritual work has been measured by Dr. Cade of England, who invented a machine called "The Mind Mirror" which measures the four levels (there are more) of Beta (awake), Alpha (meditative), Theta (sleep), and Delta (deep sleep) according to the brain cycles which identify each of these stages. It was found by Dr. Cade that good healers entrain the healee and bring his brain cycles down to a lower level identical to the healer's. Then healing occurs. Unfortunately, the level of Alpha has little significance in healing. Proof now is that Alpha is more a passageway to the more significant levels of Theta and Delta. When the healer is able to achieve these levels and then is able to entrain the healee and bring him down into these levels that he would not be otherwise able to enter, he is then open to healing.

Advanced healers are of a joyous and hopeful character. If a patient is extremely negative, it is a hardship for the healer to move that patient's vibratory levels into healing since all negativity, either on the part of the healer or the healee, will adversely affect the healing event. Worry, fear, anatagonism must be dispelled through private consultation and through stressing the partnership aspects of the healing. The patient must know that he will be healed only to that extent that he accepts. If he accepts 10 percent, he will be healed 10 percent. If he accepts 100 percent, he will be healed 100 percent. Christ did not heal everyone. At times when he healed, he would say, "You have healed yourself" stressing the deep significance of the healing act. Divine Right of Freedom of Choice is not interfered with by anyone, not even God, except in dire circumstances. Therefore, a professional attitude and comfortable surroundings devoid of bizarre gestures, strange music, chants, etc. and an explanation of the safety, quickness, and comfort of the healing act needs to be done.

Those healers who do not learn from their mistakes are most certainly doomed to repeat them. Mistakes must never be repeated because of the sacred quality of the trust placed in the healer by sacred beings. Therefore, it is essential to investigate the reason for the failures in healing. This close self-examination by the healer and of the healee and of all other stresses often leads to wondrous new methods of healing.

So long as we adhere to truth in our investigation and master our ego, the miracles continue. Every excellent healer I know has an insatiable curiosity to learn more about healing. We recommend to all aspiring healers the need to be informed about anatomy, chemistry, nutrition, and diseases because of the increasing need to communicate intelligently with members of the medical profession who are increasingly seeking our assistance. In the very near future healers will need to be well informed in all healing aspects to be viewed with respect by other healing professionals.

The ability to heal is not restricted to any ethnic group, race, or religion for in God's eyes we are all equal. Whether a healer has a Ph.D. or is a shaman in a primitive tribe in Africa, the same rules of love, truth, and joy apply, although the Ph.D. has a far better chance to rise to excellence because of his disciplined intellect.

Many healers express an experience they refer to as the Resurrection. Often, this occurs in middle-age and is accompanied by inspired dreams; the ambivalence of a deep sense of contentment and an urge to rapidly move forward in some as yet unknown directon; psychic experiences and a pursuit of an investigation of our spiritual heritage. Renunciation of long-cherished values and beliefs may be rapid. A new sense of ownership results with material aspects viewed as temporary only. Knowledge and an understanding of invisible universes begins. As healers progress, they are called upon to be invisible helpers where time and space are not existent in the accepted sense on earth. The healer will be limited in his work only as far as he limits himself. If he feels he should specialize in headaches, he will have stopped his growth and will continue his life on this level. If he leaves his horizons unlimited, he will have experiences he would never had thought possible.

All the foregoing could be interpreted to mean that healers are "goody Two Shoes." Far from it. Healers have employed expletives (Christ swore at the fig tree), lost their tempers (Christ turned over the merchant's tables in the temple), smoked cigarettes (Harry Edwards—the great English healer—was a chain smoker), and enjoyed wine or scotch. The renunciation is of a different form on the basis of the material aspects of life, maintaining and reinforcing their love of life forms, joyousness, pursuit of truth, and overcoming burdens and problems with honor and nobility. These great healers are realistic, stable, and perceptive individuals without eccentricities. Their wholesome attitude tends to add greatly to every healing event. They seek out other healers and other sources and are on a constant spiritual quest which often leads them into other creative forms of expression. We have found that many healers are also sculptors, musicians, dancers, etc. of considerable talent. The courage that comes from the act of healing another seems to trigger these abilities with many healers stating that gifted masters are working through them.

What is most exciting is the many people with healing ability that can be spotted in a crowd who have no idea at the present time of what rich resources are within them. However, no one can do it for them. They must earn it themselves through the foregoing procedure and the described necessary qualities for effective healing.

The Technique of Healing

Request for Permission to Heal Can Be Received From:

1. God, Christ, Holy Ghost.
2. The High Self of the person—comatose, babies (hand on stomach), Divine Right.
3. The person himself.
   You will be stopped if the healing is not allowed.

The Healing Act

1. Visualize the person or self as being whole and healthy without infirmity or disease and manifest it.
2. Prayer should not be negative . . . Do not ask to be delivered from disease, do not ask to be healed, but ask to be made whole and healthy and to express harmony and realize abundance.
3. Recognize disease as false thought. When all energy is erased from the disease, it will disappear. Diseased people concentrate all energies on their disease. When a healer appears, the energy begins to be transmuted.
4. Realize your body is a generator—that you can project a magnified ray of energy that can transmute harmful energies, that can protect you from harm and that can be endowed with God energies.
5. *Need*—Healers should be discriminating in accepting certain requirements from others and not involve themselves in cosmetic

improvement . . . We cannot accept *want* in place of *need.* This can be harmful to both the healer and the healees.

6. *In self healing:* Be silent. Achieve an altered state, then transmute the energies of the disease into healing energies by sending the generated white light. *Do not concentrate.* Recognize the body as being a manifestation of the spirit. If your spirit then can manifest the magnificence of the body, it has enormous power and can manifest harmony and health.

Reasons For Healing Failures:

1. There was an incorrect interpretation of the healing act by the healer. At times when a healing may appear to be very effective, the person moves through the death transition and the healer is bewildered. The healing was for the transition and results in a joyous, serene experience filled with wonderment. The healing was not to remain on this level.
2. Negativity exists on the part of either the healee or healer. Healers have positive vibratory levels. They have been forged by the fire of adversity and they have *understood the positive dynamics of the adversity.* They are unable to merge their vibratory levels with negative people.
3. The healee has not assumed responsibility for this disease and/or healing.
4. The healer healed at wrong times for that particular person. There is a window in time perhaps determined by biorhythms, or other influences.
5. The healee returns to negative influences of environment, family, and negative attitudes.
6. The healer has personal problems resulting in unstable energies.
7. The healer has not investigated past failures—thus has not learned.
8. The healer has biases against the healee.
9. The healer has burned out.

Each person is a melody—a special vibratory unification with truth—each song is unique, resonating at its own color, strength, and lyricism. This is spirituality in essence.

Catherine Ponder

PRAYERS, WHEN SPOKEN IN LOVE, ARE THE MOST POWERFUL TOOLS AVAILABLE. This short maxim was communicated to me one morning as the incisive arrows of dawn began to pierce night's veil of obscurity. As time passed and the wisdom of the maxim was put to the test, I came to value its intrinsic Truth more and more. I now believe this to be one of the Absolutes of Universal Law.

Synchronistically during this time period I was priviledged to acquire copies of Catherine Ponder's books entitled *The Dynamic Laws of Healing* and *The Prospering Power of Love.* Within their pages I discovered evidential proof in support of my hypothesis which took the form of cosmic healing laws based on the dynamic principles of love and prayer power. Not only were these laws presented for viable application but innumerable case studies accompanied their invocation as testimony to their unparalleled success in the alleviation of human suffering.

Catherine Ponder is a minister for the nondenominational Unity Faith Movement and has been associated with the Unity Churches since 1956. She is the author of fifteen books on the subjects of prosperity, positive thinking, love, and healing and is listed in *Who's Who in the World* and *The American Society of Distinguished Citizens.* She is head of Unity Worldwide with global headquarters in Palm Desert, California. Because of the elevated level of respect and esteem in which I hold Catherine Ponder's literary works, I deemed it an honor of the highest caliber when she kindly granted me permission to include her commentaries on the healing power of prayer in my chapter on Spiritual Healing. If writing can be included among the healing arts, then Catherine Ponder is truly one of the most gifted healers of our time.

The Dynamic Law of Healing through Prayer—
Catherine Ponder

"Most people have not yet learned the healing secret of the ages—that health is basically an inside job, mentally as well as physically. No matter how successful a treatment is in time of illness, a person often becomes sick again and again, because he has not gotten at the *cause* of his illness—ill thoughts and feelings about himself, others, his Creator, and the world in which he lives. These ill thoughts constrict the life force within him, causing disease, or lack of ease."[9]

Psychosomatic illnesses reflect the mental and emotional attitudes which caused the condition in the first place. For example, skin disorders indicate a "need for approval," headaches are symptomatic of insecurity while heart disorders personify "an unfulfilled need for love."

At times ill health appears to manifest in direct proportion to criticism of one's fellowman. "*Whatever of evil you see in others, you are inviting into your own life in some form of negation.* When you 'run down' someone else with your criticism and condemnation, you are opening the way for your own mind, body or affairs to become 'run down' with ill health, unhappiness, confusion, or financial lack."[10]

Since negative thoughts possess the power to destroy, conversely positive thinking generates the power to heal. Charles Fillmore in his book, *Atom Smashing Power of Mind,* elaborates on revitalizing one's body in this manner: "States of mind established in consciousness gather to themselves vitamins, cells, nerves, muscles and flesh itself. . . . In the mind, man can generate every medicine that is necessary for the upbuilding and restoring of the body. . . . You can literally rebuild your body cell by cell by rebuilding your thinking. By renewal of your mind, your body can be transformed, since your body is the visible record of your thoughts. *As a man thinks in his mind, so is he in his body.*"[11]

Prayer is among the strongest healing tools available both for the self and for others. It can be effectively utilized in several ways. To heal oneself "the expression of praise as thanksgiving, gratitude and joy is among the most powerful forms of affirmation.

"If you wait to be healed before you express thanksgiving, you may wait indefinitely! *One of the greatest secrets of healing is to praise and give thanks for it, right in the face of illness, before there is anything to give thanks for!*

"The reason praise is so powerful for healing is this: What you praise you increase. Praise liberates and releases the life force that is pent up in the atoms of your body.

"Words that express gratitude, praise, and thanksgiving release certain potent energies of mind and body that are not otherwise tapped. Praise also liberates the finer essences of the soul that are necessary for a complete healing."[12]

A second type of prayer that promotes physical and emotional healings for the self is an affirmation of Divine Love. "Disease often results from a violation of the law of love. Thoughts of hate generate a deadly poison in the body, which if not neutralized, can even produce death. Love cleanses the mind and body of these hates that accumulate in the form of resentment, criticism, sorrow, remorse, guilt, fear, anger, jealousy. Affirmations of love change these killing thoughts into life thoughts. Affirmations of love bring peace to the mind and body.

"Love has been described as the 'physician of the universe' because it has the power to heal all ills, when invoked silently or by spoken affirmation."[13]

"Love is the key to healing. . . . Love relaxes and harmonizes man's emotions. Love attunes the individual to the healing power within himself."[14]

Right now, today, you can begin to invoke affirmations of Divine Love to achieve personal healing. "Make it a practice to meditate daily on the thought: 'Divine love, manifest thyself in me.' There should be periods of mental concentration on the love center in the cardiac plexus near the heart. Think about love with the attention drawn with the breast, and a quickening will follow. All the ideas that go to make up love will be set in motion."[15]

Will the power of prayer in an affirmation of Divine Love work for healing others as well? **Absolutely!**

The Prospering Power of Love contains a story about a wife who was distraught about her husband's illness for many months.

"The more she tried to help him recover, the more he seemed to cling to his illness and the more confined they both were. One day she learned of the healing power of release and began to declare for her husband, 'I release you now to your highest good. I love you but I release you to complete freedom and complete health in whatever way is best. I am free and you are free.' "

When this woman had previously tried to help her husband by using various healing affirmations, he had seemed subconsciously to resist her attempts to will him to health. After she began to release him to find health in his own way, ceasing any mental effort in his direction, and began to lead a more normal life herself, her husband's health rapidly improved. Some of his former ailments disappeared completely. He experienced the healing power of love as it worked through release.[16]

"You have all the love you need for healing, prosperity and happy human relationships right *within* yourself. Divine love is one of your mental and spiritual faculties. *You do not have to search outside yourself for love. You can begin releasing it from within outward through your thoughts, words, actions and affirmative prayers.* As you do, you will experience the success power of love in all it's fullness as it works through people, situations and conditions that concern you."[17]

Last, acknowledge and experience joy in your life. "Exaltation is like a magnet for all good things in the universe to hasten to you."[18]

Charles Fillmore wrote in *Jesus Christ Heals,* "All healing systems recognize joy as a beneficent factor in the restoration of health to the sick. . . . That there is an intimate relation between happiness and health goes without question."[19]

Then, express the miracle of healing in your life through *joy,* for, "Fun, laughter and joy are among the world's cheapest and best medicines. Give yourself large doses of these often. They will not only save you expensive medical bills, they will make your body healthier and your life happier."[20]

THE IMPORTANCE OF INTUITIVE DIAGNOSIS AND INTUITIVE COUNSELING IN SPIRITUAL HEALING

The studious pursuit of researching and evaluating healers and their various approaches with regard to the transference of healing energies has occupied my time for the greater portion of the last five years. During this half decade I have been privileged to make the acquaintance of and become personal friends with many of the healers whose ideologies comprise the basis of this Spiritual Healing chapter. I have witnessed instantaneous physical healings, observed mental illness of long-standing simply vanish with the introduction of holistic psychotherapy, self-hypnosis, and visual imagery, and have personally worked with clients who suffered such severe handicaps that it seemed that the miracle of healing lay forever beyond their grasp. Eventually, through patience, self-understanding and faithful application of the prescribed medical, chiropractic, and counseling therapies, many on the physical merry-go-round caught the "brass ring." Some never did.

What have I myself learned from all of this theorization and intensive research? After considerable sifting of factual information from fantasy, after the accrument and open-minded ingestion of an incalculable number of books on the subjects of counseling and healing, and *most important,* after sixteen years of personal and professional experience within these fields, I have arrived at the point of origination of my own formulized theory of spiritual healing. This is what I would like to share with you.

It is my firm conviction that intuitive diagnosis and intuitive counseling should become an integral core-tool in the futuristic counseling process. The major points in connection with this intuitive counseling-healing philosophy (the words counseling and healing can be seen as interchangable) number three. They are:

1. Physical symbology is a reflective measure of a mental and/or emotional imbalance. Therefore, the use of intuitive diagnosis as a technique for identification of the causal factors

could most probably reduce by half the long arduous hours of conversation required for problem analysis. Intuitive diagnosis is the procedure explained in the *Advanced Techniques for the Enhancement of Intuitive and Healing Abilities* and is the basis of the *Holistic Life Reading.*

2. The treatment program should be a cooperative effort between allied health professionals for the benefit of the client. Each modality of treatment has its advantages and disadvantages inherent within its discipline.

3. The assuming of self-responsibility for personal healing is the key to radiant physical, mental, and spiritual well-being. Intuitive counseling can serve as a reference for sources of self-choices for self-healing.

Intuitive Diagnosis and Problem Identification

In focusing on point one, it is a fallacy to believe one can avoid stress completely. Our bodies are designed to respond physically whenever we are exposed to stresses regardless of their origin or strength of intensity. Our adrenal glands react by producing an abundance of adrenline which heightens the blood-clotting response. The pancreas pours glucose into the bloodstream to provide our bodies with additional fuel in the face of an impending crisis. Free fatty acids tend to raise the blood fat levels higher and higher. In primitive times these changes were vital if an adversary stood before us his club in hand ready to bludgeon us to death. Present day life modes dictate less stringent needs for such exaggerated physical reactions. Moreover, our sedentary life style inhibits the burning off of excess energies expended as a result of physical responses to stress. Continued stress over prolonged periods is a causatory factor in blood thickening (strokes, heart attacks), excessive glucose (diabetes), and plaque buildup in the arteries (arteriosclerosis). The duration and acuteness of the disease as well as the moment of onset are reciprocally related to the current condition of the body, the age of the individual, the prospect of stress relief, and the willingness of the patient to accept responsibility for his role in the attunement of his mind-body connection to self-healing. Measures such as physical exercise, a healthy diet, vitamin supplementation, and adequate rest are of inestimable value in the prevention of illness. Emrika Padus states in *The Complete Guide to Your Emotions and Your Health* that thoughts and emotions are the nutrition of the mind. According to this statement, there is little room for doubt that the mainstay for the acquisition and maintenance of radiant health is optimal mastery of individual attitudes and emotional reactions.

Disease usually strikes the body's weakest organ—*However, the weakest organ usually symbolizes the emotional or mental seat of the conflict.* This is where intuitive diagnosis enters in. If through The Holistic Life Reading process which encompasses Physical Symbology, Current Issues, Future Trends, Character Analysis, Past Lives, and Soul's Purpose the origin of one's infirmity can be addressed, then alternative self-choices begin to crystalize that can affect self-healing. What attitudinal posture in your career is "eating away at you" through ulcers? Why do you feel suffocated by an asthma attack when being jostled by a crowd? (Were you trampled under foot in a past life?) Does chronic loss of voice through laryngitis depict the current issue of marital subordination? Is the character trait of repressed anger continually turned inward on self reflected in the fist-like clenches of gnarled arthritis? Pin-pointing the core of the conflict, acknowledging the chief characters in the strife, and receiving medical, chiropractic, or natural prescription for the alleviation of the physical symptoms are the first creeping steps toward wholeness. It is with the resolution of these conflict questions that the unique talents of physicians, psychologists, counselors, and chiropractors can provide invaluable insights.

Cooperative Healing Treatments

This brings us to the second point. Healing isn't just the adherence to one particular creed or mode of treatment for no one method is a panacea to all. Healing is, of course, a matter of personal choice but it is also most effective when two or three processes are combined. Cooperating minds and accrued knowledge brought to bear intensify the healing energies to a far greater degree than would the sole utilization of one healing resource. It has always been my policy throughout my counseling career to seek the best possible professionals for referral. If the client was hearing-impaired, I had the name of the most respected audiologist. If sinus problems were evident, help was just a phone call away to a neighboring allergist. If a good physical examination was required, I could refer with confidence to local medical specialists. In short, seeking optimum treatment for your client is the first prerequisite to becoming an effective health professional. In order to identify a competent healing colleague one needs to appraise him or herself of the advantages and disadvantages connected to the different forms of the healing arts. Let's examine these one by one.

Medical Treatment An appointment with a medical doctor usually assures one of a proper diagnosis. The advantage of the correct medical diagnosis is the formulation of an appropriate medical program including a remedial drug prescription. These, in turn, speed the healing process. If the primary physician does not possess sufficient expertise to treat the condition adequately, the patient can then be referred to a specialist for further tests and evaluation. Psychiatrists are specialists in mind-body connection and therefore can be an excellent resource for identification of the mental-emotional source of the disease.

On the negative side you may encounter a physician who attributes your problem to nerves and subsequently writes a prescription for tranquilizers. These have their place in medicine, but pill-popping will never uncover the root of the illness. An additional source of concern is frequent adverse side-effects of prescribed drugs. A third disadvantge is unnecessary surgery. A second opinion should always be sought before this step is taken.

Counseling Counseling is one of the most effective healing modalities for fine attunement of the mind-body connection. The counseling process itself provides the client with a mirror for self-reflection and self-examination in an atmosphere of non-judgmental acceptance. Within the security of this intimate relationship, negative personality characteristics can be identified and changed, the dynamics of social conflicts can be understood, and alternative plans can be formulated for future goal-achievements. As with the medical field, counseling has its own specialties. Among these are family counselors, substance abuse counselors, rehabilitation counselors, educational counselors, and occupational counselors. Therefore, individual problems can be matched to professional expertise with optimum success for resolution anticipated. The prime advantage of counseling as a healing art is that at a subconscious level the client possesses knowledge of the root of his problem as well as its resolution. If he accepts this challenge, personal life mastery is then almost assured in all aspects of his total life pattern.

On the negative side counselors are not doctors and should never pretend to be. There is always the possibility of a physical problem masking as a mental disorder. Referral for a thorough physical examination should always be uppermost in a counselor's mind to confirm or deny the presence of a physical illness as a contributing factor. Beware also of *long term* therapy. Therapy sessions that extend over several years defeat the aim of counseling which is self-confidence, independence, and a healthy decisiveness in personal choice-making.

Chiropractic Treatment The main advantage of seeking chiropractic healing is the aligning of bodily energies. When this is achieved, physical healing is almost total. As compliments of chiropractic intervention, nutritional regimens and vitamin supplementations can provide long-term protection against any physical reoccurrence or deterioration. Chiropractors are especially knowledgable in cases of muscle spasms and vertabrae misalignments which cause back pain.

Disadvantages with regard to chiropractic treatment are the lack of a diagnosis of or the misdiagnosis of obscure but serious medical problems. If a client is simultaneously under both medical and chiropractic care and does not inform the physicians about one another, prescribed regimens may be in opposition to one another with adverse reactions resulting.

Massage One of the main advantages in connection with massage is the draining of the lymphatic system. For those under extreme tension and stress, massage is unequalled for deep relaxation and muscle release. Through the hand contact of massage, healing energies are passed from masseuse to patient.

Undesirable side effects of massage are the presence of unevolved therapists who unknowingly may transmit their unresolved angers to the bodies of the patients on whom they are working. Massage may also prove undesirable if one suffers from high blood pressure or infection as too much pressure on the circulatory system can be deleterious. Questions in connection with this should be asked before massage is instituted.

Contact or Absent Healing The prime advantage of contact or absentee healing is the possibility of instantaneous cure. With absentee healing, lack of face-to-face contact is an added bonus as far as traveling over distances is concerned. Healers are usually gifted with highly intuitive natures. This gives them easy access to their patient's subconscious. Through their own sensitivity they can hone in on the very core of the disharmony. These practitioners are usually loving in nature. This quality makes them superior counselors.

One should always make an appointment with a medical doctor before working with a healer to ascertain the exact nature of one's affliction. Professional healers will recommend a medical evaluation during the initial interview. Egotistical contact healers or absentee healers often want to take full credit for the cure. Working in isolation courts the worst possible type of disaster.

Prayer The advantages of resorting to prayer as part of the healing process is that one can tap into the Highest Source of Power available. This Source is the Possessor of All Knowledge. Thus, it provides whatever is ameliorative and essential for the individual to be healed. One can specifically petition for the desired type of healing and the response may be tailormade.

There are, however, a few negative aspects connected to prayer treatment. One is *non-action*—leaving everything up to God. This is not only non-productive, it is non-progressive. The other negative mind-set is since God heals *completely,* it is not necessary to seek medical advice. The answer to that is spiritual physicians have access to the God-Source also. If an appointment is made with this type of physician, perhaps a "three-way conference call" can be arranged to obtain optimum spiritually oriented medical information for healing.

We all possess the healing energies within ourselves. If our soul energies enter into conjuncture with the combined health resources made available through a total cooperative effort of other healing therapies, just imagine the 'miracle cures' that could be achieved.

Intuitive Counseling and Self-Responsibility

There is a definite place for intuitive counseling in the healing arts. Through the medium of intuition the focal point of the client's dilemma becomes crystal clear. If, within the security of the counseling relationship, the dynamics of the conflict can be presented for discussion, the client is then afforded a chance to squarely confront the issues. Over the years Personal Development Services, Inc. has employed counseling techniques such as dream interpretation, age and past life regression, meditation, development of intuitive skills, Holistic Life Reading information, and therapeutic group dynamics as adjunct healing tools. These have proved extraordinarily successful in the accomplishment of personal self-healing and goal-realization.

Intuitive counseling offers clients unfaltering support as well as a variety of self-choices. Albeit, in the final analysis it is the client himself who must bear the responsibility of self-renewal. Self-assertion is a prerequisite for loosening the bonds of marital subordination. Positive visual imagery in combination with a goal-oriented, physician-approved plan of action can be the mental medicine for the shrinking of a cancerous tumor. *Whatever the physical manifestations of the mental disharmony, the healing cloak of soul-responsibility is the deciding factor.*

A summarization of my personal healing ideology lies within these thought-provoking lines:

The attitude one adopts toward his illness is the crucial factor in it's termination or continuance. Medical treatment, chiropractic intervention, laying-on-of-hands, absentee healing, and even the efficacy of the medicinal action are all indeterminate unless the patient is willing to review the instigators of his particular disease. These are unique unto himself for the choice of the debilitating condition is representative of the internalization of the soul's core personality conflicts. The lack of resolution between self-esteem and self-depreciation is stated in the physical symbology of deteriorated or atrophied muscles. The unabated pulsation of a migraine headache is a reflection of the sufferer's willing acceptance of a potentially destructive force of subatomic negative build-up which, if left unchecked, can lead to the ultimate extinction of substantial life energies.

So, colleagues, in attempting to work with individual clients within the framework of this healing philosophy, realize that the most potent medical prescription, the most complicated physical regimen, the most advanced techniques of psychotherapy and electrical medicine are rendered powerless in the face of self-elected deterioration. There is no form of healing that possesses the potential to save such an individual from self-annihilation if the soul continues in a course of a self-willed disintegration of the Mind-Body Connection.

Then choose life, my soul companions! The choice is yours! For the course of true healing lies within the grasp of those who possess the inner strength to confront the deal effectively with their debilitating soul conflicts at the most basic personal level. To them is awarded the Crown of Life, *a vibrant physical, mental, and spiritual being.* In the over-soul view of life, this, above all, is the greatest gift. This, in essence, is the sole lesson to be taught through the healing process and it is pregnant with blessings. What is spiritual healing? All forms of healing are spiritual when performed as an act of love.

CHAPTER 11

Intuitive Counseling

The prayers and requests of life are most likely to be answered if there is an inner, emotional enthusiasm powering the prayer.

Alan Vaughan—*Incredible Coincidence*

Counseling is one of the most heartrendering professions that one can elect to pursue. It can also be (and often is) one of the most rewarding. It is the life-career to which I committed myself more than twenty years ago, when I enrolled in the Guidance and Counseling program offered by the College of William and Mary. Counseling learning-disabled children and adults has ultimately afforded me the rare opportunity of assembling the fragmented pieces of my client's lives, thus transforming them from academically devastated and emotionally-drained shells into educationally functioning and mentally balanced individuals. The counseling process which I utilize is not a panacea for all educational and behavioral ills, but it does seem to provide sufficient insights and self-awareness for our clients so that at some point, through remediation and self-motivation, they arrive at a position where scholastic achievement, intellectual potential, and emotional mood variations are more in balance.

Although the counseling process employs standardized tests assessing cognitive, academic, emotional, and perceptual development, and a considerable amount of background information is gathered from the client's relatives, physicians, and if they are children, their teachers, by far the most important component of the entire treatment is the face-to-face encounters between counselor and parents and between counselor and client. It is through *both verbal and non-verbal interactions and communications* that the intuitive practitioner is able to bypass the superficial facade that is evident at the lower levels of physical and intellectual involvement, and successfully begin to unravel the riddle that lies at the heart of the client's troubled psyche. In recent years I have come to regard these encounters as *mind-to-mind,* rather then *face-to-face* communications.

It is my considered opinion that 95 percent of counselors, psychologists, and psychiatrists chose their professions because of an avowed intention to be of service to mankind. If this *intent toward service* is the primal force that motivates their professional lives, they then become mental healers. Going one step further, however, many of our legion possess keenly honed intuitive minds and can, with special instruction and training, refine our healing skills to an even greater degree. If those that are so endowed begin to attune themselves through continuous study and practice, they will eventually evolve into such accurate and receptive practitioners, with regard to their client's needs, that the process of counseling takes on a new dimension and we enter the domain of *intuitive counseling.* That is what this chapter is all about.

The objective of intuitive counseling is the restoration of the client to the highest state of physical, mental, and spiritual health possible. This is accomplished through mind-to-mind communication and non-verbal assessments, as well as by traditional methods.

Over the past fifteen years I have developed a variety of counseling methods that are not found in traditional textbooks. These were acquired through personal experiences, "synchronistic events," or long arduous study. Continuous experimentation with novel techniques helped to confirm or deny their validity. While many were discarded as fruitless and unproductive, a good number have met the requirements for validation, and were subsequently added to my repertory of successful counseling techniques. I do not utilize them all continually, but rather select one or two tools that are tailor-made for the particular client with whom I am working.

When applied in this manner, the client involved displays more rapid improvement than otherwise would have been accomplished through the use of more traditional methods of treatment. I would like to share these alternative modes of "healing" with all fellow counselors, psychologists, and physicians who are destined to read this book. (Keep in mind that each of us is a potential counselor to someone else where strong bonds of friendship exist.) I present them with the hope that they will provide succor and balm to suffering souls that the Creator has entrusted to your care.

Intuitive counseling techniques or ways of gathering information or insight can be categorized under four basic headings:

1. Physical
2. Mental
3. Psychical
4. Spiritual Healing

Note that there are various subtopics under each classification. While the informational materials may run crosscurrent rather than concurrent at times, broad applicability of these counseling techniques and/or these means of gaining insight combined with assiduous attention toward individualizing treatment according to need will frequently effect "miracles" in the shortest possible period. Moreover, techniques used in combination tend to exert a more powerful healing force than those singularly applied. Study all subtopics scrupulously in order to familiarize yourself with the general concepts promoted, then broaden your scope of knowledge through indepth and intensive exploration of those subjects you find most intriguing, or with which you are truly adept.

PHYSICAL TECHNIQUES

Diet

More and more of our population has come to discover, through the acquisition of bodily ills, that dietary habits exert a tremendous influence on our physical and mental states of being. The salvation: A drastic change in diet.

In my practice I have observed literally thousands of children and adults with stuffy noses, frequent ear infections, tubes in their ears at an early age, short attention spans, concentration problems, digestive disorders, and a multiplicity of other physical and mental aberrations too numerous to mention. These anomalies cut across all boundaries playing havoc with crucial relationships involving classmates, teachers, friends, and relatives. The family unit suffers the most. Continuing indulgence in an improper diet eventually culminates in major illness of one sort or another at critical periods in an individual's life when stresses become too great to withstand. *The answer*—Nutritional counseling and a dramatic improvement in the daily menu. Here again, resolutely followed, this approach has proved lifesaving.

Since many of my readers are not plagued with the serious disabilities that physically drain my clients, nor do they have the inclination to visit a competent nutritionist, let me cite some general rules to be adhered to for the establishment and maintenance of vibrant bodily health.

1. Avoid red meats, ham, and pork. Use fowl, fish, or lamb.

2. Eat at least three vegetables per day. Raw vegetables are preferable, but steaming or stir frying is permissible. Special attention should be paid to the ingestion of raw green vegetables such as spinach, broccoli, cabbage, collards, and kale, as they are a treasury of nutrients in themselves.

3. Eggs are a good source of protein, but should be consumed infrequently. Seeds and nuts, especially almonds and peanuts, are almost exclusively protein. White cheeses are also advised.

4. Foods high in fiber promote healthier eliminations. Suggestions include bran, wheat germ, dried figs, dried dates, and artichokes.

5. "Fruits should be eaten raw, but because of the carbohydrate content they should be eaten with some protein to aid digestion. For instance, an apple with cheese, raisins with peanuts, dates with almonds."[1]

6. Milk should not be drunk on a daily basis, as this stresses the body. (Milk allergies are among the most common observed in learning-disabled children.) When consuming milk, select the low fat 2 percent type.

7. Avoid all sugars, white flour, commercially baked foods, and "junk" foods. Never allow children (or adults for that matter) to ingest large amounts of chocolate, tea, coffee, or soft drinks containing caffeine. Caffeine often raises the level of "nervous excitability" to intolerable heights.

Following these simple guidelines, energy levels should increase substantially within three weeks time.

Vitamins

The first question to ask is, "What are they?" "Quite simply, vitamins are organic substances necessary for life. Vitamins are essential to the normal functioning of our bodies, and save for a few exceptions, cannot be manufactured or synthesized by our bodies. They are necessary for our growth, vitality, and general well-being. In their natural state they are found in minute quantities in all organic food. We must obtain them from these foods or in dietary supplements."[2]

The second question to ask is, "Why are they important?" "Vitamins regulate our metabolism through enzyme systems. A simple deficiency can endanger the whole body."[3]

I was first introduced to vitamins through chronic personal illness. When standard medical practices seemed powerless to forestall continuing growth of breast cysts, I turned to vitamin therapy along with other natural remedies in desperation. A regimen of carefully selected vitamins and minerals consumed daily not only achieved a reduction in cystic growths but other bodily ailments that had plagued me for years disappeared as if by magic.

I realized that if these procedures worked for me, I could apply them to selected clients who display a number of the illnesses described in the previous diet section. *I did just that* by referring them to the proper professionals. Many clients became well.

The third question one should now pose is, "What are the most common types of vitamins, and how do they function?" Listed below is a short guide to familiarize the reader with basic vitamin and mineral information.

VITAMINS

Vitamin A Vitamin A is essential for the promotion of healthy skin and membrane functioning, strong bones, hair, teeth and gums, and good vision. It aids in healing respiratory, eye, ear, and genital infections. It assists in the treatment of acne, boils, open ulcers, and hyperthyroidism. Natural sources are carrots, sweet potatoes, squash, peaches, liver, eggs, milk and dairy products, and yellow fruits.

Vitamin B_1 or Thiamine Vitamin B_1 energizes the depressed, calms the hyperactive, and keeps the nervous system, muscles, and heart functioning efficiently. B_1 is found in pork, oatmeal, peanuts, and avocados.

B_2 or Riboflavin B_2 helps heal sore mouths, lips, and tongues, eliminates eye fatigue and, with other substances, assists in the metabolization of carbohydrates, fats, and proteins. Optimum sources are cheese, eggs, and oysters.

B_3 or Niacinamide This substance appears to reduce the degree of depression associated with hypoglycemia. It can improve concentration. B_3 is found in mushrooms, legumes, fish, fowl, and pork.

B_6 or Pyridoxine B_6 is used in the treatment of adrenal gland exhaustion. It also eliminates nausea due to pregnancy or sea-

sickness. Reduction of muscle spasms, leg cramps, and stiffness in hands, fingers, and feet is noted with increased intake of B_6. It can improve dream recall and memory in general. Look for B_6 in Brewer's yeast, liver, cantalope, molasses, wheat germ, and wheat bran.

Pantothenic Acid This is a cortisone precursor which will improve allergy problems if taken in combination with other B's, A, and C. It fights infection by building antibodies. Duodenal ulcers and the majority of intestinal disorders respond well to pantothenic acid. Sources are legumes, mushrooms, eggs, broccoli, cauliflower, and beef.

Folic Acid Folic acid builds blood. A deficiency results in fatigue, insomnia, and constipation. It wards off anemia. Prime sources are apricots, pumpkins, avocados, dates, and tuna fish.

B_{12} (Cobalamin) This is essential for healthy blood cell formation and a finely-tuned nervous system. It controls allergies, fatigue, appetite loss, shingles, insomnia, and stress. Liver, beef, eggs, milk, cheese, and kidney meats all contain B_{12}.

Biotin Biotin is used in the treatment of dry skin, eczema, and baldness. Sources are egg yolks, brewer's yeast, nuts, fruits, and unpolished rice.

Inositol Falling hair needs inositol. It also aids in lowering cholesterol levels and redistributing body fat. Brewer's yeast, citrus fruits, raisins, peanuts, and cabbage have inositol present.

Para-amino benzoic acid (PABA) PABA as a lotion is an effective sunscreen. It will also restore color to greying hair. PABA is found in organ meats, brewer's yeast, and wheat germ.

Choline This has been found to improve memory deficits. It eliminates poisons and drugs from the liver and generally produces a calming effect. To ingest choline eat green leafy vegetables, liver, and egg yolks.

Vitamin C—(Ascorbic Acid) Vitamin C is one of the most diversified vitamins. It heals wounds, burns, and bleeding gums. It prevents viral and bacterial infections, is a natural laxative, prevents and/or treats the common cold, and lengthens life by holding protein cells together. Vitamin C is found in abundance in citrus fruits, berries, green leafy vegetables, tomatoes, cauliflower, and sweet potatoes.

Vitamin D Properties connected with this vitamin are assisting in the assimilation of Vitamin A, proper utilization of calcium and phosphorous for strong bones and teeth, and prevention of colds with A and C. Natural sunlight is the best source of Vitamin D, but fish liver oils also are a primary source.

Vitamin E or Tocopherol Vitamin E is an antioxidant, a blood thinner, and a diuretic which lowers blood pressure. It accelerates healings of burns and eliminates muscle cramps and restless legs. Vegetable oils, broccoli, wheat germ, brussel sprouts, whole grain cereals, and eggs contain Vitamin E.

Vitamin K Internal bleeding and hemorrhages are prevented, and proper blood clotting is achieved by the use of Vitamin K. The best foods are yogurt, alfalfa, safflower oil, kelp, soybean oil, and egg yolk.

MINERALS

Calcium Sufficient calcium is necessary for strong bones and teeth, regulation of heart rhythm, sound sleep, iron metabolization, and proper nerve impulse transmission. Calcium is found in milk and milk products, all cheeses, sardines, sunflower seeds, dried beans, peanuts, and walnuts.

Magnesium Magnesium is also required for strong bones and teeth but is essential for normal nerve tissue reactivity. To ingest magnesium eat lemons, grapefruits, yellow corn, almonds, seafood, apricots, apples, and dates.

Phosphorus Phosphorus is present in almost all physiological chemical reactions. Vitamin D and calcium must be present for proper phosphorus functioning. Wheat germ, seeds, nuts, and meat possess abundant phosphorus.

Iron Iron is a primary ingredient in the production of red blood cells. Liver, prunes, raisins, parsley, almonds, and leafy vegetables all supply iron.

Zinc A zinc deficiency is indicated by eczema, dwarfism, slow healing wounds, white spots on the nails, and acne. It is important in the growth of all reproductive organs. Oysters contain the highest amount of zinc.

Manganese Memory improves with ingestion and nervous irritability is minimized. Some epileptics have been found deficient in manganese. Sources are wheat germ, seeds, legumes, and nuts.

Copper With copper the body converts iron to hemoglobin. It is essential for adequate Vitamin C utilization. Seafood, liver, and legumes provide this mineral.

Chromium Coupled with insulin it works to metabolize the body's sugar. Rye, wheat germ, brewer's yeast, and green peppers supply good chromium levels.

Iodine Without iodine, thyroid function will decrease resulting in fatigue and body sluggishness. Kelp and seafood should be eaten frequently to assure adequate iodine intake.

Sodium Sodium is necessary for normal growth in combination with potassium. It prevents sunstroke and aids in proper nerve and muscle functioning. High intakes of salt can result in migraines, seizures, and nervous tension. Meats, olives, and cheese contain liberal amounts of sodium.

Potassium Potassium works with sodium to normalize the water balance of the body and regulate the heartbeat. Hypoglycemia causes potassium loss as does diarrhea. Benefits include sending oxygen to the brain for improved thinking, reducing blood pressure, and disposal of body wastes. Nuts, seeds, and fruits possess potassium.

Space does not allow for an all-inclusive list of vitamins and minerals. Readers who are interested in expanding their awareness of this subject are encouraged to read *Feed Your Kids Right* and *Feed Yourself Right* by Dr. Lendon Smith and *Vitamin Bible* by Earl Mindell.

Hypoglycemia is one of the most insidious diseases with which mankind is afflicted. Although nearly half a million Americans are afflicted with it, it often remains undiagnosed. Sudden mood swings, fatigue, fainting spells, light-headedness, confusion, memory impairment, insomnia, rapid heart beat, blurred vision, and hunger attacks all characterize this disorder. Often a feeling of "impending doom" descends without warning or cause.

Dr. Earl Mindell defines hypoglycemia as, "a condition of low blood sugar, and like diabetes, presents a situation where the body is unable to metabolize carbohydrates normally. Since the hypoglycemic's system overreacts to sugar, producing too much insulin, the key to raising blood sugar levels is not by eating rapidly metabolized carbohydrates, but by eating more protein."[4]

In addition to suffering from a borderline case myself, in the course of fifteen years of counseling practice, I have encountered numerous adults and children who fell victim to this disease, and were literally rendered immobilized until some enlightened physician, chiropractor, or nutritionist came to their rescue and discovered the underlying cause. Such suffering has sharpened my awareness to the point that, during all intake interviews, I question the client intensively to determine the presence of telltale symptoms.

The glucose tolerance test is the prime diagnostic tool used by physicians to diagnose hypoglycemia. However, this test is not entirely infallible and oft times borderline cases remain undiagnosed due to the lack of sufficient scientific data for an accurate documentation.

Hypoglycemia can be treated with a combination of diet and vitamin therapy. If any of the symptoms cited above appear to apply to you, or any of your clients, the following suggestions will prove invaluable:

1. Make an appointment with a competent physician, or chiropractor, who has been schooled in vitamin therapy. Through this contact you will be assured of securing the correct vitamin and mineral supplements tailored for your own unique metabolism.

2. Eliminate white sugar, brown sugar, corn syrup, and maple syrup from your diet. Frutose and Tupelo honey as sweeteners are permissible. Fruit is allowable if accompanied by nuts, seeds, or cheese.

3. Vegetables should be eaten raw or barely cooked. Try raw vegetables, raisins, nuts, and seeds as snacks. When dining out, order broiled fish, fresh fruit salads, and cottage cheese. Never order cakes, pies, or other pasteries for dessert, but substitute fruit and/or cheese.

4. Eliminate all processed food from your diet. These contain hidden sugars, salts, and preservatives that can prove harmful.

5. Foods that cause allergic-addictive reactions such as corn, wheat, coffee, beef, eggs, and milk may need to be eliminated from the diet. They can be responsible for temper outbursts, headaches, rapid pulse, insomnia, and muscle cramps. An alternative to complete elimination would be ingestion of a small amount every four to seven days. This can be done when you have stabilized your diet.

6. Avoid white flour products, spaghetti, macaroni, colas, soft drinks, coffee, alcohol, and chocolate. These wreak havoc with the hypoglycemic physiology.

7. When all of these regulations are in force, take time to note just how *unbelievably lovable* family members have become in recent weeks. (Or is it, perhaps emerging from the beclouded world of hypoglycemic fog, you are the one who truly has been transformed?)

One of the axioms that I have internalized during the course of my "spiritual education" alluded to the principle, "Symbolism in all things." In other words, physical problems are usually symbolic of personality characteristics. This rule has remained in the upper levels of my subconscious, surfacing periodically, as the occasion warranted, to re-emphasize its singular importance. As time went by, more and more evidence was introduced in support of "symbolism in all things." Not only did I observe specific incidents in connection with my counseling practice, but, in an ever-broadening scope, exemplifications intruded on a continuing basis until they encompassed almost every avenue of daily existence. Again and again the point was reiterated—"The personality manifests itself physically." Through repetitive observations of verifiable cases I have come to accept the wisdom of this statement. I would like to share the lessons I have learned with you. As you read through these examples, consider the possibility that these theories might have merit.

Deafness A hearing deficiency means a person does not hear all the fine nuances that everyone with auditory acuity perceives. It logically follows, then, that the hearing impaired tend to not listen as well, and need specially designed amplification systems to accurately receive normal conversations. Generally, good listeners are quite attentive and perceptive in discerning the difference between important and non-important aspects of ongoing discussions and respond appropriately in accordance with oral cues and information received. Conversely, at times, the hearing impaired may be caught up in a world in which their own thoughts and ideas dominate, and, perhaps, "turn a deaf ear" toward the petitions and proposals initiated by others. The amplification system could symbolize the need for *intensification of overtones* (i.e. richness of suggestions, associations, and connotations) so essential for productive two-way conversations.

Vision Problems The most common visual deficits are nearsightedness, which is an interference with distance vision, and farsightedness, which is an interference with close vision. For those persons afflicted with farsightedness, logic suggests the existence of an inability to discriminate, or view accurately, all the fine points connected with issues. They are, however, immensely successful in comprehending and implementing long range plans and broader policies. For people who are nearsighted, the converse applies. *Case in point—me!* I view the future, and counsel my clients, with relative ease, but find it extremely difficult to apply the energies essential for work with minutia. *I am a farsighted individual.* The magnification through glasses possibly could be indicative of a necessity for broadening, or narrowing one's views.

Stomach Upsets "I have a stomachache Mommy. Can't I stay home from school today?" This is the plea heard in thousands of households across the land with children who are experiencing academic or social problems. This plea is not limited to children in the least. We adults universally respond with "butterflies in the pits of our stomachs" when faced with the unpleasantries of life. Some of us, like our learning-disabled counterparts, take to our beds rather than squarely facing up to the lesson life is about to teach us. What we are really saying is, *"I cannot stomach this situation!"* All things considered, it is generally advisable for both children and adults to muster up their courage and pass the test required of them, rather than cower in the corner of the bedroom, awaiting another "stomachache."

Pain in the Neck You have often heard one of your friends remark, "Oh, Allison is a pain in the neck." There may be more truth than fiction hidden in this statement. Many of our subconscious tensions and anxieties surface as muscle spasms in various parts of our body. "Oh, my aching back," you moan when faced with a no-win situation where you actually have your back to the wall.

The same principle applies to neck pains. If close friends of Allison consider her "a pain in the neck," think what type of vibrations are emitted by Allison in her home situation. Therapeutic adjustments of both the neck in question *and Allison* are needed to remedy this situation.

Back Problems Back problems assume two forms. Either the spine is too rigid for optimum range of motion or softness is present in the backbone that makes it painful to stand erect. These two exemplify opposite ends of the scale. Upon examination, the personality of the patient with rigidity will undoubtedly prove to be inflexible, stubborn, and unbending. Those with "soft spines" are highly unlikely to take strong stands on ideas which are emotionally threatening. Thus, the expression, "Have you no backbone?"

Another issue connected to back problems is sagging stomach muscles. We Americans have largely been a nation of sitters and eaters, although there is a healthy trend toward exercise and proper nutrition sweeping the nation today. Sagging stomach muscles mean gluttony and little exercise. Exercise requires self-discipline, self-discipline means straightening up one's psyche and *Voila!—through self-discipline a strong backbone is acquired.*

Broken Bones In times of extreme crisis when the entire universe seems to be askew, to add insult to injury, one takes a fall and breaks a bone, or two. Through this unfortunate (or fortuitous) act of Fate, the person who has cracked can retire from life's activities for a period of time and revel in the attention and sympathy showered on him or her because of the break. This might be labeled, "Taking a Break." Circumstances have *truly crippled.* It is only through withdrawal and re-marshalling of forces that one is able to recoup sufficient energies and self-esteem so that strength will return. Note the limb affected. It describes the type of problem. Breaking a finger, or toe means, "I took a false step," or, "I can't put my finger on the problem." Breaking a leg means, "I won't *stand* for that!"

I once evaluated a thirteen year old who was continually breaking arms and legs. She absolutely hated school! As I was testing her vision, she remarked, "Wouldn't it be nice to wear glasses?" This was just another manifestation of trying to "cripple her body" in order to avoid attending school because of the devastating effects of her learning disability.

MENTAL TECHNIQUES

Body Language

In counseling, physical gestures and non-verbal cues often say as much, or more, than the spoken word. Thus, it is expedient that the counselor focus on both body and spoken language. According to Julius Fast, a body-language expert, "Spoken language alone will not give us the full meaning of what a person is saying, nor for that matter, will body language alone, give us the full meaning."[5]

What are some of the telltale movements and stances that broadcast to the world our subconscious attitudes and behaviors?

HAND GESTURES AND MOVEMENTS Movements involving our hands indicate how we are "handling" the situation. *Open hands* are associated with sincerity and forthrightness. *A touching gesture* carries with it an effort toward calming. It reassures the recipient that all will be well. *A hand to chest movement* is representative of loyalty, honesty, and devotion. *Hands on hips* depicts an action-oriented individual. Evaluative gestures are those which include *stroking the chin* and the *hand to cheek gesture.* The latter pose is struck when the thinker places his chin in his palm and rests his index finger on his cheek.

Negative hand movements can be monitored through *hand-wringing,* which connotes anguish, and *clenched hands,* which suggest extreme tension. *The fist* signifies determination, anger, and possible hostility.

Examination of finger movements is also helpful in evaluating non-verbal behaviors. A *pointed index finger* says, "Do you understand my meaning?" with strong emotional components attached. *Steepling* is done "when people join their fingertips and form what might be described as a 'church steeple.' It immediately communicates that person is very sure of what he is saying."[6]

ARM AND LEG POSITIONS *Open arms* imply the same attitude as open hands—*Openmindness.* Arms crossed on chest announce defensiveness. This may be a habitual way for some people to sit, however. *Locked arms in back* convey self-control, or perhaps some pressure.

Leg motions and positions say more than ten sentences which are intended to communicate the opposing attitude. A person may affirm his good intentions and nod his head in agreement, but, if he has *locked ankles,* chances are slim for reaching an agreement. This connotes a locking in, or holding back. *Crossed legs* frequently reveal a competitive stance.

Different types of walkers relay different types of emotions. "Adults who walk rapidly and swing their arms freely tend to be goal-oriented and readily pursue their objectives."[7] Walkers with droopy shoulders and lead shoes are a depressive sort. A preoccupied person may walk with hands behind his back in a meditative state.

If a person tends to stand above you and "lecture," addressing you while you remain seated, he is trying to assume a position of dominance. Personal conversing at the same level represent equality positions.

The Eyes and Facial Expressions

"Of all the parts of the human body that are used to transmit information, the eyes are the most important, and can transmit the most subtle nuances. Does this contradict the fact that the eyes do not show emotion? Not really. While the eyeball itself shows nothing, the emotional impact of the eyes occurs because of their use, and the use of the face around them."[8]

There are eyes and eyes and eyes. *Defiant* eyes stare straight at you and say, "I dare you." *Awkward blinking eyes* convey a message of doubt and insecurity. *Downcast eyes* reveal subservience.

On the positive side, *wide eyes* display amazement and awe. *A winking eye* expresses a secret known to both persons, or perhaps approval. A *straightforward look* bespeaks honesty and truthfulness. *Sparkling eyes* transmit the joy of the soul.

A dream I had on January 2, 1985, succinctly expresses the importance of eyes.

The Eyes Have It (January 2, 1985)

> I am engaged in a discussion with a learned man. I ask him about the importance of the eyes revealing the personality of the soul. He responds, "The Eyes Have IT!"

With regard to head positions and facial expressions, one can infer from a *tilting head* that the person is listening attentively. A *bowed head* bemoans a broken spirit. A *head held high* implies pride and assurance.

A counselor can deduct a considerable amount of useful knowledge from a person's mouth and type of smile. A *droopy mouth* means, "I'm down in the mouth." *Tight lips* mean restricted psyche. *Lip-biting* shouts, "I am eating away at myself." Beware of the *crooked smile.* Behind it hides a devious mind. A *semi-smile* means the client is half there. A *trusting smile* means, "I know you are my friend and will help me." A *broad grin such as the one John Hollis always wears,* tells the world *"I love you!"*

Colors

Color is vibration or movement. It is a property of matter. Our souls are atomic patterns which project these colors. "All bodies radiate those vibrations with which it, the body, controls itself in mental, in physical and such radiation is called the aura."[9]

The aura is not visible to everyone, but there are those among us who are able to witness its emanations. Through reading the aura, one is able to gain impressions of the person's mental, emotional, physical, and spiritual conditions.

Color is light. The colors observed in the aura run in a spectrum sequence progressing from short to long wave lengths of light: Violet, indigo, blue, green, yellow, orange, and red. The pituitary gland is the master gland of the body which regulates the secretions of other major glands. The eyes are the vehicles which absorb vibrational color patterns. These are then transmitted through bundles of nerve fibers to the pituitary gland and ultimately affect our physical, mental, and spiritual behavior. Understanding this concept allows one to understand the dramatic impact color exerts on our personalities.

It should be stated that different shades of the same colors take on different meanings in accordance with the brightness or muddiness present. Bright colors reflect goodness, happiness, and positive vibrations. Muddy or dark colors in auras reveal depression, illness, and negativity. In addition, specific colors predominate depending on the condition of the body at the time of viewing.

Aura reading is a skill that can be developed. There are publications which contain exercises on how to develop auric vision. If as counselors you do wish to invest the time and energy required to acquire this skill, let me offer a practical suggestion. A client's choice of color in clothes often is a reflection of those colors that are prevailing in the auric field at that moment. A glance at your client's outfit will furnish you with invaluable knowledge concerning his current mental state. Consistent choosing of the colors over a long period of time certifies the major shades that predominate in his or her auric vibrational pattern.

Now that we know these colors exist in the aura, what information can be inferred about the individual when his aura "pops into view"?

1. **Red**—Red represents powerful energy. On the positive side, red is stimulating, energizing, and sexual. Negative qualities include anger, frustration, and lack of moderation in physical desires.

   Shades should be noted. Dark red suggests nervous tension. Scarlet suggests egotism. Pink is found in persons who are immature. Pink also indicates changes in growth patterns.

2. **Orange**—Orange is the color of illusion associated with magic and the occult. Robes of a saffron hue are donned by Buddist Monks. Positive attributes associated with orange are thoughtfulness, self-control, endurance, and consideration. Orange is connected to creative expression.

   When a brownish orange emanates from the aura, laziness, or lack of ambition exists.

3. **Yellow**—Yellow is the Sun color. Bright yellow projects optimism, cheerfulness, courage, self-confidence, and strength of character. It is expansive and aspiring.

   When yellow is ruddy, timidity exists. Red-heads with a ruddy yellow in their auras exhibit inferiority complexes and indecisiveness of will. Dirty yellow reflects cowardice.

4. **Green**—Green in the aura reflects growth, harmony, and balance. Emerald green with a touch of blue symbolizes healing. Physicians elect to wear green and usually have an abundance of this color in their auras. A splash of blue, in association with green, establishes trustworthiness.

   Negative properties concomitant with green are envy and jealousy. A lemon-green which leans more toward yellow shouts deceit.

5. **Blue**—Blue is a highly spiritual color. It is connected with the intellect and striving to attain a higher level of mind. Blue is also the color of communications. Almost all shades of blue are positive. However, there are degrees of depth reflected in the intensity. Pale blue suggests struggling toward maturity. Medium blue indicates the person applies more energies than his pale blue co-worker, but the level of talent is equal. Workers who exhibit deep blue are certain of their task in life and are engaged in fulfilling it. They may be unusual and moody, but they are steadfast and spiritually minded, and almost always dedicated to service to others.

   Less desirable blue connotations are present when a state of depression exists either because of defective communications between self and others, or a sense of being overwhelmed by current life circumstances is present.

6. **Indigo**—Indigo or midnight blue has the power to draw us beyond ourselves. Traditionally, it is associated with wisdom, loyalty, piety, and saintliness. With emanations of blue coming from one's aura, the counselor can be assured this person is searching for a cause, or a religious experience.

   Negative characteristics of indigo are impetuosity and argumentativeness.

7. **Violet or Purple**—Violet and purple are among the least common colors. Therefore, a distinctiveness exists. Persons with this auric color possess a high sense of integrity and are sensitive and introspective.

   When too much purple exists, there is a tendency toward being overbearing. Pale violet is indicative of aloofness, indecision, and vacillation.

   The colors black and white deserve mention. Black either denotes mysteriousness or evil. White which is inclusive of all colors of the rainbow communicates innocence, purity, and centering of the Christ Consciousness.

Not all persons possess the ability to see and read auras. It is, however, a useful skill to cultivate due to the fact that an auric pattern broadcasts a visually descriptive representation of the client's mental and physical state of being.

PSYCHICAL TECHNIQUES

Precognitive Dreaming and Dream Incubation:

In my own experience, one of the most fascinating applications of precognition has been in my own counseling practice. It is not uncommon for me to be interviewing a client or testing a child, and in the midst of the session, recollect some tidbit of information or insight from the previous evening's dreams that, through proper synchronistic energy, is transformed into an insightful clue that assists in assembling the fragmented pieces of that puzzle into a meaningful whole. For instance, let me tell you about Judith, a sullen, depressed eight year old, whom I was testing. Although we had been together for more than an hour, communication and rapport were at a low ebb. I had used every technique at my command to break through the protective shield with which she surrounded herself, to no avail. At our most depressive point a vision of a huge black and white rabbit flashed in my consciousness. He was being fed and cared for with love. I recalled that this was one of the last dreams I had recorded in my dream journal this morning.

"Do you like rabbits?" I inquired hesitantly. The listless expression vanished, and from behind that emotionless mask, a cautious face appeared. "Do you own any rabbits?" she ventured carefully.

"Not any more," I remarked regretfully. "But my son used to." Delighted with a topic with which we had some basis to establish a closer relationship, I eagerly recounted several stories involving my son Jimmy, being particularly sure to include a description of that large, black and white rabbit that had "paid me a visit" 5:30 AM that morning.

"Oh," she exclaimed, her eyes glistening with excitement and pride. "He sounds just like Midnight. He's my pet rabbit, you know." From that moment on, I became her trusted friend.

In addition to employing precognitive dreams as an effective tool, therapists have at their disposal another dream technique, dream incubation,* that has proven invaluable with regard to programming "healing information" on clients. *It is advisable to seek the client's permission before formulating the request,* however. In this procedure the counselor incubates a dream containing the sought-after answers to his client's personal problems by formulating a specific question or noting a clearly defined problem, in his mind, before going to sleep. Several counselors of my acquaintance have been enormously successful over the years in retrieving solutions to a wide variety of inquiries. This has always worked to their benefit and contributed to the rapidity of their client's mental healing.

Client Dreams

One of the most fruitful areas into which to delve, as a counselor attempting to determine the underlying causes of his client's dysfunction, is the personal dreams of the client himself. The symbology intricately woven within the framework of his dreams accurately depicts the agents at work. Hidden away in the protective layers of the dreamer's subconscious, these can only be uncovered through skillful and painstaking analysis of the self-revealing portrait created by the dream symbols themselves. This is a worthwhile venture infused with healing overtones, if the time is taken to properly learn the fundamentals of dream analysis and dream interpretation. Clients' dreams are alive with clues which portray their dilemmas, but it requires a proficient counselor to decipher the heavily veiled messages broadcast from the dark mysterious recesses of his client's subconscious. But the effort is well worth it considering dreams are almost always concerned with the theme of self-preservation.

* Further detailed information can be read in my previous book, *The Inner Eye* (Prentice-Hall Inc., 1985).

An illustration in support of this statement might be in order here. When treating a case of school phobia, I was utterly amazed to note how clearly the boy's dream delineated the root of the problem. Tommy was stuck in an elevator between floors (grades) and the individual who had her finger on the "Up–Down Control" was none other than Mrs. Smith, his current third grade teacher. She refused to move her finger and, as he gazed at her, horns grew out of her forehead. The diagnosis here was—"Caught!" The prescription—"Move to another third grade."

Telepathy

The thoughts you dwell upon create your own destiny. Those thoughts that are clothed in the most energy serve as the primary foundation upon which you build your life. Where do these thoughts originate? It is generally accepted that the conscious mind is the source of thought, but the power source is rooted in the subconscious. "The subconscious mind is beyond space and time, and it is fundamentally a powerful sending and receiving station with a universal hook-up whereby it can communicate with physical, mental, psychic, and according to many investigators, spiritual worlds, past, present, and future, as well."[10]

The process whereby one subconscious mind communicates with another is termed telepathy.

Telepathy can be *spontaneous* or *purposeful.* Hunches or flashes of intuition are the result of accidently or spontaneously tuning into another person's thought transmissions. Purposeful telepathy is accomplished through *intent.* In other words, the sender determines to convey a selected idea or concept, energizes that thought, and then transmits it to a previously selected receiver. Through the utilization of this process, the sender *purposefully* directs his thoughts in such a way as to influence strongly the views or opinions of the receiver.

Spontaneous Telepathy As the counseling process progresses, powerful emotional ties are forged between client and counselor. The sympathetic mind of the counselor reaches out in a compassionate and healing manner toward the anguished soul of his client. Almost immediately, random mental pictures, or strong emotional impressions flood the counselor's empathetic awareness. Through spontaneous telepathy, answers and guidance are received without the counselor, silently or orally, expressing a specific request for the desired information. Needs are anticipated and met on other levels.

Let me present an example here related to my own counseling practice. Approximately two years ago, a beautiful blonde eight-year-old girl was brought to Personal Development Services, Inc. for an educational evaluation. The parents were most cooperative during the initial interview and described her educational problems extensively. After the parents left, I began the testing process. Almost immediately I began receiving a mental picture of cherub eyes spitting forth flames of fire. A second impression that intruded in my consciousness was that of considerable stamping and yelling which terminated in a full-blown temper tantrum. I gazed into those blue eyes in utter disbelief. This child appeared too innocent for such formidable outbursts of emotion. I filed these impressions away mentally and proceeded with the evaluation. During the informing interview, I inquired as to the possibility of temper tantrums.

"Why, yes," replied the mother in a surprised tone. "She is quite strong-willed, but isn't that just a part of growing up?" The parents had misjudged the seriousness of the child's behaviors. Her manipulative behaviors were consistently rewarded, thus reinforcing the likelihood of their reoccurrence. Both parents and child were subsequently referred to a child psychologist for behavior counseling.

Purposeful Telepathy In the Bible, Paul tells us that personal transformation can take place through the renewing of our minds. When counterproductive thoughts and attitudes are replaced by healthy new mental concepts, personal transformation is brought into being.

Spiritual counselors who are skilled in the use of purposeful telepathy possess a potent healing tool indeed. To be able to send forth healing energies and implant the seeds of healing within agonizing minds, is to don the mantle of the spiritual physician.

Three elements must be present to successfully energize purposeful telepathy. According to Shakti Gawain in *Creative Visualization* these are:

1. *Desire*—"You must have a true desire to have, or create, that which you have chosen to visualize. By desire I don't mean addictive, grasping desire, but a strong feeling of purpose."[11]
2. *Belief*—"The more you believe in your chosen goal and the possibility of attaining it, the more certain you will be to do so."[12]
3. *Acceptance*—"You must be willing to *accept,* and *have,* that which you are seeking."[13]

Ms. Gawain calls the sum total of these three elements *intention.* If the client's attitude becomes goal-oriented and the counselor uses healing visualizations and affirmations, the process of purposeful telepathy can regenerate unhealthy minds. Perhaps personal transformation, such as that spoken of by the Apostle Paul, can become a reality after all.

Although I am accomplished in sending healing thoughts and energies to my learning-disabled clients, the virtuoso in our family is my husband Jim. Over the years, as we have conducted a joint counseling practice, I recall witnessing countless clients of his transformed from fragile and emotionally damaged human beings into highly productive and self-confident individuals. I often wondered how he effected such rapid attitudinal changes. It remained a mystery until 1981 when I began studying visualization and telepathic thought. As I became more and more well-versed in the concepts of thought-transference and spiritual healing, it gradually dawned on me that all these years Jim had been planting healing seeds in the minds of his clients. These then took root and blossomed forth into self-understanding and self-selected goals that the clients perceived to be their own and from which they could begin rebuilding their lives in terms that were meaningful to them. When confronted with my theory, Jim turned to me with a twinkle in his eye and chuckled, "What took you so long to catch on?"

SPIRITUAL TECHNIQUES

Healers

The use of human hands to heal the sick extends back to ancient times. The most commonly used term for such a practice is laying-on-of-hands. Healers exist today the same as they did in Biblical times. Researchers today have begun to take a renewed interest in healers possessing this skill. In an article published by the New York *Times* in April of 1985, the results of a scientifically designed study conducted in a New York hospital concluded that "therapeutic touch goes beyond the well-known placebo response, in which patients improve because they believe the therapy is beneficial. In this and other studies, therapeutic touch was found to have health benefits even without direct contact between healer's hands and the patient's body, and even if the patient had no knowledge of what the technique was suppose to achieve."[14] (Therapeutic touch is similar but not exactly like the laying-on-of-hands.) Among the benefits cited were pain relief, reduction of anxiety, increase in oxygen-carrying hemoglobin, and pronounced relaxation response as indicated by a change in brain waves.

Who are these healers and what type of personality characteristics do they possess? According to Harry Edwards, one of England's foremost spiritual healers until his death in 1976, the most likely candidates to develop the capacity to become spiritual healers are "People who have a deep inner yearning to give of themselves in healing the sick, take away pain and stress, who possess compassion and sympathy for those afflicted and are willing to sacrifice their time without any pecuniary reward; people who are generous in their nature and who render willing service for good causes are those who possess the spiritual qualities which mark the healing gift."[15]

How is laying-on-of-hands executed? The hands of the healer are positioned four to six inches above the patient and are moved over the body from head to toe. While the movement takes place, the healer attempts to determine the condition of the patient through the detection of hot spots where energies have accumulated due to tension or illness. These energies are then redirected or redistributed, thus alleviating the symptom or symptoms. The healer mentally directs the healing force for this purpose.

Healers also visualize themselves as clear channels with an abundance of healing energies flowing through them from a Universal Source. When this mode of healing is used, powerful therapeutic energies are transferred from healer to patient in an effort to restore the weakened physical vehicle to a state of balance and harmony. (See pages 248–249 for further details on this subject.)

Both Jim and I have used healers for ourselves and our clients with varying degrees of success depending on the efficiency of the healer and openness of the patient to the concept of spiritual healing. This form of healing is worthy of consideration by counselors.

Scientific Prayer

Emmet Fox refers to prayer as the Golden Key to harmony and happiness. He is not talking about simple prayer but a more highly developed concept recognized as scientific prayer. Scientific prayer refers to the lifting up of thought processes to a level above that of the problem being faced. If one is able to elevate his level of thinking high enough, the problem will solve itself.

In Fox's opinion it is useless to try and extricate oneself or other people from the problems in which they are emersed by manipulating circumstances or thought. If through praying scientifically the degree of consciousness is raised to a level where negative patterns of thinking are negated and confidence and faith in the Almighty is foremost in one's mind, God will take over and resolve the difficulty in ways our menial minds could have never conceived. He feels the simplest and perhaps the prayer most likely to produce the desired result is "God is with me." It was his experience that incurable maladies were healed when a prayer such as this was offered in faith and humility.

As for myself, I am in total agreement with Dr. Fox's philosophy. My personal view on the utilization of prayer as a healing technique can be summarized in the following message dream statement:

Prayers, when spoken in love, are the most powerful tools available.

Is it not paradoxical that, after seeking the ultimate answers to our problems by delving into the most learned of treatises and working toward their resolution by traveling through a maze of self-created thorns, we eventually arrive at the realization that the simplest answer of all is the most infinitely powerful? That answer, sincerely prayed, is "God is Love."

Counselors, why not begin scientific prayer for your clients as a first rather than a last resort? Prayers are always answered.

CHAPTER 12

Cosmic Contemplations

Love is the key to healing—Love relaxes and harmonizes man's emotions. Love attunes the individual to the healing power within himself.

Dr. Catherine Ponder—*The Dynamic Laws of Healing*

At the conclusion of each Psychical Research Project reading there is a section entitled *Soul's Purpose.* Contained within that paragraph is a concise commentary on the constructs and types of studies each cosmic pupil has elected to master during the course of his or her sojourn on the Earth Plane. The ideals chosen afford a kind of spiritual yardstick with which to measure the level of soul success attained when compared with the actuality of daily living. These commentaries are imbued with ethereal knowledge flavored with piquant humor rendering more palatable life's most bitter spoonfuls.

Just as each entity has been assigned his or her soul's purpose, so too do the creative works of individuals manifest an essence unique unto themselves. Thus, it would seem fitting that this book not be finalized without the inclusion of *Cosmic Contemplations.* These inspirational communications were transmitted either in the hypnotic state between waking and sleeping or channeled while in trance. The ideas touched upon during these communiques appear to be drawn from multi- rather than uni-dimensional resources with subjects under discussion including the importance of meditation, the elimination of fears, the benefits of prayer, the challenge of happiness, and the all-enveloping power of love. Laced with plaudits of encouragement these maxims offer beginning and advanced students of cosmology a variety of Universal Truths and Directives from which to formulate their personal philosophical posture toward life.

I cannot lay claim to the authorization of *Cosmic Contemplations* for, as with *The Inner Eye,* I am firmly convinced that the spiritual orators for whom I serve as faithful recorder list their residence far beyond realms envisioned by man's limited mentality. Having been privileged to be the recipient of these scintillating discourses, I feel a strong sense of obligation when serving as their intermediary to disseminate these insightful communications to the broadest possible audience. By so doing, it is my fervent prayer that the ideals reflected upon within these pages will provide the impetus for a concerted movement on the part of self-actualizing souls to extricate themselves from the shadowy twilight of life's darkest corners and evolve upward in an ever-expanding multidimensional progression, but with a singularity of purpose—*The Unification of Individuality with the Illumination of the Light.*

IDEALS FOR THE UNIFICATION OF INDIVIDUALITY WITH THE ILLUMINATION OF LIGHT

The unifying precepts selected for inclusion under this heading are a continuation of the Universal Truths initially presented in *The Inner Eye.* Their incorporation into one's personal belief system and patterns of action will provide a concise and viable religious philosophy for seeking logical resolutions to life's most demanding challenges.

On Internalizing Truth: Meditation, manifestation, and faith bring truth.

Endure and Endear: When conditions are not ideal, have the patience to endure and endear.

On Measuring Love: You should not measure love for those who need it most do not get it in abundance.

Faith Seekers: Those who seek in faith will always find answers.

Needs: Look upon these as opportunities.

Growing Humanity: People are like trees—they grow!

On Blessing Those Less Fortunate: God blesses those who bless others.

The Value of Readings: Readings are valuable only in terms of the creativity for the recipient.

Slow-Learning Souls: Slow learners depend upon general judgements and not critical experience.

Miracles: Life is made for miracles.

Prosperity: You will receive in accordance with the measure given others.

The Quest for the Rainbow: Beauty forms in the quest for the rainbow.

A Divisible Soul: When unhealthy situations are avoided, divisible portions of one's soul remain intact. If the soul becomes divided, the time is then opportune for hellish influences to enter in.

Beliefs: Ye who do not believe fall victim to your own deceit.

Blessed Vicissitudes: We provide you with blessed vicissitudes.

Bound By Love: When bound by love, can anything but absolute success transpire!

The Importance of Envisioning: Once an idea or ideal is envisioned, it should then be understood and adhered to.

A Christian Viewpoint: If the viewpoint is underscored by the cross, all is well.

Manifestation: The law + the energies = the event.

The Four Bes for Readings: Be still. Be aware. Be perceptive. Be assured.

On Praying: In preparation for all things, *pray!*

The Qualities of Faith: In all cases faith proves to be either the anodyne or the antidote.

Petitioning: There is never anything that you petition that is not answered in a fashion more appropriate than your original supplication.

THE PURPOSES OF INCARNATING SOULS

The passages below were included because of their global applicability regarding the personality quality discussed. These were selected from personal Holistic Life Readings the basic themes of which were all-pervasive throughout the entire commentary. The ideals expressed therein suggest their wisdom might prove educational and beneficial for humanity as a whole.

Self-Sacrifice

This entity is generally a loving and caring soul. The disharmonies that are expressed through the disease symbology are the result of past-life karmic ties, as well as an element of self-sacrifice again in this existence which has extruded into a physical manifestation of the personality deficiency to a greater degree in both mental and physical realms than should exist.

The task chosen for this incarnation is to understand that one can love and live in harmony with individuals in family and close associations without sacrificing completely for their mental, physical, and spiritual needs, replacing the element of self-sacrifice with an awareness of confidence in one's own true worth. This sets the soul of this individual upon the correct spiritual course so that she may pilot herself and steer a clear and steady course through troubled waters, keeping the Light in mind. The Light of the Christ Consciousness provides spiritual guidance through these troubled times so that at a future point calmer waters will be traversed and a feeling of tranquility and achievement of peace and spiritual serenity will ultimately be achieved through the understanding of the personality deficits. Thus, with the elimination of these, the realization of the soul's true purpose will be arrived at and maintained and through this fashion many of life's spiritual laws and ultimate truths will be at last internalized.

Self-Forgiveness

The soul of this entity has knots of unforgiveness extending outward and inward damming up energies which could otherwise be used in the healing of others, which is one of the main purposes for her incarnation. Prior to the maximum use of the healing ability, the entity must begin to unravel the knots of the past and refocus the dammed up energies that have laid dormant within her physical being for a period of ten years.

The investing of positive . . . visual imagery and a change of ideology with regard to the physical deficits are the course to the healing of the soul during the current time period. Thus completed, the entity may then focus maximum energies on the realization of her excellent healing potential and energize the second portion for her current incarnation. The first and most important, however, is to learn to love self and release feelings of despondency, the tendency toward frustrated ambition, and the pools of unshed tears that have so long played havoc with the physical self. When the forgiveness occurs, revitalization ensues.

Beauty

This beauteous soul has elected for her primary lesson in this incarnation the bestowing of gracious gifts from her own material resources to enhance the life pleasure of others. With the understanding and internalization of a viable philosophy of life a score of years ago, the fulfillment of the soul's purpose is gradually being achieved. The provision of spiritual knowledge to those less evolved, as well as physical bestowals are material proof the existence of these truths. Many a life of those closely associated with her, and moreover, those of a less personal status in her circle of acquaintances, have come to the realization of their own reasons and lessons for the evolution of their souls. The general purpose elected of immersing other souls into beauty and truths of the Source of our soul's existence has been and ever will be the primary root of pleasure for this spiritual entity. The harvest reaped is more abundant than the seeds sown due to the energizing process provided by this entity during the growth process.

Healing

This is one with healing hands who is just beginning to set her course on avenues that will lead spiritually to rewards and opportunities that are unparalleled and inconceivable at the present moment. Becoming a channel of healing blessings to others, both physically and spiritually, is the purpose this entity has selected for her current incarnation. Although confusion has surrounded this one in the past, the current and future ideologies will so pervade and mesh themselves within the life tapestry of this entity that the outpouring of energies which have tended to delight associates of hers in the past, will be intensified to the point where she may literally become the light in the lives of many a person who is fortunate enough to come in contact with her healing illuminations.

Transformation

This entity crosses back and forth between realms of higher vibrations on a daily basis carrying to and fro psychic and healing knowledge of benefit to both living and discarnate beings. The scope of her talents is numinous. Psychic instruction, intuitive knowledge, and healing vibrations are the gifts that this soul has elected to develop as she trods the spiritual path toward enlightenment of self endeavors. This soul is the personification and appropriator of the greatest power the universe has known—Love.

THE SIGNIFICANCE OF MIND-BODY INTEGRATION

The final two essays in *Dreams and Healing* express concisely, and in unmistakable terms, the importance of unifying the mind-body connection with regard to illness and healing. Attunement of the mind-body connection is an absolute if one is to acquire and remain in a physically fit, mentally astute, and spiritually progressive state of being.

On Illness

Illness is the harbinger of disharmony between physical and mental states of being. The upsurge of vibratory discordants reverberates throughout the body alerting the afflicted entity to the existing disquietudes. Clashes between powerful vibratory forces are evidenced in those portions of the soul's physical replica that project the most indolent energy patterns. These are but reflections in the Mirror of Life of irresolvable perplexities of long-standing which have taken root in the fertile soils of despair.

Note carefully the site of the malady which oft times broadcasts the nature of one's grief. Does the selfishness of avarice curl gnarled arthritic fingers inward portraying the ever present Clutch of Greed? Are the gnawing pangs of green-eyed jealousy responsible for repetitive stomach ulcers whose searing fires can be quenched neither by diet nor knife? Is there a possible link between progressing deafness and the proverbial "turning of the deaf ear" to loved one's woeful pleas? Do the wasted limbs of Parkinson's

Disease symbolize an all-too permissive attitude on the part of the patient to acquise to ever-mounting pressures of authoritarianism, thus inevitably resulting in the complete domination of one's self-will and individual density? *Physical symbolism annotates mental anguish.*

The depth and duration of the illness merit staid contemplation as well for both allude to the gravity of the bodily condition. The fisty, fleeting nip of an Oriental Flu Bug is far more tolerable than the deadly talons of life-ebbing emphysema or steathily creeping lung cancer. And who among us would not prefer the maddening itch of a fortnight of poison ivy to the soul-scarring ravages of disfiguring psoriasis? *Passions unleashed and unabating continue to etch themselves ever more deeply into the very core of our being until, at last, death claims victory and the final decimation is complete.*

Thus, when the scourges of ill health come upon thee, peer deep into thy soul to unravel the tangled web of these self-destructive disharmonies. Then, with Faith as thy constant companion, lay claim to physical perfection and spiritual well-being for these are the birthrights of all God-imaged souls who dwell within the Omniscient Consciousness of our multidimensional universe.

On Healing

Just as disease is the manifestation of submerged fears, conversely, healing is the substantive representation of the explusion of these demonic forces. The explanation of these avenues of thought is the primary consideration of any dissertation involving healing principles.

Why does a God so full of love and forgiveness permit the degree of suffering that persists among the peoples of the world? The response is simple and concise—*the exercise of individual free will.* Free will is the most valuable possession bestowed upon us by the God Force. We can choose to be or not to be spiritually unified with Our Creator. The latter choice invariably culminates in a violation of Universal Laws, and from these resultant behaviors spring rapidly breeding emissaries of disease. If, however, through meditation and prayer, we align our soul's purpose with the life plan co-created by each living soul with the God Force, then absolute harmony, perfect health, and total contentment will become our natural state.

Why do we want to be healed? It is an unbelievably exhilerating experience to witness the crippled made whole and hear the mute shout with joy. Albeit, the crucial issue is to what avail is the healing if stalwart limbs and loosened tongues fail to enter into future spiritual service in direct proportion to the blessings that have already been so abundantly provided. Physical healing is, of course, essential but it is the spiritually oriented goals the healee seeks to pursue subsequent to the physical healing that are the signposts indicating the direction the individual is following in his ensuing steps toward soul evolution. *With purposeful direction the healing process augments itself.*

What exactly comprises the source of universally healing energies? There is absolute agreement among healers on this point regardless of their position on the use of spirit physicians, laying-on-of-hands, or absentee healing. *All healing is divine in nature and originates from The Well Spring of God.* The healer simply serves as a tool for the Divinity to submit proof of his Omnipotent Power and Healing Grace. Spiritual healing is freely distributed to all mankind irrespective of race or personal religion.

How is the healing process accomplished? There is a cosmic connection between the process of healing and the process of thought. Each bodily cell composing the human form is interconnected with all other bodily cells. These forms, in turn, are bound together by invisible cosmic skeins based on the principle of the Oneness of All Force. In His Infinite Wisdom the Almighty has set no limitations on the dispersement of universally healing energies. Thus, the act of healing merely requires that the healer tap into the vast cosmic reservoir, and through the power of thought and mental supplication, transmute the diseased cells into healthy functioning organisms. *This being fulfilled, the ultimate task of maintaining the healing is placed directly on the shoulders of the healee. The decision to remain in this state of harmonious well-being is singularly dependent upon the degree of faith exhibited and the spiritual productivity of future actions and endeavors.*

FINAL COMMENTS

It is mid-winter of 1986. Jack Frost left his signature upon my window pane this morning. As I gaze from my dining room window, I can observe icy crystalline formations bejeweling the shoreline of my beloved James River. Is it truly possible that eighteen months have elapsed since the initial word of *Dreams and Healing* was penned and, once again, I find myself composing the final lines of another book?

I approach the ending with feelings of both joy and loss—joy in the sense that bonds of solitude imposed upon a writer will soon be loosened; loss in that I shall no longer be privileged to experience the exhilaration of co-creativity that accompanies the finis of a well-turned phrase or the channeling of universal precepts conveyed from the consciousness of far more highly developed minds than the finite one I possess.

It is impossible to conduct research with healers and their erudite philosophies without being the recipient of their remarkable beneficence. Accordingly, innumerable physical, mental, and spiritual healings have transpired for me personally as my limited theorizations were expanded. Therefore, the greatest single reward granted to me for the authorship of *Dreams and Healing* is the powerful realization that I am undoubtedly the greatest beneficiary of its healing principles.

If I could encapsulate all I have learned in the past eighteen months, it would be summarized thusly: *All healing is but a reflection of God's Smile as the chains of self-inflicted torment are at last unfettered and the blessings of the transforming miracle re-splendorize the soul. Healing is truly His Acknowledgement of life's lessons well learned.*

Epilogue

THE HEALING PHYSICIAN

The physician of the future will have two great aims. The first will be to assist the patient to a knowledge of himself and to point out to him the fundamental mistakes he may be making, the deficiencies in his character which he should remedy, and the defects in his nature which must be eradicated and replaced by the corresponding virtues. Such a physician will have to be a great student of the laws governing humanity and of human nature itself, so that he may recognize in all who come to him those elements which are causing a conflict between the Soul and the personality. He must be able to advise the sufferer how best to bring about the harmony required, what actions against Unity he must cease to perform and the necessary virtues he must develop to wipe out his defects. Each case will need a careful study, and it will only be those who have devoted much of their life to the knowledge of mankind and in whose heart burns the desire to help, who will be able to undertake successfully this glorious and divine work for humanity, to open the eyes of a sufferer and enlighten him on the reason of his being, and to inspire hope, comfort, and faith which will enable him to conquer his malady.

The second duty of the physician will be to administer such remedies as will help the physical body to gain strength and assist the mind to become calm, widen its outlook and strive towards perfection, thus bringing peace and harmony to the whole personality. Such remedies there are in nature, placed there by the mercy of the Divine Creator for the healing of comfort of mankind.

Heal Thyself
by Edward Bach, M.D.

Appendices

APPENDIX A

Brewing Parsley Tea

Parsley is a very reliable diuretic remedy. It is a remarkably effective healing treatment in cases of cystitis, difficult urination, kidney infections, and kidney stones. Parsley is high in Vitamin A and B and contains three times the amount of Vitamin C as citrus juice.

Parsley tea may be brewed in the following manner: If the parsley is dried, use 1 tsp. to each cupful of hot water. If it is fresh, use a handful in a pint of hot water. Cover and let steep for several minutes. When the tea is sufficiently strong, one cupful should be sipped slowly. This should be done every 3 hours until relief is obtained.

(This information was taken in part from *School of Natural Healing* by Dr. John R. Christopher.)

APPENDIX B

Human Potential Attitude Inventory

Dr. Norman Shealy

As you read each of the following items to yourself, get a sense of whether your emotional response is agreement or disagreement. If you get strong agreement, mark ++. If you get mild agreement, mark +. If you get no response at all, mark it 0 for neutral response. If you get a mild argument, mark −. If you are aware of strong disagreement, mark −−. It sometimes happens that people are in agreement in general (which would be a +), and are simultaneously aware of an uneasy feeling that argues, or their brain shows them a single exception. In such a case, it is permissable to answer +, −, to reflect this conflict; this would be preferable to marking 0 if you are really getting a mixed response.

Strong agreement ++ Neutral 0 Mild disagreement −
Mild agreement + Strong disagreement −−
Remember mixed responses are possible

____ I have forgiven everyone who has wronged me.

____ I forgive those who unintentionally wrong me.

____ I forgive those who purposefully wrong me.

____ When I tell those who have wronged me what they have done, I expect them to apologize or repent.

____ I have sometimes wronged or harmed others.

____ I apologize when I wrong others.

____ I expect others to forgive me when I apologize.

____ I helped someone else within the last week.

____ I walked and talked with someone I love during the last week.

____ I attend church regularly.

____ I believe that my *attitude* each day is more important than *attending* church.

____ I believe my affliction(s) was given me by God for his honor and glory as part of a divine plan.

____ I believe God is wrathful and punishes sinners.

____ I have lots of friends and see/visit them often.

____ I pray regularly for myself and others.

____ I believe the most important goal of life is service to God or others.

____ I prayed for someone else yesterday or today.

____ I often (more than once a week) watch sunset and sunrise with a feeling of reverence.

____ I read the Bible or inspirational materials at least once a week.

____ I attend a *fun* event or listen to good music at least once a week.

____ I meditate, pray or think about the beauty of life regularly.

____ Everyone is born a sinner.

____ Mankind is basically bad.

____ I believe hypnosis is the work of the Devil.

____ I believe everyone has a right to his or her beliefs.

____ I believe that those who do not share my religious beliefs are sinners and likely to go to Hell.

____ God does not forgive sinners unless the debts of sins are paid.

____ If your beliefs are different from mine, you cannot help me. My spiritual/religious beliefs are: a. strong ____b. correct and right ____

____ I feel calm and serene most of the time.

____ When I become frustrated, I pause and calm myself.

____ I feel compassion for all other human beings.

____ I go out of my way to help other persons.

____ I know I can attain my goals.

____ I believe *I* can accomplish anything to which I apply myself adequately.

____ I *will* apply myself enough to accomplish my goals.

____ I feel great joy in my life.

____ I can face whatever life offers.

____ I believe I learn from my problems.

____ I willingly or lovingly contribute to help others less fortunate than I.

____ I believe tomorrow will be a better day.

____ I believe in a benevolent God.

____ I believe in life after death.

____ I believe I have a soul which survives death.

____ I believe one dies and goes to Heaven or Hell.

____ I believe in reincarnation.

____ Reincarnation is an evil concept.

____ I have the will power to accomplish my goals.

____ I am wise enough to make the right choices.

____ I make rational, reasonable choices.

____ I feel love for all other human beings.

____ I bless all other human beings.

____ I bless all who have wronged me.

____ I bless all who have helped me.

____ My life is meaningful.

APPENDIX C

Human Potential Development Scale

Dr. Norman Shealy

Throughout history, philosophers and religious leaders have emphasized that there are certain characteristics that represent the highest potential for service to and interaction with humanity. There is no test that we know of which measures this development, although the Human Potential Attitude Inventory gives you some hints. We'd like to offer you here an opportunity to measure your feelings of your development at this point in time. We suggest you take the following test in your ordinary state of consciousness, just by reading it. Then get into a deep state of relaxation, ask yourself the same question, and rate yourself from that point of view. Zero means total lack of the quality; 100 implies the maximum any person could possibly achieve.

HUMAN POTENTIAL DEVELOPMENT

Love	0	5	10	15	20	25	30	35	40	45	50	55	60	65	70	75	80	85	90	95	100
Reason	0	5	10	15	20	25	30	35	40	45	50	55	60	65	70	75	80	85	90	95	100
Wisdom	0	5	10	15	20	25	30	35	40	45	50	55	60	65	70	75	80	85	90	95	100
Will	0	5	10	15	20	25	30	35	40	45	50	55	60	65	70	75	80	85	90	95	100
Faith	0	5	10	15	20	25	30	35	40	45	50	55	60	65	70	75	80	85	90	95	100
Hope	0	5	10	15	20	25	30	35	40	45	50	55	60	65	70	75	80	85	90	95	100
Charity	0	5	10	15	20	25	30	35	40	45	50	55	60	65	70	75	80	85	90	95	100
Courage	0	5	10	15	20	25	30	35	40	45	50	55	60	65	70	75	80	85	90	95	100
Joy	0	5	10	15	20	25	30	35	40	45	50	55	60	65	70	75	80	85	90	95	100
Motivation	0	5	10	15	20	25	30	35	40	45	50	55	60	65	70	75	80	85	90	95	100
Confidence	0	5	10	15	20	25	30	35	40	45	50	55	60	65	70	75	80	85	90	95	100
Compassion	0	5	10	15	20	25	30	35	40	45	50	55	60	65	70	75	80	85	90	95	100
Serenity	0	5	10	15	20	25	30	35	40	45	50	55	60	65	70	75	80	85	90	95	100
Tolerance	0	5	10	15	20	25	30	35	40	45	50	55	60	65	70	75	80	85	90	95	100
Forgiveness	0	5	10	15	20	25	30	35	40	45	50	55	60	65	70	75	80	85	90	95	100

APPENDIX D

A Condensed List of Common Dream Symbols

The following short list of common dream symbols is presented only as a guide from which to begin formulating your own dream associations. Your personal symbology is by far the most important component for accurate dream interpretations.

Airplane: (Sun, moon, stars, comets, planets) represent spiritual ideals.
Baby: A new birth. Rebirth of self to higher and nobler ideals if the baby is beautiful and often able to speak. It can also represent a real individual.
Bed: Rest or sex.
Bird: At the highest level, related to beauty, joy, and love. These are frequently in dreams at a critical period in one's life. Note the type of bird.
Boat: The voyage of life. "Smooth sailing," "stormy crossings," "shipwrecked individuals."
Bridge: State of transition.
Car: The physical body. The driving mechanism of the car can represent the various anatomical parts of the dreamer. *Use of brakes:* use of will. Driving the wrong way is a warning concerning health as is a car out of control. A *truck* is a work vehicle.
Cat: Independence but often uncooperativeness and isolation. Petting a cat often suggests pleasure in a negative emotion. Note cat's color and disposition. Also "cattiness."
Climbing: Movement upward. Note how difficult the ascent is.
Clock: Time. *Clock with hands still:* Death. *Clock with hands racing:* Time running out.
Clothes: Representation of activity or attitude of the dreamer. *Work clothes:* Work; *Swim clothes:* Relaxation; *Formal attire:* Formality; *Quality*

material and beautiful color: Positive qualities; *Disheveled clothes:* Disorderliness; *Tight clothes:* Ill-fitting characteristics.

Darkness: Subconscious, unknown, lack of awareness. "In the dark."

Dawn: A second choice, new understanding, an enlightenment.

Department Store: Things stored. A selection from various items.

Dining: Watch what you are eating. The dream may give a clue.

Dog: Faithful companion. The dog can represent both faithful and unfaithful aspects of self in a relationship of trust given to you. Note the manner and type of dog.

Door: Entrance into self. *Locking a door:* Locking out unpleasant conditions. *Opening the front door:* Receiving spiritual help. *Closed door:* Negative attitudes that close out people and help.

Eyes: The windows of the soul. It shows the intelligence of the individual as well as often revealing his spiritual state. Spiritually-minded people may even dream of having three eyes. *Blindness:* A refusal to face certain realities. *Glasses:* Enable one to see more clearly. *Dark glasses:* Seeing less clearly.

Father: Enbodiment of authority, law, order, social conventions, patterns of behavior, as well as masculine protectiveness. He can be seen as an oppressive person who commands the dreamer to mold to conformity. He can also represent the father archetype in himself or an actual relationship with the dreamer's own father.

Fire: It represents the heart of man. All great forces in nature have a duality. Fire may either purify or destroy. It can signify uncontrolled temper, jealousy, vengeance, hatred and unbridled zeal, patriotic fervor, patience, and enthusiasm. Dreams of fire that suggest carelessness should be taken literally.

Fish: This is often related to the spiritual side of life because a fish was the early symbol for Christ. A beautiful fish represents growth of the self. An ugly fish signifies spiritual weakness. Fish eyes represent perpetual attention because they never close. Eating fish suggests renewal.

Flying: Wishful thinking. Astral projection. Suggestions to rise above the problem. Sex.

Food: Appetites. Food for the spirit. Specific foods may be those one has a need for or should avoid. *Ice cream:* Special items "frozen" for future use and delight. This may also carry the suggestion to use immediately.

Game: The game of life. A reluctance to become involved in life. A conflict in life. The two opposing sides may represent parts of the conflict. Note how the game is played and what it takes to win.

God: When the image of God appears in dreams, it may point to the dreamer's need to realize his fullest inner potential. A person may feel his ego is destroyed by "an experience resembling death," but the result is he will be at one with the enduring spirit of which he is a part.
Grave: Death. Thoughts about someone who is dead. The past, what is dead and buried.
Hair: Thoughts. *Kinky hair:* Straighten out thinking. *Bald head:* Do more thinking. *White hair:* Wisdom or maturity. *Golden hair:* Golden or spiritual thoughts. *Bright, shiny black hair:* Ever-intriguing mysteries of the mind. *Black dull hair:* Mental depression. *Red hair:* Temper. *Golden red hair:* Constantly active mind. *Stiff hair:* Rigidity. *Disheveled hair:* Mental imbalance. *Dirty hair:* Cleanse one's thoughts. *Combing of the hair:* Reasoning.
Hands: Beautiful hands mean beautiful service. *Hands applauding:* Approval unless accompanied by negative symbols which then mean self-applause. *A wagging of the index finger:* A warning or reproach. *Trembling hands:* Lack of gentleness in one's approach. *Clawlike hands:* A grasping or holding on.
Hats: Mental conditions. *High silk hat:* Thinking. *Straw hat:* Mental telepathy.
Hallways: Transition. Change.
Horse: Tempestuous emotions. Message. *White horse:* Master creative energies, which can lead to genius, ESP, creativity that enables one to serve well. *Red horse:* Persistence, patience, drive. May also mean "Stop!" *Black horse:* Necessity to balance male and female qualities of the soul.
Hotel: A temporary or transitory state.
House: The activities of self. The condition of the house, building, or room represents the dreamer's own state and his recent relationships or activities to people in the dream or those in the background.
Jewelry: (Gold, money, valuables): Symbols of spiritual graces at their highest level. A beloved person. *Diamond:* Center of consciousness is shifted from the ego to the original source. *Pearl:* The mind. *Ruby:* Rose color or mystic rose; highest form of true love.
Journey: The journey through life.
Keys: The solution to a problem. They key to happiness. Safety.
Legs: Spiritual foundation or support.
Light: Directing force. Spiritual light.
Marriage: Literal marriage. Union with higher self. Integration.
Medicine: Actual treatment. Treatment to cure a problem.
Mirror: Reflection of oneself. Look at yourself.

Money: Anything of value. Exchange. This can be at the highest spiritual level, at the practical everyday level as a necessity to have or its lowest level as in "money is the root of all evil."
Mother: The archetype representing wholeness or potential wholeness in a woman. One's own mother. Basic family relationships as they affect one's current life.
Newspaper: Daily activities.
Nudity: Undressed and exposed.
Ocean: The moods and mystical powers of the psychic. The cosmic unconscious. *Deep versus shallow water:* Profound versus superficial. *Waves:* Waves of emotion. The ocean itself.
Office: The meaning depends on the activity carried on there. One's own office means one's work.
Pearls: "Pearls of wisdom." The whole self.
Pen and Pencil: Communication. Writing.
Photograph: Reflection of the person. *One's own photograph:* Self-examination required.
Pregnancy: Potential new life. Anything full of possibilities and hopes.
Radio: Message from the unconscious.
Railroad: A trip or change. *Single track:* One-track mind. *Getting derailed:* Going off the track. *On the right track:* Literal interpretation. *Arriving at a station:* Death.
Rain: A cleansing process within. Rain provides for richer growth.
Road: The individual way or destiny that leads to the culmination of one's aims or objectives. *A stretch of road:* A period of time. *A choice of roads.* Alternate courses. *Turn in the road:* New events lie ahead. *Dead end:* Road leads to nowhere. *Going downhill:* Literal interpretation. *Going uphill:* State of tension.
Sand: Poor foundation or poor building materials.
School Classroom: Lessons to be learned. Note the level of education.
Shoes: Foundations.
Snake: Temptation or evil. Wisdom. Sneakiness. Note the manner and type of snake.
Snow: Cold. Frigid emotion. Trouble or warning.
Soap: Purity indicated or a need for cleansing.
Stairs: A moving upward or downward.
Stars: Destiny. Whatever gives life its direction and guides to an inner goal. *Bright star:* Mystical achievement. *Falling star:* Failing hopes.
Storm: Outburst of emotion, desire, or instinct. Extreme mental agitation. Difficulties encountered in life.

Sun: Light of consciousness. Intellect. *Sunrise:* Dawn of consciousness. *Noon:* Maturity. *Sunset:* Decline of creative energy. Old age. *Black sun:* Death or profound depression.
Teeth: Speech.
Telephone: Message or communication coming.
Test: Some new "test" in life.
Train: Journey. "Trains of thought." Death.
Veil: Something only partially recognized by the dreamer. Veil to the unknown or future.
Water: Mother of creation. Spiritual symbol. Symbol of unconsciousness. "Water of life." Note beauty of water. *Clearness:* Purity, spirituality. *Muddy water:* Uncleanliness. Death.
Window: Light, perception, eyes, awareness.

Colors
See section on Auras

Numbers
One: Universal Force, Creative Energy, God.
Two: Weaker number than one. Two is a combination of 1 and 1 but is a division of the whole.
Three: Combination of one and two. The Trinity. Great strength.
Four: Elements of earth, air, wind, and fire. The body. *Forty:* Cleansing, preparation, or testing.
Five: Activity. An immediate change in activity from whatever it is associated with.
Six: Beauty and symmetrical forces of all numbers. It may also represent Satan.
Seven: A healing number. The spiritual forces in all ritualistic orders. A mystical relationship.
Eight: Double weakness of form. Vacillation.
Nine: A completion or finish. A termination of the order of things.
Ten: A completion of all numbers in a strength seldom found. From ten all numbers return to one.

Further detailed dream symbology is presented in my previous book *The Inner Eye* (Prentice-Hall, Inc. 1985).

Notes

Chapter 2

1. Mary Ann Woodward, *Scars of the Soul.* (Fair Grove, Missouri: Brindabella Books 1985) p. 30.
2. George Chapman with Ray Stemman, *Surgeon from Another World.* (Wellingborough, Northamptonshire, England: The Aquarian Press 1978. Revised and expanded 1984) p. 86.
3. Mary Woodward, *Scars of the Soul.* p. 155.
4. Harry Edwards, *A Guide to the Understanding and Practice of Spiritual Healing.* (Burrows Lea, Shere, Guildford, Surry, England: The Healer Publishing Company, Ltd. 1974) p. 17.
5. Ibid. p. 14.
6. Ibid. p. 15.
7. George Chapman and Ray Stemman, *Surgeon from Another World.* p. 101.
8. Ibid. p. 172.

Chapter 5

1. Ronald Beesley, *Substance of Thought.* (Tunbridge Wells, Kent, England: White Lodge Publications 1975) p. 10.
2. Phyllis R. Koch-Sheras, E. Ann Hollier, and Brooke Jones, *Dream On.* (Englewood Cliffs, New Jersey: Prentice Hall, Inc. 1983) p. 77.
3. Ibid. p. 148.

Chapter 6

1. Stephen La Berge, Ph.D., *Lucid Dreaming: The Power of Being Awake and Aware in Your Dreams.* (Los Angeles, California: Jeremy P. Tarcher, Inc. 1985) p. 206.
2. Ibid. p. 225.
3. Ronald Beesley, *The Emergence of Cosmic Forces.* (Tunbridge Wells, Kent, England: White Lodge Publications 1979) p. 57.
4. Richard Bach, *The Bridge across Forever.* (New York, New York: William Morrow and Company, Inc. 1984) pp. 301–302.
5. Elizabeth Hollis, *Correspondence.* (Winston Salem, North Carolina: May 1983).

6. Elizabeth Hollis, *Correspondence.* (Carrollton, Texas: May, 1985).

Chapter 7

1. Phyllis R. Koch-Sheras, E. Ann Hollier, and Brooke Jones, *Dream On.* (Englewood Cliffs, New Jersey: Prentice Hall Inc. 1983) p. 102.
2. Stephen La Berge, Ph.D., *Lucid Dreaming: The Power of Being Awake and Aware in Your Dreams.* (Los Angeles, California: Jeremy P. Tarcher, Inc. 1985) p. 156.

Chapter 8

1. Mary Ellen Carter, *Edgar Cayce on Prophecy* (Virginia Beach, Virginia: Association for Research and Enlightenment Press 1968) p. 143.
2. Richard Bach, *The Bridge Across Forever.* (New York, New York: William Morrow and Company, Inc. 1984) p. 27.
3. Harmon Bro, Ph.D., *Edgar Cayce on Dreams.* (New York, New York: Paperback Library Inc. 1968) p. 210.
4. Emmet Fox, *Find and Use Your Inner Power.* (New York, New York: Harper and Row Publishers 1941) p. 104.
5. Joan Windsor, *The Inner Eye* (Englewood Cliffs, New Jersey: Prentice Hall, Inc. 1985) p. 145.
6. Emmet Fox, *Power Through Constructive Thinking.* (New York, New York: Harper and Row Publishers 1940) p. 230.

Chapter 9

1. William A. McGarey, M.D., *The Edgar Cayce Remedies.* (New York, New York: Bantam Books 1983) pp. 60–61.
2. Paul C. Bragg, ND, Ph.D., *The Miracle of Fasting.* (Santa Barbara, California: Health Science 1983) p. 29.
3. Ibid. p. 57.
4. Ibid. p. 65.
5. Ibid. p. 77.
6. Dr. Harold J. Reilly, *The Edgar Cayce Handbook for Health through Drugless Therapy.* (New York, New York: Jove Publications Inc. 1977) p. 301.
7. Litany Burns, *Develop Your Psychic Abilities* (Englewood Cliffs, New Jersey: Prentice-Hall Inc. 1985) pp. 85–86.
8. Ibid. pp. 87–88.
9. Ibid. p. 88.
10. Dael, *The Crystal Book* (Sunoi, California: The Crystal Company 1983) p. 71.
11. Wally and Jenny Richardson and Lenora Huett, *The Spiritual Value of Gem Stones* (Marina del Rey, California: Devorss and Company 1980) p. 90.
12. Shakti Gawain, *Creative Visualization.* (San Rafael, California: Whatever Publishing, Inc. 1978) p. 21.
13. Ibid. pp. 24–25.

14. Joan R. Windsor, *The Inner Eye.* (Englewood Cliffs, New Jersey: Prentice Hall Inc. 1985) pp. 168–169.

Chapter 10

1. Harry Edwards, *A Guide to the Understanding and Practice of Spiritual Healing.* (Burrows Lea, Shere, Guildford, Surry, England: The Healers Publishing Company, Ltd. 1974) p. 75.
2. Ibid. p. 131.
3. George W. Meek, *Healers and the Healing Process.* (Wheaton, Illinois: The Theosophical Publishing House 1977) p. 123.
4. Ibid. pp. 131–132.
5. Norman Shealy, MD, *Self-Healing through Love Energy.* (Springfield, Missouri: February 1986).
6. Dr. Genevieve Haller, *A Philosophy of Health.* (Virginia Beach, Virginia: March 1986).
7. Mrs. Margit Nassi, *Massage Therapy.* (Virginia Beach, Virginia: March 1986).
8. Mrs. Virginia Light, *The Process of Spiritual Healing: Its Essential Components for Success and Failure.* (Great Falls, Virginia: November 1985).
9. Catherine Ponder, *The Dynamic Laws of Healing.* (Marina del Rey, California: Devorss and Company. Copyright 1966. Revised and updated by author 1985) p. 2.
10. Catherine Ponder, *The Prospering Power of Love.* (Marina del Rey, California: Devorss and Company. Copyright 1966. Unity School of Christianity: 1983 Catherine Ponder) p. 34.
11. Charles Fillmore, *Atom Smashing Power of Mind.* (Unity Village, Missouri: Unity Books 1949) as quoted in Catherine Ponder's *The Dynamic Laws of Healing* p. 11.
12. Ibid. pp. 97–98.
13. Ibid. p. 115.
14. Ibid. p. 120.
15. Ibid. p. 121.
16. Catherine Ponder, *The Prospering Power of Love* p. 44.
17. Ibid. p. 13.
18. Ibid. p. 68.
19. Charles Fillmore, *Jesus Christ Heals.* (Unity Village, Missouri: Unity School of Christianity, 1939) as quoted in Catherine Ponder's *The Prospering Power of Love* p. 69.

20 Catherine Ponder *The Prospering Power of Love* p. 69.

Chapter 11

1. Lendon Smith, M.D., *Feed Your Kids Right.* (New York, New York: McGraw-Hill Book Company 1979) p. 31.
2. Earl Mindell, *Vitamin Bible.* (New York, New York: Rawson Associates 1979) p. 22.

3. Ibid. p. 23.
4. Ibid. p. 241.
5. Juluis Fast, *Body Language.* (New York, New York: Pocket Books 1970) p. 108.
6. Gerald I. Nierenberg and Henry H. Calero, *How to Read a Person Like a Book* (New York, New York: Pocket Books 1971) pp. 94–95.
7. Ibid. p. 37.
8. Julius Fast, *Body Language* pp. 129–130.
9. Roger Lewis, *Color and the Edgar Cayce Readings.* (Virginia Beach, Virginia: Edgar Cayce Foundation 1973) p. 8.
10. Claude M. Bristol, *The Magic of Believing.* (New York, New York: Pocket Books 1948) p. 45.
11. Shakt Gawain, *Creative Visualization.* (San Rafael, California: Whatever Publishing, Inc. 1978) p. 37.
12. Ibid. p. 37.
13. Ibid. p. 37.
14. Jane Brody, *Healers Develop Special Touch.* (New York, New York: Copyright New York *Times* Company April 17, 1985) p. 1.
15. Harry Edwards, *A Guide to the Understanding and Practice of Spiritual Healing.* (Burrows Lea, Shere, Guildford, Surry, England: The Healer Publishing Company, Ltd. 1974) p. 11.

Bibliography

1. Bach, Richard, *The Bridge across Forever.* New York, New York: William Morrow and Company, Inc. 1984.
2. Beesley, Ronald, *The Emergence of Cosmic Forces.* Tunbridge Wells, Kent, England: 1979.
3. Beesley, Ronald, *Substance of Thought.* Tunbridge Wells, Kent, England: 1975.
4. Brody, Jane, *Healers Develop Special Touch.* New York, New York: Copyright New York Times Company. April 17, 1985.
5. Bragg, Paul C., *The Miracle of Fasting.* Santa Barbara, California: Health Science 1983.
6. Bristol, Claude M., *The Magic of Believing.* New York, New York: Pocket Books 1948.
7. Bro, Harmon, Ph.D., *Edgar Cayce on Dreams.* New York, New York: Paperback Library Inc. 1968.
8. Burns, Litany, *Develop Your Psychic Abilities.* Englewod Cliffs, New Jersey: Prentice-Hall Inc. 1985.
9. Carter, Mary Ellen, *Edgar Cayce on Prophecy.* Virginia Beach, Virginia: Association for Research and Enlightenment 1968.
10. Chapman, George with Ray Stemman, *Surgeon from Another World.* Northamptonshire, England: The Aquarian Press 1978.
11. Deal, *The Crystal Book,* Sunoi, California: The Crystal Company 1983.
12. Edwards, Harry, *A Guide to the Understanding and Practice of Spiritual Healing.* Burrows Lea, Shere, Guildford, Surry, England: The Healer Publishing Company, Ltd. 1974.
13. Fast, Julius, *Body Language.* New York, New York: Pocket Books 1970.
14. Fillmore, Charles, *Atom Smashing Power of Mind.* Unity Village, Missouri: Unity Books 1949.
15. Fillmore, Charles, *Jesus Christ Heals.* Unity Village, Missouri: Unity School of Christianity 1939.
16. Fox, Emmet, *Find and Use Your Inner Power.* New York, New York: Harper and Row Publishers 1941.
17. Fox, Emmet, *Power through Constructive Thinking.* New York, New York: Harper and Row Publishers 1940.

18. Gawain, Shakti, *Creative Visualization.* San Rafael, California: Whatever Publishing, Inc. 1978.

19. Haller, Dr. Genevieve. *A Philosophy of Health.* Virginia Beach, Virginia: November 1985.

20. Hollis, Elizabeth, *Correspondence.* Winston-Salem, North Carolina: May 1983.

21. Hollis, Elizabeth, *Correspondence.* Carrollton, Texas: May 1985.

22. Koch-Sheras, Phyllis R., E. Ann Hollier and Brooke Jones, *Dream On.* Englewood Cliffs, New Jersey: Prentice-Hall Inc. 1983.

23. La Berge, Stephen, Ph.D., *Lucid Dreaming: The Power of Being Awake and Aware in Your Dreams.* Los Angeles, California: Jeremy P. Tarcher Inc. 1985.

24. Lewis, Roger, *Color and the Edgar Cayce Readings.* Virginia Beach, Virginia: Edgar Cayce Foundation 1973.

25. Light, Virginia, *The Process of Spiritual Healing: Its Essential Components for Success and Failure.* Great Falls, Virginia: November 1985.

26. McGarey, William A., M.D., *The Edgar Cayce Remedies.* New York, New York: Bantam Books 1983.

27. Meek, George W., *Healers and the Healing Process.* Wheaton, Illinois: The Theosophical Publishing House 1977.

28. Mindell, Earl, *Vitamin Bible.* New York, New York: Rawson Associates 1979.

29. Nassi, Margit, *Massage Therapy:* Virginia Beach, Virginia: March 1986.

30. Nierenberg, Gerald I. and Henry H. Calero *How to Read a Person Like a Book* New York, New York: Pocket Books 1971.

31. Ponder, Catherine, *The Dynamic Laws of Healing.* Marina del Rey, California: Devorss and Company. Copyright 1966. Revised and updated by author 1985.

32. Ponder, Catherine, *The Prospering Power of Love.* Marina del Rey, California: Devorss and Company. Copyright 1966. Unity School of Christianity. 1983. Catherine Ponder.

33. Reilly, Dr. J. Harold, *The Edgar Cayce Handbook for Health through Drugless Therapy.* New York, New York: Jove Publications 1977.

34. Richardson, Wally and Jenny and Lenora Huett, *The Spiritual Value of Gem Stones.* Marina del Rey, California: Devorss and Company 1980.

35. Shealy, Norman, M.D., *Self-Healing through Love Energy.* Springfield, Missouri: February 1986.

36. Smith, Lendon, M.D., *Feed Your Kids Right.* New York, New York: McGraw-Hill Book Company 1979.

37. Windsor, Joan R., *The Inner Eye.* Englewood Cliffs, New Jersey: Prentice-Hall Inc. 1985.

38. Woodward, Mary Ann, *Scars of the Soul.* Fair Grove, Missouri: Brindadella Books 1985.

Index